CHILD MALTREATMENT IN THE UNITED KINGDOM

A STUDY OF THE PREVALENCE OF CHILD ABUSE AND NEGLECT

Pat Cawson

Corinne Wattam

Sue Brooker

Graham Kelly

NSPCC

Cruelty to children must stop. FULL STOP.

THE AUTHORS

Pat Cawson is Head of Child Protection Research at the NSPCC

Corinne Wattam is Professor of Child Care at the University of Central Lancashire

Sue Brooker is Director of Social Research at BMRB International

Graham Kelly is Associate Director of Social Research at BMRB International

The National Society for the Prevention of Cruelty to Children (NSPCC) is the UK's leading charity specialising in child protection and the prevention of cruelty to children.

The NSPCC exists to prevent children from suffering abuse and is working for a future for children free from cruelty.

First published 2000 by the NSPCC, reprinted 2002.
Weston House, 42 Curtain Road,
London EC2A 3NH
Tel: 020 7825 2500 Fax: 020 7825 2525
Email: infounit@nspcc.org.uk
Website: www.nspcc.org.uk

Registered charity number 216401

Director and Chief Executive: Mary Marsh

ISBN 1-84228-006-6
Design by Red Stone

FOREWORD

Research must be an integral part of any strategy for stopping cruelty to children. Only when we have a good knowledge base can we hope to succeed in preventing the harm suffered by children. However, both research and prevention are long-term activities and it can be a considerable time before the results are known. Research can also seem costly. For these reasons there has been a reluctance to invest in research into child abuse. Such a view is very short-sighted if we are intent on understanding the needs of children. The NSPCC is committed to undertaking and promoting research into the nature, causes, and consequences of child abuse and neglect.

In March 1999, the NSPCC launched its FULL STOP Campaign, which has ending cruelty to children within a generation as its objective. In order to achieve this ambitious goal, the NSPCC developed a long-term strategy which comprised a range of initiatives including the provision of services, awareness raising and public education, research, and influencing law, social policy, and professional practice. The FULL STOP Campaign has got off to a good start but there is still a long way to go. Quite rightly, the question has been asked "how will we know what progress has been made in ending cruelty to children?"

In part, it was to answer questions like these that the NSPCC embarked on a major study of the prevalence of child abuse in the United Kingdom. We believe that because of the size and representative nature of the sample, this is the most authoritative prevalence study of child abuse ever to have been conducted in the United Kingdom. It contains a wealth of information on the childhood experiences of 18 to 24 year olds. The NSPCC intends to repeat the study within ten years and that will enable us to chart changes in the treatment of children and young people over a period of time. The prevalence study will provide us with a benchmark against which to assess the success of our campaign to end cruelty.

The research reported here has, however, a wider significance because its findings will have a relevance to the community of professionals, policy makers, and researchers. It is a cause for concern that we have surprisingly little good research on the scale and nature of child abuse and that we almost seem to be in a position of making policy and planning services from a position of potential ignorance. In part, this study will help fill that gap and we hope that the findings will be considered very carefully by all those who have a responsibility for the care and protection of children.

A common understanding of how children are harmed will help improve responses to child abuse. Professionals from different disciplines need a common language if they are to work together. The findings of this study will help create a base of knowledge for multi disciplinary and agency working. This is crucial if we are to end cruelty to children. The NSPCC alone cannot achieve this goal. It can only be secured if agencies work in partnership together. The NSPCC is therefore committed both to working with other organisations and to sharing our experience, including that of research. This will enable us to critically examine the ways in which we respond to the needs of children and their families and encourage new and creative thinking in our provision of services.

We hope that this will lead to a fundamental shift in how our society treats our children. We wish to see a significant change in our culture so that all children are loved, valued, and able to achieve their full potential. Much greater priority needs to be given to children if we are to eliminate the types of maltreatment described in this study. One important way in which children could be accorded improved status would be if the government were to appoint national Children's Commissioners for each of the United Kingdom countries. These Commissioners would be independent, powerful advocates for all children. They would also have a key role in the promotion of research into children's needs and the dissemination of findings. A national

Commissioner who could act on and progress the findings of this prevalence study would be providing an invaluable service to us all. The NSPCC is campaigning for the establishment of independent Children's Commissioners who can take an overview of the needs of children and young people and identify ways of meeting them. Research has a vital role to play in this.

The results of this study are complex and we plan to publish a series of reports and papers over the coming months which will discuss specific aspects of the findings. To be most useful research needs to be critically assessed and the NSPCC would very much welcome feedback and comment on the issues raised in this study. Such a debate can help inform both the future analysis of this prevalence study and the commissioning of new areas of research.

Mary Marsh

NSPCC Director and Chief Executive

ACKNOWLEDGEMENTS

A number of individuals helped in this project. Particular thanks are due to the following people:

the staff of the Social Research and Operations Departments of BMRB International, in particular the fieldwork interviewers and those who carried out the data processing and statistical analysis;

those who helped with comments at design and report stages, including Professor Nigel Parton and Dr Brid Featherstone, Huddersfield University Centre for Applied Childhood Studies; Professor David Finkelhor, Crimes Against Children Research Center, University of New Hampshire; Professor David Gough, Social Science Research Unit, London University Institute of Education; Dr Deborah Ghate and Dr Patricia Moran, Policy Research Bureau, and Dr Penelope Leach;

there are too many staff of NSPCC to name everyone individually, but Phillip Noyes, Bruce Clark, Sue Creighton, Peter Dale, Enid Hendry, Ilan Katz and Caroline McGee were particularly helpful in commenting at design and drafting stage and in providing encouragement. Sarah Smith grappled with typing the complex report and the NSPCC library staff gave considerable time and patience to supporting our numerous requests for documentation;

above all, we thank the young people who gave their time to be interviewed for the study. They are the ones who made it possible.

CONTENTS

TABLES

FIGURES

1. INTRODUCTION

This report gives the first results of a major national study undertaken to explore the childhood experience of young people in the UK, including their experience of abuse (physical, sexual and emotional) and neglect, collectively described as maltreatment. The research described here is the only UK study, and one of the few world wide, to have addressed the issue of maltreatment comprehensively, in a large random probability sample of the general population. It is also the first UK general population study to cover all kinds of abuse both inside and outside the family. Reliable baseline data on abuse and neglect, in the context of knowledge of normal family behaviour, is a prerequisite for the formulation of a long term child protection policy which would have public support, and for development of effective services for children and families.

This first report describes the young people's experiences with parents and carers, other relatives, adults in their neighbourhood, professionals in positions of responsibility towards them, and age peers at school and elsewhere. It seeks to establish measures of abuse and neglect which are transparent, robust and replicable, based on the best available knowledge from previous research and practitioner experience in the UK and elswhere. The measures incorporate both what is known about public opinion on the acceptability of behaviour towards children in the UK, and what behaviour is likely to be harmful to children, immediately and in the long term. Later reports will link the young people's experience of maltreatment to other aspects of their childhood, and examine the interrelationships between different types of maltreatment.

The survey of 'childrearing and children's experience'

The present study aims to redress the deficiencies in existing data as far as possible by providing credible and reliable measures which will be robust in the context of social and cultural differences due to social class, ethnicity and region. It attempts to establish benchmarks for the measurement of child abuse and neglect from which it will be possible to monitor future changes and trends in the maltreatment of children, and in public attitudes to child abuse and neglect. To achieve these objectives the research had to be:

■ based on definitions of abuse and neglect which have credibility as indicators of social consensus on acceptable behaviour towards children, and can be operationalised in measurable and reliable form

■ informed by what is currently known about the levels and nature of child maltreatment, especially as related to age and gender of victims and identity of abusers

■ designed to allow for the possibility of abuse both inside and outside the family

■ designed to tackle the borderline areas where there is known to be uncertainty and public debate about what is acceptable care of children, and what is generally recognised as abuse or neglect.

It was important to base the research in a context of broader aspects of childrearing. Pathological behaviour towards children can only be understood in relation to 'normal' treatment of children in our society. Child protection practice and legislation has to operate in a context of cultural acceptance of its values, if laws are to be enforceable and public support for services retained. Furthermore, available evidence suggests that circumstances in which maltreatment occurs represent points on a continuum of behaviour towards children, and that judgements of the acceptability of that behaviour vary in different times, places and contexts. In trying to eliminate child maltreatment, there is little reason to believe that what has been termed the 'BSE approach' - find infected families or abusers and zap them - would be a successful strategy (Katz, 2000). Instead, consideration of maltreatment must take place as part of our thinking about the way in which all children are cared for.

Results from this survey will help agencies planning and providing child protection services to direct their resources to better meet the needs of children, particularly by addressing the under-reporting of the various types of maltreatment. By providing baselines for abuse and neglect, the findings will assist monitoring of change in the treatment of children over the next decade.

This research has been conducted amongst people born between 1974 and 1980 who were at the time of the survey 18–24 years old. Their childhood experiences are therefore very recent, and reflect the experiences of children growing up in the United Kingdom in the latter quarter of the 20th century. The study has been conducted amongst a group of people who, if they are not already parents, may become so in the near future. Their views on what does and does not constitute child abuse are therefore of particular importance.

What do we know about child maltreatment?

The term child maltreatment is used to refer to all forms of child abuse and neglect. Abuse is generally categorised into three types: physical, sexual and emotional (sometimes referred to as psychological) abuse. All definitions of maltreatment have at least three aspects: the action responsible, the person responsible, and the harm incurred (Gough, 1996). Child abuse refers to acts of commission: things done to children, whereas neglect refers to acts of omission: things not done. In official statistics neglect is treated as one category although like abuse, it can take different forms, such as physical, emotional and educational neglect. Child maltreatment cases which hit the headlines are typical of the most severe types of harm, but child maltreatment as seen by social workers and other professionals in their daily work, and recorded in official statistics, is complex. Children can be badly treated in a range of different ways within their own home environment by those responsible for their care, and can also experience many forms of harm and exploitation outside the home.

We know surprisingly little about the true extent of child abuse and neglect in the UK. The main sources of information are official statistics or specially commissioned research. Official data only records what is brought to the attention of the authorities and what is important for the organisation to know. For example, child protection registers in the UK record the numbers of children for whom the likelihood of future significant harm is high. These are children who are made known to child protection agencies and are in need of future service. Registers do not record the numbers of children who are known to have been subjected to maltreatment in the past, and therefore give no estimate of prevalence or incidence. The Home Office reports data on crimes against children and these statistics represent the incidents that are reported to the police for which there is sufficient evidence. Evidence in cases of child abuse is often difficult to obtain. Children and their families may be reluctant to talk, physical injuries can be hidden and there are rarely other witnesses. In general we know that crimes against children are highly underreported (Morgan and Zedner, 1992). It is still very difficult to know how many children die as a result of abuse or neglect because of the way in which the cause of death of an infant or child is diagnosed, recorded and assessed (Stangler et al., 1991). Official homicide statistics suggest that currently around 70-80 children are killed in the UK each year. This is likely to be an underestimate as it only reflects cases where there is absolute certainty of the cause of death. Between five and ten of these homicides are carried out by strangers, the remainder by those known to the child, usually a parent or carer (Home Office, 2000).

With the exception of prevalence studies, of which there have been few in this country, very little research examines child maltreatment in relation to those who do not come to the notice of the child welfare or protection services. Almost everything we know is based on that small group of cases reported to the official agencies. Reported cases, and statistics from Child Protection Registers, are known to incorporate many sources of bias, including a greater likelihood of identifying risk in working class families than in middle class families, and a tendency for families, already known to agencies because they have social problems, to attract more attention than others. Inclusion on Child Protection Registers is also known to show considerable variation between local authority areas, which does not reflect differences in the nature of the populations or the levels of harm experienced by children(Department of Health, 1995). There is also evidence that the much greater concern for risk to very young children, reflected in registers and other official data sources, seriously underestimates the levels of abuse of adolescents (Rees and Stein, 1999). Sources of bias in official figures have a 'knock on' effect on the availability of help to children and families, because service planning is built around demand from existing service users. Unrecognised demand will not be met, clients whose needs do not fit existing service patterns will be unable to locate the help they need, and in consequence will never become part of the official figures, creating a cycle of ignorance on the part of service providers. In order to help children, now and in the future, it is crucially important to know more about the wider phenomenon of abuse and neglect. We need to know whether there are differences between children whose cases are reported and those who never see a social worker or police officer; or whether there are differences between those who tell others and those who don't, or between those who suffer serious and long term effects and those who seem to be less affected by the abuse. These questions are central to the development of prevention strategies and also to the development of sensitive and accessible services. A first step in reaching answers is to provide an overview of the population of children and young people who have been maltreated, one that is genuinely representative and from which valid conclusions about the total child population can be drawn.

Defining child maltreatment

Three problems in particular affect the attempt to determine the prevalence of maltreatment:

- identifying the boundaries between maltreatment and other forms of harm, including harm from less than optimal parenting, or from social factors such as poverty

- the known variation which exists between cultures, countries and generations over acceptable ways to treat children

- achieving 'single measures' of abuse or neglect which have any meaning, given the great variety of harms that children can experience, the possibility of both primary and secondary harm, and the variation in experience throughout childhood.

Boundaries between maltreatment and other harm

Children can be especially vulnerable to harm in many contexts, including those of child labour, armed conflict, polluted and physically dangerous environments, as well as in their normal domestic or social environments. There are many potentially damaging ways of treating children in personal relationships, such as excessive discipline, teasing, bullying, poor standards of care, or adults not liking individual children very much and showing it.

The boundary issues concerning the line to be drawn between harm and abuse or neglect over questions such as physical punishment, verbal aggression or adequate supervision, raise fundamental issues about childrearing standards, linked with ethical judgements about the right way to treat children, and whether different rules should apply to adults and children, for example over the acceptability of hitting them. It is clear that there can be no definition of maltreatment which will meet with universal acceptance because these are questions on which public opinion is divided, but there are indications from general population research that on some aspects it is possible to achieve measures of the acceptability of behaviour towards children which would achieve substantial public support from most (80% – 95%) of the adult population (Creighton and Russell, 1995).

We know that in the UK and other western countries there is general agreement between professionals about what constitutes serious abuse (Barnett et al., 1993; Hallett, 1995). There is a high level of consensus where actions cause actual or likely physical or psychological harm to the child, where these actions and harms are serious or frequent (Portwood, 1999). There is less agreement in law and in child care and child health practice about the acceptability and seriousness of behaviours such as hitting children, exposing them to sexually explicit films, not giving them a healthy diet or allowing them to witness domestic violence.

Part of the reason for this is that very little is known about the consequences of such actions. We know from individual cases and from research that serious physical and sexual abuse can lead to long term mental health problems, physical health problems, problems in relationships and even to death, but that some people seem to have great resilience and the ability to overcome the most adverse of experiences (Department of Health, 1991; Beitchman et al., 1992; Kendall-Tackett et al., 1993; Briere and Elliot, 1994; Wattam and Woodward, 1996; Bifulco and Moran, 1998; McCauley, 1999. However, there is less evidence about the effect of other forms of abuse or harmful treatment. It may be that the effects vary according to context and also to factors which foster resilience in the child which may be influenced by relationships, generation or culture. Wider effects on society may be just as important as individual effects. For example, Straus and Paschall (1998) report a small but measurable lower rate of cognitive development for children who are physically punished. If this rate is generalised out to the level of the population, given that it is also known that the majority of parents smack their children at some point, it represents a far more significant loss of cognitive potential for a nation. It is an established principle in epidemiology that a widely prevalent risk factor with small effect size, e.g. spanking, can have a much greater impact on public health than a risk factor with a large effect size, but low prevalence, such as child homicide (Rose, 1985). Findings from recent longitudinal studies and overviews of research (Thompson, In press) suggest that the benefits of reducing levels of physical punishment are far wider than the individual child or family. It is maintained that effects would be seen in levels of juvenile delinquency, adult depression and substance use, increased probability of completing higher education and earning potential (Straus and Paschall, 1998).

Cultural differences in the definition of child abuse

In 1995, the Department of Health summarised the findings of twenty research studies on child abuse and concluded that the definitions of child abuse changed over time and varied according to culture, and in any particular culture depended on social agreement (Department of Health, 1995). So, for example, practices which were in the past considered quite normal punishments such as locking children up or rubbing their faces in the sheets if they had wet the bed, although we know that they still happen, seem from recent research to be unusual now. The use of corporal punishment is also a topic on which views have varied between cultures and generations. Sometimes there are differences in what is considered acceptable according to where the behaviour takes place, or by gender. For example, using the cane on adolescent boys in school was still common and accepted in the United Kingdom long after studies showed that this was a rare form of punishment at home. In contrast, it is now illegal to punish with the cane in publicly funded schools – but the cane may be used legally by parents in the home.

Today some countries have legislation banning the physical punishment of children whereas in others it is generally acceptable to beat children with sticks or straps as long as no permanent injury is caused (see for example, Enzmann et al., 1998, with reference to law and practice in relation to physical punishment in Germany). Indeed, some parents may feel that physically disciplining a child is an integral part of being a 'good' parent. In studying the abuse of children in multi-cultural societies Korbin (1993) proposes that it should not be assumed that behaviour harmful to children can be explained away by culture, whilst promoting a difference rather than a deficiency model. We therefore require a more representative picture of different childhood experiences on which to base assessments of harm and maltreatment.

Attitudes towards childhood sexual relations are subject to cultural and historical variation in a similar way to attitudes towards physical discipline, supervision and methods of child rearing more generally (see, for example, Foucault, 1987). Sexual assault is clearly defined in penal codes as being against the law, however, sexual relations with and between children and young people are more difficult to define in relation to abuse. The age at which it is legal for children to engage in sexual relations varies, even in the contemporary world, across countries and between cultures. There is a growing consensus that sexual relations between adults and children are morally wrong and can be extremely damaging. This has evolved with an understanding that children are unable to give fully informed consent to sexual practices with adults and that adults are by definition in a position of power and trust (Schecter and Roberge, 1976). This consensus is now formally recognised in the UN Convention on the Rights of the Child (1989) which specifies the child's right to be protected from sexual abuse and sexual exploitation of all kinds, and which has been ratified by all countries in the world except the USA and Somalia.

Achieving single measures of abuse

The conventional approach to prevalence studies results in obtaining a series of single figures representing the proportions of the population who have been abused, physically, sexually or emotionally, or have been neglected. The process of achieving the figures requires the concentration of very varied experiences - of being beaten, or kicked or burned for example - into the single experience of being 'abused'. An overall figure masks the differences in severity, frequency and duration of abusive experiences, which may range from life threatening or even fatal injuries on a single occasion to a whole childhood of regular severe beatings, or from rape to taking pornographic photographs of children. The argument made earlier, that maltreatment occurs along a continuum of ways of treating children, illustrates the difficulty of identifying generally accepted cut off points at which neat divides from 'acceptable' to 'unacceptable' to 'abusive' may be made. In research terms, it is preferable to measure how many respondents were beaten over and over again rather than to state that 7% were physically abused. Statements about specific adult child interaction are clearer and allow for the development of more precise prevention measures (Dingwall, 1989).

Attempting to achieve single measures also creates problems in dealing with overlap and avoiding double counting when children experience more than one form of maltreatment, or maltreatment from more than one source. There is also the problem, particularly in relation to emotional or psychological abuse, that there may be distinctions between 'primary' and 'secondary' abuse. All forms of abuse and neglect can potentially include associated emotional abuse, whether from the induced guilt and secrecy commonly associated with sexual abuse, or the tendency of all kinds of abusers to 'blame the victim' and for victims to blame themselves. The methodological problems of non response, recall of events in early childhood and loss of sample populations of those most at risk, mean that any gross figure is likely to be an underestimate. All of these difficulties raise the question of whether working towards single measures is a useful activity.

Yet the range of possible abusive or neglectful treatment is so wide that planning coherent service development is made difficult. A total figure makes it possible to estimate the proportion of the population who are in need of some specialised service, at a level which enables estimates for the purpose of resource allocation. Provided that the measures are replicable, it also means that over time it is possible to assess, albeit crudely, whether the treatment of children is improving or deteriorating in general, rather than in specific ways. It does seem important however that measures attempt to allow for the severity and frequency of abusive or neglectful behaviour, as well as giving a simple account of whether it ever happened.

Self-assessed abuse

Research comparing rates of abuse assessed by professionals and by the victims has also found considerable differences (Steele, 1987; McGee et al., 1995). This reflects the different criteria adopted. Professionals judge by what was actually done to the victim, by whether the victim suffered harm or by a mixture of these factors. Victims take other things into account, such as their relationship with the person harming them, an understanding of the health problems or pressures on that person which might have affected their behaviour, or by comparison of their treatment to that of other children in the family and neighbourhood (Bifulco and Moran, 1998). They also consider their own role in what happened. They may assess underage sexual activity as not abusive because they consented to it, even though the activity is illegal, or those responsible for their care might think them too young to give informed consent. They may think that they provoked a beating or other attack by bad behaviour, and that what they experienced was deserved (Bower and Knutson, 1995). This perspective does not necessarily reflect a realistic assessment that they have misbehaved. Both research and clinical experience have found that victims of abuse by parents or other loved or respected people will often seek to minimise the abuse by taking the blame upon themselves. This reflects the extent to which any kind of abuse is also an attack on the self-esteem and self-confidence of the victim. Since it is a deeply rooted assumption in most cultures that parents love and care for their children and that adults in general will protect children, to be attacked by parents or other adults can seem incomprehensible to victims except in terms of punishment for misbehaviour or other 'badness'. Abusers often exploit this feature of children's understanding by telling them that they have misbehaved or caused what has happened to them (Bifulco and Moran, 1998).

Patterns of overlapping abuse

Emotional or psychological abuse is a comparative newcomer to the research literature on child maltreatment, though accounts of children suffering rejection, denigration, hostility, imprisonment and isolation inflicted by adults in their families and elsewhere are staples of both adult and children's literature from many cultures and ages. Garbarino, Guttman and Seeley (1986) point out that aspects of psychological abuse and neglect had been identified in child development literature for many decades, but that problems of clear, legally enforceable definition have hindered the recognition of this form of maltreatment in the child protection canon. They note the difficulty of separating psychological abuse or neglect from other forms with which they are frequently associated, and suggest that psychological abuse is in fact the only form which is likely to occur as the sole form of maltreatment. 'Rarely if ever does a child experience physical abuse or neglect, or sexual assault or exploitation, in a relationship that is positive or nurturing' (p.8) whereas children can experience psychological maltreatment without suffering physical or sexual harm. They suggest that far from being regarded as an 'ancillary issue, subordinate to other forms of abuse and neglect, we should place it as the centrepiece of efforts to understand family functioning and to protect children'. This view has gained increasing support from research in several countries (Brassard, Hart and Hardy 1993; Grayson 1993; McGee et al., 1995, Department of Health, 1995). It has major implications for any assessment of prevalence, since it suggests that all other forms of maltreatment should in effect be regarded as multiple maltreatment. Emotional or psychological maltreatment has even greater capacity for cultural variation than other forms, and previous research shows relatively low consensus on its definition even within a single culture and generation.

The issue of definition is therefore a central one in research on the prevalence of maltreatment. There is divergence between approaches to definition which are based exclusively on parental or other behaviour towards the child and those which incorporate an assessment of how much the child has suffered harm. Iwaniec (1997) argues that definition must take into account the effect of parental behaviour on the child. The National Commission of Inquiry into the Prevention of Child Abuse (1996) for example, defined emotional abuse as: 'the severe adverse effect on the behaviour and emotional development of a child caused by persistent or severe emotional ill treatment or rejection.' Bifulco and Moran (1998) point out that approaches such as this are tautological, by confusing the nature of the abuse with the effects on the child and defining abuse as that which causes damage. Since any kind of abuse can cause damage, but does not always do so, it is essential to define abuse by the perpetrator's behaviour which has the potential for causing harm. Grayson (1993) points out that the extent of damage to the child may not become apparent for many years, and that the lack of short term behavioural problems should not be taken to mean that no harm has occurred. Waiting until the child demonstrates problems may leave children in an unacceptable situation for many years and mean that intervention comes too late. Most American approaches to the measurement of abuse now focus on behavioural measures rather than assessment of harm. The USA 3rd National Incidence Study takes both dimensions into account by assessing behaviour towards the child and giving separate measures of 'harm' (where damage to the child has occurred) and 'endangerment' (where it might occur but has not yet done so) and recording all three measures (Sedlak and Broadhurst, 1996). Definitional issues will recur as a constant theme throughout this report.

A further central issue in measuring the prevalence of abuse is the role of the family in relation to child maltreatment, and perceptions of when treatment inside and outside the family setting are abusive. In the UK the family is the primary context in which maltreatment can occur undetected. Because the family is where physical punishment of children is legally permitted and culturally sanctioned it is easier for abusive physical treatment to be hidden, and child homicides, particularly of young children, are most likely to occur in the family home. The family is the primary context in which neglect and psychological maltreatment can take place, by the very nature of the child's physical and emotional dependency on parents or parental substitutes. In contrast, it is also the setting where sexual behaviour between children and other family members is generally illegal and regarded as abusive. British child protection services are largely organised to deal with maltreatment in the family. Yet a number of recent scandals have demonstrated that the family is not the only environment where maltreatment can occur: sexual abuse frequently involves family friends and neighbours, while schools, children's homes, foster care, churches, sports and youth clubs are also places where relationships of trust with adults can be abused. Child protection research says very little about this, and even less about the problems of bullying in schools, though this has been established as a common experience and common fear faced by children (Creighton and Russell, 1995; Ghate and Daniels, 1997) and at times has driven children to suicide. (Smith and Sharp, 1994)

Sample design

For practical and ethical reasons, it would have been problematic to interview children on this subject (Ghate and Spencer, 1995), especially so in a survey involving 'cold calling', interviews predominately held in the respondents' homes, and with very limited follow up support available for those reporting maltreatment. It was therefore decided to interview very young adults aged 18 – 24 years. This subgroup was selected on the grounds that their experience of childhood was sufficiently recent. Additionally, they were less likely than older adults to have experienced other major trauma and stress which would make it more difficult for them to isolate the impact of any childhood experiences on their lives.

A random probability sampling technique was employed, using the Postcode Address File as the basic sampling frame. While this is representative of households throughout the UK, inevitably it under-represents young people living in institutional settings such as prisons, hospitals or large hostels, and omits young people with no fixed abode. Young people in these categories represent a very small proportion of the age group, but some of these settings may be expected to contain a higher proportion than average of young people who had adverse childhoods. A total of 2,869 interviews were achieved with a response rate of 69%. Further detail on the sampling and response rate is given in Appendix 1.

Characteristics of the sample

The sample consisted of 1,235 men and 1,634 women. The response rate amongst women was a little higher than amongst men. The data have been correctively weighted to allow for this and also for regional differences in response and for the proportion living in households where more than one person would have been eligible for the sample, so that findings are representative of the total UK population of 18 - 24 year olds. In order to be eligible for interview, all 18 - 24 year olds had to have spent the majority of their childhood (a minimum of 10 years) in the United Kingdom.

Over half (56%) of those interviewed were still living with their parent(s) in the family home. Just under a fifth (18%) had moved on to live with a partner and just under one in ten (8%) were living alone. Just under a sixth (15%) had children of their own, rising to over a fifth (22%) amongst 21- 24 year olds. Most parents of this age had just one child (11%), though a minority had two (4%) or even three or more children (1%). Most had become parents at 18 or older (8% 18 - 20 and 4% aged 21 or older) but 1% had been 16 or younger, and 2% were 17 at the birth of their first child. Almost all these young parents (89%) had their child(ren) living with them.

Ethnicity was recorded using the census classifications. The majority of the sample (92%) described their ethnicity as white. The 8% from other groups were predominately Asian (5%) or black (2%). Most Asian respondents identified their ethnicity as Indian or Pakistani and most black respondents as Black Caribbean or Black Other. Proportions of other ethnic groups were all less than 1%.

Assessment was made of the sample's social status using the standard Market Research grading. This was considered a better option for this age group than the Registrar General classification of socio-economic groups because it allows inclusion of economically inactive groups such as students and the unemployed. With a sample in this age range there are issues which must be considered in interpreting socio-economic data. A sample of 18 - 24 year olds will contain a high proportion of students, whose socio-economic status while studying is by convention assigned as C1 in the grading system used. For many this will bear no relationship to their eventual position after graduating or completing a vocational course. Many employed young people at the threshold of their careers will be in junior posts which do not reflect either the social status of their families of origin or that which they will attain. The effect of these factors is to inflate the proportion of the sample classified as C1 ('skilled non-manual') and 38% of the sample were in this group. Of the remainder, 15% were assessed as AB (professional and managerial), 21% as C2 (skilled manual) and 26% as DE (semi and unskilled occupations).

The assessment of social status in relation to childhood experience was clearly going to present some problems. Although there is much continuity of status through generations, some level of social mobility would be expected. Furthermore children's educational achievement, closely related to social status, is particularly vulnerable to suffering from adverse childhood experience. Maltreated children would be expected to suffer reduced chances of higher education and reduced employment prospects, depressing their social grade and giving an increased risk of downward mobility. Respondents' present group would not be a fully reliable guide to their childhood situation, but it is also difficult to obtain reliable assessment of parents' employment status from their children. Instead it was decided to obtain parents' educational background, closely related to socio-economic status, which children do usually know. Two thirds of the sample (64%) reported that their parents' highest educational attainment was either GCSE, A Level or an apprenticeship (most likely to lead to either C1 or C2 occupations); 17% had at least one graduate parent and 19% said that their parents had no formal qualifications. This presents a picture similar to that of the young people but with more of the respondents being in manual grades than of their parents.

A small proportion of the sample (7%) reported that they had a disability or long term illness. Most reported mobility impairment or a learning disability, with very small numbers reporting sight impairment or hearing impairment, and almost half of the disabled respondents reporting other conditions.

The questionnaire

The study aimed to overcome the limitations of previous research by using descriptions of behaviour that were compatible, wherever possible, with previous studies but that did not pre-define behaviour as abusive. It examined a range of experiences during childhood and attitudes towards the way in which children should be treated. The study also examined what forms of behaviour are not considered acceptable in the United Kingdom today and probed the prevalence of child maltreatment using a retrospective approach to definition. It is not solely an attempt to define maltreatment and give overall levels of prevalence. Rather, it specifies a range of behaviours, some of which respondents have condoned or rejected, and gives prevalence levels for each one.

Interviews were carried out using CAPI (Computer Assisted Personal Interviewing) so that respondents could enter responses directly without having to discuss sensitive topics aloud. The questionnaire was introduced as being about 'experiences in childhood' and began by collecting some general background information about respondents' current circumstances and their family background, before moving on to obtain some attitudinal information about child rearing. The second half of the interview addressed respondents' own experiences in their childhood. Respondents completed this part of the interview themselves, reading the questions on the computer screen and typing in their answers. Thus they were able to provide information without the interviewer (nor anyone else who might be present in the room) knowing the questions asked nor their answers. All sections were introduced with broad, general questions about aspects of their care in childhood, gradually moving to more sensitive and detailed questions.

This part of the questionnaire covered:

- family relationships
- amount of supervision and freedom
- physical care
- verbal, physical and violent treatment
- bullying and discrimination
- emotional or psychological treatment
- sexual experience

Responses which indicated that the young people may have had abusive or potentially abusive experiences were followed up in detail with those respondents. The questions themselves did not define abuse and neglect. Instead, respondents were asked whether or not they had experienced any of a range of behaviour towards them (some of them positive, some negative). If they had some of the more negative experiences, they were asked a number of further questions to put that experience in context. At the end of each section, these respondents were asked if they considered the treatment they received to have been child abuse. Questions allowed multicoding unless the answers were mutually exclusive. The text of the questionnaire is included at Appendix 3.

At the very end of the interview, after demographic information had been collected, respondents were asked how worthwhile the interview had been. After an average of over 45 minutes answering these sensitive questions, just 2% felt it had not been a worthwhile use of their time. 85% said they would be prepared to help the NSPCC with further research on this subject, with an additional 7% saying that they might help, depending on the circumstances.

This is a very large scale research enterprise, and work is still continuing on the analysis. The present report is the first of several and covers the basic population figures for the prevalence of physical, sexual, emotional abuse and neglect. Later reports will explore the relationships between the different forms of abuse and neglect and other aspects of child rearing. The study will also seek to establish the relationship between young adults' childhood experience, their present day views on child abuse and neglect, and between self assessed abuse and the ratings which others might make.

Summary

- This is the first report from the only UK study to have addressed the issue of child maltreatment (including physical, sexual, emotional abuse and neglect) comprehensively, in a large random probability sample of the general population.

- Respondents were young people aged 18-24 years, who were young enough to be close to their childhood, for whom the effects of childhood experience on the young adult would be assessible, but relatively uncontaminated by later stresses of adult life. The young people entered their answers to sensitive questions about personal experience directly onto computer, to protect confidentiality.

- A sample, drawn from all parts of the UK, comprised 2,869 young people. Of these 92% recorded their ethnicity as white, with 8% from minority ethnic groups, predominantly Asian; 7% reported that they had a disability, usually of mobility or a learning disability. The study achieved a 67% response rate.

- This study focuses on the extent and effects of child maltreatment in the general population, rather than children reported to the police or social services who are known to be unrepresentative of the general population. This knowledge is essential for the development of prevention strategies, and of sensitive and accessible services for all children who might need help.

- Child maltreatment is inherently difficult to define, since children can be harmed in many different contexts, of which assault, whether physical, sexual or psychological, is only one. Maltreatment of children can generally be seen on a continuum, rather than there being an organic difference between 'abusive' and 'non abusive' families or situations.

- Although there is evidence of consensus about what constitutes serious harm, there are some areas where there are much publicised disagreements, such as the age of consent to sexual intercourse, the use of physical punishment and the appropriate levels of supervision of children at different ages. For this reason, a prevalence study must obtain data on whether specific acts or omissions have occurred, rather than restrict data to behaviour which is predefined as maltreatment.

- Attempting to achieve a single measure for the prevalence of any type of maltreatment is a relatively crude process, ignoring the immense diversity of experience represented by the term 'maltreatment', but it enables population estimates which can be used as a basis for policy and service development.

- Like all child maltreatment prevalence studies, this study is likely to underestimate abuse and neglect because events in very early childhood may not be remembered.

- The questions did not define abuse and neglect but asked respondents if they had experienced specific behaviour, some positive and some negative. Those whose accounts indicated that they might have experienced maltreatment were asked more detailed questions about that experience.

- Asked their opinions at the end of the interview, 98% of respondents thought the survey was worthwhile and 85% said they would definitely be willing to take part in further research.

2. FAMILY LIFE

It is important that child abuse and neglect are placed in the context of what it is more typical for children to experience as they grow up. This chapter therefore discusses young people's experience of family life, family relationships, the amount of freedom, independence and responsibility they had while growing up, and their own attitudes towards bringing up children. It also looks at the ways in which the majority were 'disciplined' and treated during childhood.

Family life is one of the least studied areas of our society. We take it for granted that we understand families because we have experience of our own and those of our friends and assume that most other families are broadly similar. The few studies which have examined family life in general population samples have had a specific focus, but even so are revealing of the very great differences found within the range of 'normal' family life and childrearing patterns (Wilson, 1980; Creighton and Russell, 1995; Smith and Grocke, 1995; Ghate and Daniels, 1997). Creighton and Russell reviewed research on childrearing over a period of 30 years. Studies showed the importance of social class in affecting patterns of supervision, discipline and the way affection was demonstrated between parents and children. They also showed the persistence of traditional nuclear family patterns for the majority of families, and of gender-linked roles, behaviour and attitudes. The central position of mothers in supporting and socialising children was marked. It was possible to identify a core of belief about acceptable ways of treating children which was subscribed to by more than 90% of the population from all social groups, and to identify common patterns in behaviour towards children. Ghate and Daniels' (1997) findings showed that these features were still true for children today. They also showed the continued importance of the extended family to children, and the extent to which children were aware of the stresses which their parents often faced, and shared in their worries. Many of those findings were replicated in the present study.

Living arrangements experienced as a child

Nine in ten of respondents in the present study had at some point in their childhood lived with their birth mother and birth father together and seven in ten had spent their whole childhood with birth parents. One fifth of the sample had spent at least part of their childhood in a single parent family and 13% had lived at some time in a reconstituted family with a birth parent and the parent's new partner. Where birth parents were not together the absent parent was nearly always the father: one in six had lived with their birth mother but not their birth father for some time during their childhood and around one in ten had lived with a birth mother and her new partner. Less than one in ten had lived with their birth father and not their birth mother (either with or without a new partner), and few had lived with other relatives and not their birth parents. A small number had lived with foster carers (1%) or adoptive parents (1%).

Over a fifth (21%) gave more than one answer to this question and these respondents were asked with whom they had spent most of their childhood. Results are shown in the second column of the table below. In the vast majority of cases, those who had not spent most their childhood with both their birth parents said that this was because their parents had separated or divorced (89%), rather than because they had been bereaved (9%). At a different point in the interview 1% said they had been in residential care, and 4% said they had attended boarding school.

Table 1 Adults lived with as a child

Base: All respondents

	Ever	Most of childhood
Unweighted base	2,869	641
Weighted base	2,869	613
	%	%
Birth mother and birth father together	89	43
Birth mother only	17	23
Birth mother and stepfather(s)	11	20
Birth father only	5	4
Birth father and stepmother(s)	4	3
With other relative(s) (without parents)	6	2
Foster parents	1	1
Adoptive parents	1	2

Childhood experiences of family life

Respondents were asked whether they agreed or disagreed with statements concerning their family life. Table 2 shows that three quarters of respondents agreed strongly that they had a warm and loving family background, and over nine in ten agreed at least to some extent that this was so. Most of the sample agreed that they were 'a happy child', though in this case the proportion agreeing strongly dropped to two thirds.

Response to the statement 'there was a lot of stress in the family home' was more mixed. Over a third said this was the case, one in ten agreeing strongly that this had been their experience. Similarly, a third agreed that there had been worries about the shortage of money, and a similar proportion agreed that most other children had things which their family could not afford. A quarter said that there were things in their childhood that they found it difficult to talk about. Around one in six said that they had problems making friends.

Table 2 Experiences in childhood

Base: All respondents

		Strongly agree	Slightly agree	Neither agree nor disagree	Slightly disagree	Strongly disagree
Unweighted base	2,869					
Weighted base	2,869					
I had a warm and loving family background	%	77	15	3	2	3
I was a happy child	%	67	23	3	4	2
There was a lot of stress in the family home	%	11	26	15	19	28
There were always a lot of worries about the shortage of money	%	9	24	12	21	33
Most other children had things which my family could not afford	%	8	22	14	23	32
There are things that happened in my childhood that I find hard to talk about	%	10	15	11	13	50
I often had problems making friends	%	3	13	8	18	58

Praise and affection

One question probed the ways that families show that they care for each other, using items concerned with things additional to basic physical care . Respondents were asked 'in your family did people do any of (these things) to show that they cared about you?'

- Praise you or tell you that you did something well

- Give you money/extra pocket money

- Hug you, cuddle you, kiss you

- Give you sweets or nice things to eat

- Say nice things to you or tell you they cared about you

- Buy you presents or special treats

- Help you do things e.g. homework

- Take you out on trips to places you liked

- Something else (type in .....)

- None of these things

Because these had been used in a previous study of childhood which interviewed a national sample of children aged 8-15 years (Ghate and Daniels, 1997) it was known that they represented normal ways of behaving to children across the social spectrum. Although there were gender, socio-economic and regional differences on individual items, Ghate and Daniels showed that only 1% of children answered 'none of these things' while 95% named two or more ways that they were shown affection.

Almost nine in ten of the present respondents had been praised or told that they had done something well. Over three quarters had been hugged, cuddled or kissed. Only a slightly smaller proportion in each case had been told nice things, such as that they were cared for, or had been taken out on trips to places they liked. Just under seven in ten were helped with difficult tasks, such as their homework. Just under two thirds were bought presents or treats and just under six in ten in each case were given sweets and pocket money. Responses were very similar to those found by Ghate and Daniels. Only 1%, the same proportion as that found by Ghate and Daniels, indicated that they had not experienced any treatment that showed they were cared for.

All those who said they were hugged, cuddled or kissed (77%) were asked how often they were shown affection by each of their parents (or their step-parent if they had spent the majority of their childhood with this parent rather than their birth one). Around two thirds of mothers (68%) and just under half of fathers (46%) were reported to have frequently shown affection. Two thirds described their relationship with their mother as 'very close' and a further quarter described it as 'fairly close'. In total, then, nine in ten had at least a fairly close relationship with their mother, under one in ten saying that they were not close to her. Fewer (four in ten) said that they had a very close relationship with their father, though in total over three quarters said that they were at least fairly close to their father. One in ten had grown up without a father figure.

Table 3 Closeness of relationship with parents

	Mother	Father
Unweighted base	2,869	2,869
Weighted base	2,869	2,869
	%	%
Very close	65	42
Fairly close	26	36
Not very close	5	9
Not close at all	1	4
No mother/father	2	10

Role models

All respondents were shown a list of various types of people and asked: "Thinking now about the adults you knew when you were growing up, were there any from this list that you particularly respected or looked up to?" From the same list, they were also asked to select those 'who set a particularly good example of the sort of adult they wanted to be.' More than one person could be named in response to both questions.

Over three quarters said that they particularly respected their mother and an only slightly smaller proportion named their father. Half particularly respected a grandmother and slightly fewer than this, a grandfather. Almost half particularly respected a teacher. When asked to select the adult who provided a good example of how they wanted to be, fewer selected each type of adult, though again mothers were mentioned most often, followed by fathers, and with grandparents and teachers also being mentioned more than other categories of adults. Over one in ten said that no adults that they knew provided them with a particularly good example of what they wanted to be like.

Table 4 Role models

	Respected	Example
Unweighted base	2,869	2,869
Weighted base	2,869	2,869
	%	%
Mother	78	51
Father	71	45
Grandmother	52	14
Grandfather	47	15
Teacher	46	17
Older brother/sister	33	9
Aunt	30	9
Uncle	30	11
Neighbour	15	3
Youth leader	12	5
Priest	8	2
Doctor	5	2
None	2	11

Advice and support

Respondents were asked to select the adults who helped them especially with advice when they needed it and who gave them a helping hand when they were in trouble or things were going wrong. Mothers were considerably more likely (69%) to have provided advice and help than fathers (40%). Next most frequently turned to was a teacher (21%) or older brother and sister (18%).

Openness about sex

Respondents were asked about young people obtaining help and advice about sex. The question was introduced as follows:

"In the past many people found it too embarrassing to talk about sex to young people. This sometimes made it difficult for young people to get the help and advice they needed with relationships or if someone was putting pressure on them to have sex. How easy did you find it to talk to your parents about sex?"

Table 5 shows that slightly over a third of respondents (35%) had found it quite difficult or very difficult to talk to their parents about sex. Young women were more likely to have found it easy to talk to parents than were young men.

Table 5 How easy did you find it to talk to your parents about sex?

Base: All respondents

		Male	Female	Total
Unweighted base	2,869			
Weighted base	2,869			
		%	%	%
Very easy		12	16	14
Quite easy		22	26	24
Neither easy nor difficult		25	20	23
Quite difficult		19	19	19
Very difficult		16	16	16
Don't know		4	1	3
Do not wish to answer		2	2	1

Freedom and responsibility

All respondents were asked how much freedom they were allowed in their childhood in terms of expressing their views and having them taken into account, of being allowed to think and believe what they wanted, and of being allowed to meet and mix with other people. These are rights included in the United Nations' Convention on the Rights of the Child.

Over half said that they had complete freedom in thinking and believing what they wanted on matters such as politics and religion, and in total, around eight in ten had quite a lot of freedom on these sorts of issues. While fewer had complete freedom to meet and mix with other people, in total almost nine in ten had quite a lot of freedom to do this. A quarter had complete freedom to express their views and to have these taken into account, and almost half had quite a lot of freedom in this respect. However, just under one in ten said they had either very little or no freedom to express their views.

Table 6 Amount of freedom

Base: All respondents

		Complete freedom	Quite a lot of freedom	A little freedom	Very little freedom	No freedom
Unweighted base		2,869				
Weighted base		2,869				
Thinking/believing what you wanted to e.g. politics/religion	%	53	30	9	4	1
Meeting/mixing with other people	%	39	48	10	3	★
Having your views considered	%	25	48	19	5	2

There was little difference between responses given by young men and young women to these questions with the exception of men being more likely to claim complete freedom to meet and mix with other people (45% of men compared with 33% of women).

A little later in the interview, after young people had been asked about any responsibilities they had to take on during their childhood (see Table 7 below), they were asked whether they felt the amount of independence and responsibility they had was appropriately balanced. Almost three quarters (74%) said that the amount of independence and responsibility they had experienced was about right. One in ten said they had too much (3% far too much) and a slightly greater proportion (13%) said they had too little (2% far too little).

Table 7 Amount of responsibility/independence

Base: All respondents

Unweighted base	2,869
Weighted base	2,869
	%
About right	74
Far too much	3
A bit too much	6
Far too little	2
Not quite enough	11
Don't know/not answered	4

The types of responsibilities that some children had to take on, together with the proportions of those affected, are shown below. In total 14% said that they regularly had some form of adult responsibilities in their childhood. Although there were some gender differences, the marked differences are in social grade, with respondents in C2 and DE grades at least twice as likely to have had these responsibilities than those in AB grades. With a sample of 18 –24 year olds, this is likely to reflect the respondents' reduced educational opportunities due to carer responsibilities (Dearden and Becker, 2000).

Table 8 Experience of adult responsibilities in childhood

Base: All respondents

| | TOTAL | SEX | | SOCIAL GRADE | | | |
		Male	Female	AB	C1	C2	DE
Unweighted base	2,869	1,235	1,634	435	944	627	847
Weighted base	2,869	1,434	1,435	416	1101	594	744
	%	%	%	%	%	%	%
Regularly had to care for someone in your family who was ill or disabled	4	4	3	2	2	5	5
Often had to look after self as parents had problems of their own e.g. alcohol, drugs etc	3	2	4	1	3	3	5
Parents regularly depended on you for support for emotional problems e.g. divorce, separation, bereavement	8	6	10	5	8	9	10
Regularly had to look after self because parents went away	2	2	2	★	2	1	3
None of the above	82	82	82	91	85	81	74

The vast majority considered that they were well cared for as a child. Over eight in ten described themselves as 'very well cared for' (84%) with a further one in ten (11%) saying that they were at least 'reasonably well cared for'.

Experience of verbal and physical treatment/discipline

Respondents were asked whether they themselves had experienced various forms of behaviour either in their family, at school or anywhere else. Inevitably their responses will be affected by their memory, particularly of events in early childhood, and this may lead to an underestimate of experiences when memory is incomplete. This is particularly likely to affect frequency of reporting physical punishment as studies of parental behaviour consistently show that the peak ages for physical punishment are between four and seven years (Creighton and Russell, 1995). **All the following figures in this report should therefore be read in the context that they are more likely to be underestimates than overestimates.**

Respondents were not asked specifically whether their experiences of the various forms of verbal or physical behaviour were 'punishment', because we did not wish to make assumptions about the cause of the behaviour or that it would only happen in response to actual or perceived wrongdoing by the child. This might have led to experiences of verbal or physical violence being omitted if they were not disciplinary. Instead respondents were asked if they had ever had specific experiences, although it is probable that most of these occurred in a disciplinary context. The report refers to 'treatment', to 'treatment/discipline', or to 'behaviours' throughout. The figures given in this chapter refer to the forms of discipline known from previous research to be the most usual, and most socially acceptable for adults to use towards children (Creighton and Russell, 1995). More severe physical behaviour using implements or causing injury was categorised separately as 'violence' and is presented later in this report. Behaviours listed are taken from the Conflict Tactics Scale (Straus,1979).

Almost nine in ten said that they had it explained to them why they were wrong; three quarters had been grounded or had their privileges stopped at some point, and over seven in ten had been sent to their room. Just three in ten reported being distracted from what they were doing that was wrong, and it seems probable that this too may be affected by memory as this tactic is likely to be used with very young children.

Table 9 Experience of various ways of treating children

Base: All respondents

Unweighted base	2,869
Weighted base	2,869
	%
It was explained to me why I was wrong	87
Grounded/stopped from going out/privileges stopped	74
Sent to room	72
Given something to distract me from what doing wrong	30

Three quarters said that they had been shouted or screamed at, at some point. Two thirds had been threatened with smacking, if not actually smacked. Four in ten had been called stupid, lazy or a similar name and over a quarter reported having been sworn at. Around a fifth in each case had been threatened with being thrown out or sent away, or made to feel embarrassed or humiliated. In total, almost nine in ten had at least one of the experiences listed in table 10.

Table 10 Experience of verbal treatment/discipline

Base: All respondents

Unweighted base	2,869
Weighted base	2,869
	%
Shouted at/screamed at	75
Threatened with smacking, not actually smacked	66
Called stupid/lazy/similar name	42
Sworn at	28
Threatened with being sent away/thrown out	22
Made to feel embarrassed/humiliated	19
Any verbal treatment	87

Young men were more likely to say that they had been shouted at, sworn at, called stupid or lazy, or threatened with smacking (on average 7% more men than women reported each of these treatments).

Over three quarters of these experiences had occurred at home. Just under a fifth had been treated this way at school and fewer than one in ten at a friend's or relative's house or in a public place. Almost two thirds (64%) had been shouted at, sworn at, called names or been embarrassed or verbally threatened by their mothers, whilst over half (52%) had experienced this form of behaviour from their fathers. Some (17%) had experienced it from their teachers and less than one in ten in each case from a brother, sister or grandparent or from any other young person. In most cases, these types of verbal treatment had been experienced irregularly or on and off over time. However, one in seven said that they had experienced them regularly, either over a certain period or for years.

Just under three in ten (28%) said that they had no experience of physical discipline, while more than seven in ten had (72%) experienced it in some form. In the majority of cases (59% of the whole sample, 84% of those physically disciplined), this had been in the form of a slap on the leg, arm or hand with a bare hand. Half of all 18-24 year olds had received a smack on the bottom at some point in their childhood, this constituting 72% of those physically disciplined. A fifth of the whole sample had been slapped on the face, head or ears and just under one in ten had been pinched.

Table 11 Experience of physical treatment/discipline

Unweighted base	2,869
Weighted base	2,869
	%
Slapped on leg, arm or hand with a bare hand	59
Smacked on bottom with bare hand	51
Slapped on face, head or ears	21
Pinched	9
Any physical treatment/discipline	72

Looking in more detail at the young people who had experienced physical treatment/discipline, most (95%) said that they had received this at home. Relatively few had been treated in this way in a public place (11%), at a friend's or relative's house (9%), or at school (8%). Over three quarters of these young people (79%), had received the physical treatment/discipline from their mother, with 58% receiving it from their father. In most cases, this sort of treatment had been administered either infrequently (65% of those physically disciplined) or irregularly: one in five experienced it 'on and off over time'. However, 10% had experienced it 'regularly over the years' and a further 4% 'regularly for a period', giving a figure of 10% of the whole sample for whom physical treatment/discipline had been a routine treatment for at least part of their childhood, usually involving both parents. The pattern of physical treatment/discipline is similar to that reported by Creighton and Russell (1995). Although they found a higher proportion of their total sample having experienced physical punishment (only 18% had never experienced it compared to 28% of the present sample) they also note that 18 – 24 year olds had experienced less physical punishment than older groups. The present findings support their contention that present day parents are less likely to use physical punishment than in the past.

Summary

- The few studies which have examined family life in general population samples reveal very great differences within the range of 'normal' family life and childrearing patterns.

- The present survey shows that the large majority of young people aged 18-24 grew up in loving homes and described themselves as well cared for. Over nine in ten agreed that they had a 'warm and loving family background'.

- Nine in ten respondents had at some point lived with both birth parents together, and seven in ten spent their whole childhood with both birth parents. One fifth had spent at least part of their childhood in a single parent family and 13% lived at some point in a reconstituted family. At some point 1% had lived with adoptive parents, 1% with foster carers, 1% in residential care, and 4% had attended boarding school.

- More than nine out of ten described themselves as having 'very' or 'fairly' close relationships with their mothers and almost eight in ten with their fathers. Almost all had someone to turn to for help and advice, mothers being most commonly mentioned (69%), followed by fathers (40%) and teachers (21%). Although most named parents and other relatives as people they particularly 'looked up to', they were rather less likely to choose them as role models.

- Between three quarters and 90% described themselves as having complete or quite a lot of freedom to develop their own values and beliefs, to mix in a wider social world and to express their views.

- Most often discipline was based on reasoning, explanation (87%) and non-physical punishment, with almost three quarters also reporting being 'grounded' or sent to their room. Almost three quarters received some physical discipline which was most often described as mild and infrequent, taking the form of a slap on the leg, arm or hand (59%) or the bottom (21%) with a bare hand.

- About a third reported there was 'a lot of stress' in their families and the same proportion reported financial pressures and worries. Almost a fifth had regularly to shoulder responsibilities at an early age because their parents were ill, disabled, had substance abuse problems or had needed emotional support through divorce or bereavement.

3. ACCEPTABLE AND UNACCEPTABLE WAYS OF TREATING CHILDREN

Attitudes are important to understand when measuring the prevalence of abuse since there may be a relationship between attitudes, perceptions, self reporting and experience of abuse. Previous studies have found that many people do not perceive childhood experiences such as 'being whipped or beaten to the point of laceration' (Steele, 1987) as abuse, because there is a tendency to believe that the discipline they experienced was normal and deserved (Bower and Knutson, 1996). Such a mediating factor would have an effect on levels of self reported physical abuse although it should not affect responses to descriptive questions such as 'has anyone ever hit you with an object?' This is reflected in discrepancies detected in studies where respondents are requested to reply to a range of selected behaviours such as those contained in the Conflict Tactics Scale and subsequently asked whether they rate themselves as abused. For example, a study of over 4,500 university students found that whilst 9% of the whole sample could be 'conservatively' classified as physically abused, only 2% self assessed themselves as abused (Berger et al., 1988). Experience of physical abuse has also been found to impact on attitudes towards the appropriateness of physical punishment. People reporting histories of physical abuse who rate their own experiences as deserved or normal rate physical punishment as more appropriate than those who have not been abused (Kelder et al., 1991) and a direct relationship has been established between childhood experience and disciplinary attitudes (Bower and Knutson, 1996).

Creighton and Russell (1995) found that people who had experienced constant or frequent physical punishment in childhood were more likely as adults to think that corporal punishment should be made illegal. However, they were also slightly more likely to administer physical punishment to their own children. A recent study which focused on children's views of smacking found that children themselves viewed smacking as negative and said they would not smack when they became adults (Willow and Hyder, 1998). Ghate and Daniels (1997) in a national sample of children aged 8 - 15 found that only 14% of 12 - 15 year olds thought that smacking was acceptable discipline for a child of their age, and only 11% of all ages thought it would make them behave better in future, though girls were markedly more likely to oppose smacking than were boys. The relationship between attitudes and assessment of abuse is further complicated by degrees of physical punishment, in that children may be more likely to accept blame and feel they deserve mild punishment but not severe mistreatment (Ney et al., 1986). Long term effects also impact on perception. One study suggested that out of a sample of 'objectively' defined physically abused women, those suffering from depression were more likely to subjectively define themselves as abused (Carlin et al., 1994).

Attitudes towards ways of disciplining a child

In the present study, all respondents were asked to consider possible ways of 'disciplining' a child, separating those they thought were 'often justified', those 'occasionally justified' and those that could never be justified. Results are shown in the table below. Almost everyone agreed that discussion of the breach of discipline and persuasion by argument was often justified. The imposition of additional chores, the withdrawal of privileges and grounding were also considered often justified by around a half, with the vast majority saying that these measures were at least occasionally justified.

Few considered all the other ways of treating children as often justified, although opinion was divided on whether or not it was occasionally or never justified to warn about fear figures, slap with an open hand, or isolate a child by sending them to their room or getting them to stand in a corner. A considerable majority felt it was never justified to use silence and not speak to a child, to verbally threaten them with a beating which was not acted upon, or to make them miss a meal or part of a meal. Embarrassing or humiliating a child, slapping with an implement or hitting with a closed fist were considered even less acceptable.

Table 12 Views of ways of treating children

Base: All respondents

			JUSTIFIED	
		Often	Occasionally	Never
Unweighted base		2,869		
Weighted base		2,869		
		%	%	%
Discussion of breach of discipline	%	87	11	1
Imposing additional chores/tasks	%	55	40	5
Withdrawal of privileges	%	53	43	4
Grounding	%	52	43	4
Warning about fear figures e.g. bogey man	%	14	41	44
Slapping with an open hand	%	10	52	37
Isolation (sending/locking child in room/standing in corner)	%	9	41	50
Silence (not speaking to child)	%	6	32	61
Verbal threats of beating or similar (not acted upon)	%	5	27	67
Making the child miss a meal/part of a meal	%	4	26	70
Embarrassing/ humiliating a child	%	3	20	77
Slapping with soft implement e.g. belt	%	2	10	88
Slapping with hard implement e.g. stick	%	1	3	95
Hitting with a closed fist	%	1	2	96

Attitudes towards care and supervision of a child

Respondents were asked some attitudinal questions concerning the care and supervision of children, ascertaining their level of agreement or disagreement with a series of statements. Two thirds of respondents agreed that 'it is easy to give a child a healthy diet even on a low income', with more women (42%) than men (29%) strongly agreeing with this statement. There was no clear socio-economic trend in responses.

A second statement, that 'a home can be happy for children even if it is not clean' met with less consensus, with only 17% strongly agreeing and 30% slightly agreeing. There were no consistent gender or socio-economic differences.

More than three quarters of the sample (77%) agreed that 'if children say they are ill they should always be taken seriously' and women were again more likely to strongly agree (46%) than men (38%) with a marked trend for lower social grades to strongly agree.

Half of all respondents (51%) disagreed with the statement that 'children don't have as much freedom these days' with no consistent gender differences, but there was a marked trend for lower socio-economic groups to be more likely to think that children's freedom was now more restricted.

Attitudes towards sexual relationships

Assessment of whether sexual abuse has occurred is dependent on beliefs about the acceptability of sexual relationships involving children and young people. It was shown earlier that there are cultural differences over this issue which are reflected in different ages of consent and expectations concerning sexual behaviour. There are many areas of dissent and debate in the UK, for example over the different ages of consent for homosexual and heterosexual acts, the provision of sex education and contraceptive advice for under 16s, and whether sexual relationships between young people and professionals working with them should ever be permitted. Views on these and other related issues would be expected to be linked to respondents' understanding of the acceptability of sexual behaviour towards them.

Views on the 'age of consent'

Respondents were asked their views on the age of consent for sexual intercourse. Initially they were asked about intercourse between a male and female. Almost three quarters of the sample (73%) thought that the present age of 16 was right, with just over a fifth wanting it higher (age 18 most commonly chosen by this group) and only 3% wanting it lowered. Only 1% thought that 'there shouldn't be any law' on age of consent. More women than men wanted the age raised, and almost all who wanted the age lowered were men.

Responses to the question were more varied when considering the age of consent for sexual intercourse between two people of the same sex. Respondents were given a choice to specify the exact age, to say that it should be 'the same as for heterosexuals', 'there shouldn't be any law' or to say that it 'shouldn't be allowed'. Just over a third of respondents (34%) thought that the age should be 18, while 36% thought 16 was right and 9% wanted age 21. Only 1% thought it should be lower than 16 and less than 1% that 'there shouldn't be any law'. A small group specified that the age should be 'the same as for heterosexuals' (4%) and 6% said that same sex intercourse 'shouldn't be allowed'.

Finally, respondents were asked for their views on the age of consent for sexual relationships between young people and an older person who has responsibility for them, such as a teacher or social worker: should the age be the same as, higher or lower than ages for other couples or should such relationships be prohibited altogether. This fieldwork was carried out at a time when some high profile cases of relationships between teachers and pupils had attracted national publicity, and results showed considerable differences of opinion. Just over half of the sample (51%) thought that for heterosexual couples ages of consent should be the same as for other couples, and 36% thought the age should be higher when one of the couple was in a position of responsibility. For same sex couples, 43% of respondents thought the age of consent should be the same, and 41% thought it should be higher. Only 8% thought the relationship 'shouldn't be allowed' between heterosexual couples if one was in a position of responsibility for the other, and a slightly higher proportion (12%) thought this for same sex couples.

In order to obtain an indication of general attitudes towards sexual relationships one question asked respondents about sexual activities which they considered acceptable between children and young people aged under 16 and adults of 18 years or older. The results showed an overwhelming consensus that adult sexual activity at any level with children of 12 or under was unacceptable and that oral or penetrative sex between adults and 13-15 year olds was unacceptable. Results on other levels of sexual activity between adults and 13-15 year olds were more mixed.

Table 13 Acceptability of sexual activity between adults
over 18 and children/young people

Base: All respondents

	With children 12 or under			With young people aged 13 -15 years		
Unweighted base	2,869					
Weighted base	2,869					
	%	%	%	%	%	%
	Male	Fem	All	Male	Fem	All
Nothing acceptable	90	90	90	46	39	43
Kissing and cuddling	5	6	5	35	46	40
Touching and fondling under the clothes	★	1	1	6	5	5
Full intercourse or oral sex	1	★	★	3	1	2
Don't know	2	2	2	7	7	7
Do not wish to answer	2	1	1	2	2	2
No answer	★	★	★	★	★	★

When respondents were asked the same question concerning sexual activity between age peers, 80% considered either that kissing and cuddling or fondling were acceptable between 13 - 15 year olds but only 5% said that intercourse or oral sex were acceptable at this age. Almost six out of ten (56%) said that any level of sexual activity between children aged 12 or under was unacceptable, but women were more likely to say this (64%) than were men (47%). Over a third (38%) considered that kissing and cuddling were acceptable for age 12 or under, but only 14 respondents (less than 1%) thought that intercourse or oral sex could be acceptable at this age.

Summary

- There is a complex relationship between attitudes to the treatment of children and experience of abuse, which may affect willingness to tolerate abuse or to report it, and may influence the likelihood of punitive or abusive behaviour towards children. Research has shown that people experiencing serious assault often do not rate their treatment as abusive because they have learned to regard it as normal or deserved.

- Respondents were asked about their attitudes to the treatment of children in a number of areas relevant to child abuse and neglect. Most of them considered that discipline should be primarily handled by verbal discussion and non-physical means such as imposing additional chores, withdrawal of privileges and grounding.

- More than six out of ten thought it never justified to refuse to speak to a child, or to threaten beatings. More than seven out of ten said it was never justified to make a child miss a meal, embarrass or humiliate a child.

- Just over half of the sample (52%) thought a slap with an open hand was sometimes justified, but only 10% thought this often justified. Using implements to hit a child or hitting with a closed fist was unacceptable to almost the whole sample (88 – 95%).

- Two thirds of respondents felt that children could be given a healthy diet, even on a low income, and 77% that children should always be taken seriously when they said they were ill. Views were more mixed on the importance of a clean home and on whether children's freedom was now more restricted than it had been in the past.

- Respondents showed a conservative approach to sexual freedom for young people under 16. Almost three quarters (73%) supported the current law on the ages of consent for heterosexuals, though there was considerable sympathy for lowering the age for homosexual couples to 16. Just over a fifth would like to see the heterosexual age of consent raised and there is almost no support for the age of consent to be lowered below 16 in any circumstances.

- While only 8% wanted to prohibit heterosexual relations between young people and professionals with responsibility for them, 36% felt that the age of consent for these relationships should be higher than for other couples. For same sex couples, 12% thought relationships between young people and professionals should be prohibited, and 41% that the age of consent should be higher than for other same sex couples.

- When asked about sexual relations between young people under 16 and adults over 18. nine out of ten thought that no sexual activity was acceptable for children under 12 with over 18s.

- Responses were more mixed concerning those aged 13-15, but more than four out of ten thought that nothing was acceptable and most of the remainder considered only kissing and cuddling acceptable. Only 2% considered that intercourse or oral sex were acceptable between 13-15 year olds and adults.

- Results show that respondents shared in a a broad consensus on the acceptability of specific treatment of children. The similarity of the results to those found in previous research indicates a social consensus which is a reliable and stable feature of values about the treatment of children, and which provides a foundation for the judgement of child maltreatment in the UK.

4. BULLYING AND DISCRIMINATION

Bullying and discrimination both from other children and adults other than parents and carers have some overlap with abuse, but were covered separately because the terms bullying and discrimination have a particular social context within which behaviour can be assigned. These terms might convey a different meaning to respondents from that of child abuse, although the actual behaviour might be identical to behaviour which in a different context would be called child abuse. The term 'bullying' in particular may be used to play down the significance of aggressive behaviour between young people, treating it as less serious than the same acts carried out by an adult.

Bullying is generally defined in terms of three components: it must occur over time, rather than being a single aggressive act, it involves an imbalance of power, the powerful attack the powerless, and it can be psychological, verbal or physical in nature (Besag, 1993). Children and young people include these elements in their own descriptions of bullying behaviour (Arora and Thompson, 1987). Rates vary according to definitions of frequency and severity. For example, in one study 27% of junior/middle school pupils reported having been bullied at sometime and 10% claimed to have been bullied once a week or more (Smith and Sharp, 1994). Children of all ages are subject to bullying, although there is an indication that younger children experience higher rates (Central Statistical Office, 1994; Creighton and Russell, 1995; Balding, 1998). Ghate and Daniels (1997) showed that more than half of a national sample of 998 children aged 8 -15 years 'sometimes' or 'often' worried about being bullied at school and that younger children worried most. Balding (1998) in a survey of 37,538 pupils aged 9 - 16 showed that a third of girls and approximately a quarter of boys said that they had sometimes felt afraid to go to school because of bullying.

The semantic issues surrounding definitions of bullying are complex, and the term could encompass a range of physical, verbal and other behaviour, some of which might be defined or labelled differently in different contexts. For this reason the questionnaire used three different concepts of bullying, discrimination and exclusion which were likely to cover a wide range of behaviours which could collectively be considered as aggressive.

Bullying and discrimination by other children

Respondents were asked:

"Thinking now about your relationships with other children, either at home, school or elsewhere, were you ever bullied, discriminated against or made to feel different, like an outsider?"

Table 14 Experience of bullying and discrimination by other children

Base: All respondents

	TOTAL	SEX		SOCIAL GRADE			
		Male	Female	AB	C1	C2	DE
Unweighted base	2,869	1,235	1,634	435	944	627	847
Weighted base	2,869	1,434	1,435	416	1101	594	744
	%	%	%	%	%	%	%
Bullied	31	33	30	36	32	29	30
Discriminated against	7	10	4	9	7	8	6
Made to feel different/ an outsider	14	15	13	20	14	10	14
None of these things	54	52	56	50	54	59	54
Don't know/not stated	3	5	2	1	3	3	4

In total, 43% reported having experienced at least one of these things. Three in ten said they had been bullied, one in seven had been made to feel different like an outsider, and over one in twenty reported that they had experienced discrimination. In the vast majority of cases (94%) this had taken place at school. There was relatively little gender or socio-economic difference except that respondents from social group AB (most of whom would be young graduate professionals) were slightly more likely to say that they had been bullied and 'made to feel different'. White respondents were more likely to say that thay had been bullied (32%) than were other ethnic groups (25%), but non white respondents were more likely to say they had been discriminated against (23% compared to 6%) or made to feel an outsider (19% compared to 14%) by other children.

When asked to say why they believed this had happened, a quarter of those bullied said it was due to their size, and just over a fifth said it was 'class' related (money, how they spoke or how they dressed, for example). Just under a fifth said it was intelligence related and one in ten said it was because they had a particular hobby or interest. Race was identified as the reason by 8% of the whole sample but by more than two thirds (68%) of the respondents from minority ethnic groups compared to 3% of white respondents. A small number of respondents cited reasons specific to their family situation such as 'parent's behaviour', or 'parent's occupation', or attributed it to the bully's problems ('jealousy' 'bully insecure'). Just over a fifth were unable to give any explanation at all. There is evidence of gender differences.

Most commonly, respondents reported that they had been subjected to name calling, insults and verbal abuse: almost nine in ten of those who said that they had been bullied or discriminated against said that this was what they had experienced, which is the equivalent of over a third (37%) of the total sample. Around four in ten (19% of all young people) said that they had been deliberately embarrassed and humiliated by other children.

Table 15 Why they think bullying and discrimination by children occurred -
reasons most commonly given

Base: All experiencing bullying/discrimination by children

	Male	Female	Total
Unweighted base	530	669	1,199
Weighted base	632	592	1,225
	%	%	%
Size	29	23	26
"Class"	20	22	21
Intelligence	23	15	19
Interests/hobbies	14	6	10
Race	9	7	8
The place you lived	7	7	7
Appearance	4	6	5
Disability	4	2	3
Sexuality	3	1	2
Don't know/not stated	19	23	22

Around a third had been lied about and the same proportion subjected to physical bullying (14% – 15% of all respondents). Three in ten had been ignored (12% of all young people) and just under a quarter had been threatened with violence (10%). Male respondents had more often been physically bullied and threatened, or had property stolen or damaged, while females were more likely to have experienced being 'ignored/not spoken to'.

Table 16 The form bullying and discrimination by children took

Base: All experiencing bullying/discrimination by children

	Total
Unweighted base	1,199
Weighted base	1,225
	%
Name calling/insults/verbal abuse	87
Embarrassing/humiliating you deliberately	44
Telling lies/spreading rumours about you	35
Physical bullying/pinching, punching, hitting etc	33
Ignoring you/not speaking to you	29
Threatening violence but not actually attacking you	23
Damaging your things	20
Didn't treat you fairly	19
Getting you into trouble with parents/teachers/older children	12
Stealing/demanding things from you e.g. money/sweets	11
Don't know/not stated	2

A fifth of those who had experienced bullying and discrimination (8% of all respondents) had experienced it regularly over the years. Around a fifth of those who had been bullied or discriminated against said that they had not been affected by this. Half had been affected at the time but had since got over it. However, a quarter (equivalent to around one in ten of all respondents – 10%) said that they had experienced long term effects.

Table 17 How often bullying by other children occurred

Base: All experiencing bullying/discrimination by children

	Total
Unweighted base	1,199
Weighted base	1,225
	%
Regularly over years	20
Regularly for a certain period	34
On and off over time	30
Not regularly	18
Don't know/not stated	1

(Note: multicoding allowed)

Bullying and discrimination by adults

A similar series of questions was asked about experience of bullying and discrimination by adults other than parents/carers. This was much rarer than bullying by children, but one in ten reported having experienced this, with fairly similar numbers reporting each of bullying, discrimination and being made to feel like an outsider. In seven in ten cases (71%) this had taken place at school. In one in six cases (15%) it had taken place at a friend's or neighbour's house, or at a youth club or somewhere similar (13%). There is no evident gender or socio-economic pattern.

Table 18 Experience of bullying and discrimination by adults other than parents/carers

Base: All respondents

	TOTAL	SEX		SOCIAL GRADE			
		Male	Female	AB	C1	C2	DE
Unweighted base	2,869	1,234	1,635	435	943	627	848
Weighted base	2,869	1,434	1,435	439	969	633	813
	%	%	%	%	%	%	%
Bullied	3	3	3	2	2	3	5
Discriminated against	3	4	2	4	3	3	3
Made to feel different	5	5	5	5	5	3	7
None of these things	85	84	87	87	87	86	81
Don't know/not stated	5	7	4	4	4	6	7

When asked why they believed this had happened, almost a quarter said it was class related and a fifth said it was due to their intelligence. Around one in seven said it was due to their size. Just under a quarter were unable to give any explanation at all.

Table 19 Why they think bullying and discrimination by adults occurred

Base: All experiencing bullying/discrimination by adults

	Total
Unweighted base	253
Weighted base	274
	%
"Class"	23
Intelligence	20
Size	15
Race	10
The place you lived	10
Dislike of family	7
Behaviour	6
Interests/hobbies	5
Gender	4
Religion	4
Don't know/not stated	24

Most frequently, respondents reported that they had been deliberately embarrassed or humiliated; half of those who said that they had been bullied or discriminated against by adults. Around four in ten in each case said that they had been unfairly treated or verbally insulted. Around a quarter had been ignored or not spoken to.

Just under a fifth (17%) of those who had experienced bullying and discrimination by adults had experienced it regularly over the years, a quarter experienced it regularly for a certain period, and a third on and off over time. Just under a quarter (23%) said that they had not been affected by this. Over a third (36%) had been affected at the time but had since got over it. However, a third (equivalent to 3% of all respondents) said that they had experienced long term effects.

Table 20 The form bullying and discrimination by adults took

Base: All experiencing bullying/discrimination by adults

	Total
Unweighted base	253
Weighted base	274
	%
Embarrassing/humiliating you deliberately	51
Didn't treat you fairly	39
Name calling/insults/verbal abuse	28
Ignoring you/not speaking to you	25
Physical bullying/pinching, punching, hitting etc	16
Telling lies/spreading rumours about you	15
Getting you into trouble with parents/teachers/older children	11
Threatening violence but not actually attacking you	10
Damaging your things	5

Just over a fifth (22%) of those who had been bullied or discriminated against by adults said that they believed that this constituted child abuse – this amounts to 2% of all respondents claiming that they had been abused in this way.

Summary

- Bullying by other children and young people was a feature of the childhood experience of almost a third of the sample. Respondents also reported experiencing discrimination and being made to feel 'like an outsider' by other young people. One or other of these circumstances were identified by more than four out of ten respondents.

- 14%–15% had been physically bullied and large minorities had experienced threats of violence, having their belongings damaged or money or property taken from them. The most usual reason given was 'size' (height or weight) closely followed by 'class' and 'intelligence'. A fifth of those who had experienced bullying and discrimination said that it had occurred 'regularly over the years'.

- One in ten reported bullying and discrimination by adults, with no gender or social trends. This most commonly took the form of deliberate attempts to humiliate or unfair treatment. Just under a fifth of those bullied by adults had experienced it regularly over the years.

- The results confirm previous studies suggesting that bullying and discrimination by young people, especially at school, is one of the most common forms of harmful aggression experienced by children and young people in the UK. The issues about which respondents were bullied – their size, intelligence, social background and race – were aspects over which they had no control.

- A quarter of those bullied by other young people (one in ten of all respondents) reported that they had suffered long term harmful effects from being bullied.

5. PHYSICAL ABUSE

Attempts have been made to measure the prevalence and incidence of physical abuse in over twenty countries. The results of some of these studies are summarised in table form in Appendix 2. As with all other areas of child maltreatment studies have a range of findings depending on the definition of physical abuse adopted and the methods used to obtain the information.

In most prevalence studies physical abuse is measured by the Conflict Tactics Scale (Straus, 1979). The scale was developed on the basis of conflict theory which proposes that all human relationship will contain conflict. This conflict can be resolved in many ways ranging from discussion to murder. The Conflict Tactics Scale rates maltreatment items as violent acts that have a high probability of causing injury. These items include kicking, biting, punching, hitting (or trying to hit) with an implement, beating up, threatening with a knife or gun or using a knife or gun. This scale was used in the US National Family Violence Survey to interview over 4,000 randomly selected parents by telephone in 1985. The results suggested that 107 out of every 1,000 children in the US experienced severe violence from their parents. The estimated prevalence rate for very severe violence, what Gelles and Straus (1987) refer to as physical abuse, was 19 per 1,000. Whilst very severe violence was found to be unrelated to age, severe violence was greater between the ages of 3-10. There was no variation according to the gender of the child but significant differences were found in relation to socio-economic status with families earning less than $20,000 per year having the highest rates of severe violence.

There have been no national random probability studies conducted on the prevalence of physical punishment and abuse in the UK. Research on community samples in this country find high levels of corporal punishment and a general acceptability of 'mild' physical punishment such as slapping with an open hand (Creighton and Russell, 1995). Studies by Newson and Newson (1989) and Smith et al. (1995) both show that approximately 9 out of every 10 children are smacked. In the latter study it was found that most children receive mild punishment but that 15% had experiences which could be categorised as severe (Department of Health, 1995).

Physical abuse and neglect comprise the largest categories of reported abuse in all countries where monitoring statistics are collected. For example, in the US in 1995, 53% of reported cases involved neglect and 26% referred to physical abuse (Daro, 1996). In the UK in 1999, 42% of children on the child protection registers were registered for neglect and 31% for physical injury, compared to 19% for sexual abuse and 16% for emotional abuse (Department of Health, 1999).

The physical abuse of adolescents

Whilst we know that younger children may be more vulnerable to physical abuse (Creighton and Noyes, 1989) and that rates for corporal punishment drop as children get older (Smith et al., 1995) growing attention is being paid to the physical abuse of adolescents. In the US it is estimated that 650,000 cases of adolescent abuse could be projected annually and that adolescents account for over 40% of known cases of maltreatment (Schellenbach and Guerney, 1987), which often concerns physical violence between parents and young people. Rees and Stein (1999) note the absence of reliable figures on the prevalence of the abuse of adolescents in the UK, in spite of the evidence from reported cases and studies of runaways that adolescents are very commonly victims of physical abuse in their families. A further type of violence experienced by adolescents concerns physical aggression in courtship. Experiences of abuse as a victim in the dating relationships of adolescents show overall prevalence rates of 59% (Jezl et al., 1996). Analyses by gender show that being a victim of physical abuse within courtship is more prevalent amongst males than females (Arias et al., 1987; Jezl et al., 1996).

Physical punishment and physical violence

Although all physical punishment involves the use of physical force, whether it is defined as 'violence' in the context of the criminal law or of public opinion is culturally determined. It was shown earlier, for example, that cultural definitions of what is reasonable chastisement of children vary considerably, in different countries, generations and local contexts. Nevertheless in the UK there is now sufficient evidence of public and professional consensus on the acceptability of some behaviour towards children to form a good basis for the assessment of when physical chastisement or other use of force becomes abusive. Creighton and Russell (1995) showed that more than 90% of a general population sample aged between 18 and 45 years considered that it was never justified to hit a child with an implement. For hitting with a closed fist the proportion rose to 99%. The data given in Chapter Three of this report shows that the present sample of young adults also endorse these views. Creighton and Russell, reviewing the literature on physical punishment, show that although its use is accepted by the majority of the population, what they consider acceptable is occasional slaps with an open hand, and that even this decreases markedly after children reach the age of seven years and becomes rare in adolescence. Yet studies also show that, for a variety of reasons, some parents and other adults do use more severe violence to children, perhaps even while disapproving of it. (Creighton and Russell, 1995; Smith et al., 1995).

In the present study it was necessary to identify the points at which the use of physical force towards children reached a level which could be considered abusive. The questions used to ascertain when respondents had experienced potentially abusive physical force used concepts from the Conflict Tactics Scale (Straus, 1979) combined with an assessment based on the UK research of when treatment was unacceptable to the majority population. Initially respondents were asked about their experience of specific behaviour towards them, and those who had experienced these were followed up with more detailed questions.

The question was introduced in the following way:

"Thinking of the ways you personally were treated as a child, did you ever experience any of the following ways of being treated, in your family, at school or anywhere else?"

Included in the list were:

- Hit on the bottom with a hard implement e.g. stick

- Hit on another part of the body with a hard implement e.g. stick

- Hit with a fist or kicked hard

- Shaken

- Thrown or knocked down

- Beaten up, being hit over and over again

- Grabbed around the neck and choked

- Burned or scalded on purpose

- Threatened with a knife or gun

All those who indicated that they had ever experienced any of these were asked where these things had occurred, who had done them, when they had first experienced this, when it had stopped, how regularly they had been treated like this, and what the physical and emotional effects had been. The table below shows the numbers of respondents who said that they had ever experienced any of these more violent forms of behaviour towards them, at any time, from anyone.

With the exception of shaking, which is usually only dangerous if it is experienced by a child under the age of two, one in ten or fewer said that they had experienced any individual form of treatment. In total, however, a quarter of the whole sample had experienced at least one of them. Young men were only a little more likely than young women to have had these experiences, mostly accounted for by their greater experience of being shaken. However, those now in Social Grade C2 (skilled manual) and especially DE (semi and unskilled manual) were notably more likely to have experienced them.

In most cases, those reporting violence said that they had been treated like this at home (78% of those respondents who had experienced violence) but 15% of them said they had experienced this at school and 13% in a public place. The person responsible was most often the mother (49%) or father (40%). Violence was reported from some stepmothers (3%) or stepfathers (5%), grandparents (3%) and other relatives (1%). Age peer violence was also reported, with 10% naming brothers, 3% sisters and 14% other young people as responsible. Very small numbers said that they had experienced violence from professionals, most often a teacher (7%) but 2% of those who experienced violence said that police behaved violently to them. Only one respondent said that he had been treated violently by a care worker. More than a fifth of those experiencing violent treatment said that they had experienced it regularly 'for a certain period' (7%) or 'regularly over the years'(16%). Although a slightly smaller proportion of female respondents experienced violence, young women were more likely to have experienced it regularly: almost six out of ten had done so compared to just under four out of ten male respondents.

Table 21 Experience of 'violent' treatment from anyone

Base: All respondents

| | TOTAL | SEX | | SOCIAL GRADE | | | |
		Male	Female	AB	C1	C2	DE
Unweighted base	2,869	1,235	1,634	435	944	627	847
Weighted base	2,869	1,434	1,435	416	1,101	594	744
	%	%	%	%	%	%	%
Ever experienced							
Hit on bottom with hard implement	6	7	6	6	6	4	10
Hit on another part of the body with a hard implement	6	7	6	2	6	5	10
Shaken	15	17	13	11	13	16	20
Hit with fist/kicked hard	9	9	9	5	8	7	13
Thrown/knocked down	9	9	10	6	7	11	14
Beaten up/hit over and over again	6	6	7	3	5	6	11
Grabbed round the neck and choked	4	4	4	2	4	4	6
Burned or scalded on purpose	1	1	1	–	1	1	★
Threatened with a knife or gun	3	4	2	2	2	4	4
Any of these	25	27	23	21	22	25	30

Respondents who had experienced any physical treatment/discipline, whether those described above or the smacks, slaps and pinches described in Chapter Two, were asked further questions about its severity. Firstly they were asked whether they had suffered effects such as pain, bruising or marks which had lasted till next day or longer. For most of them this had rarely (14%) or never (62%) happened, but for more than one in ten this had happened more often, with 4% saying that it had happened on most occasions and 1% that it happened every time. Although numbers were small at this level of analysis, respondents who experienced this severity of treatment were more likely to be in social grades DE.

Secondly respondents were asked if they had received physical injuries as a result of the treatment. The most common injury mentioned was bruising, but respondents reported a variety of other injuries, including broken bones, head injuries, bites, and burns.

Table 22 Injuries caused by physical or violent treatment

	Total	Male	Female
Unweighted base: 568 respondents reporting injury or lasting effects		259	309
Weighted base: 568 respondents reporting inquiry or lasting effects		292	281
	%	%	%
Injuries received			
Bruising	44	42	47
Head injuries	6	7	4
Broken bones	5	5	4
Bites	3	3	3
Burns	2	2	3
Genital/anal injuries	2	2	2
Internal injuries	1	1	1
Other physical injuries	9	12	6
No physical injuries	40	31	48

Defining physical abuse

The approach taken to define physical abuse for the purposes of the present study has followed that developed by Bifulco and Moran (1998) which grades the forms of abuse and neglect into various levels. These take into account the severity of what happened, whether it was continuous or long term, or a single or occasional happening. The definitions also take into account the concept of 'endangerment' used in the USA National Incidence Studies (NIS-3) to include some high risk behaviours which did not necessarily cause actual harm to the child but carried a high risk of doing so.

The definitions cover both behaviours that would clearly constitute criminal violence, and those where previous research has indicated that almost the whole population (approximately 90% or more) think it an unacceptable way to treat a child, such as the use of implements to hit children, punching, kicking, choking, knocking down and burning or scalding: those actions described above as 'violent treatment'.

Finally, behaviours which are acceptable to most of the population when used occasionally or mildly can be seen as unacceptable when used severely or continuously (Creighton and Russell, 1995). Physical behaviours such as smacking, slapping and pinching were included as abusive or potentially abusive if they were serious enough to cause effects such as pain, soreness or marks lasting at least until next day or longer, or if they were used regularly.

Physical abuse was grouped into three levels, with the first two assessed as definitely abusive, and the third a borderline category of physical treatment serious enough to cause concern about the child's well being. A fourth level of 'mild' physical treatment/discipline such as smacking with an open hand, which caused no lasting effect and did not happen regularly, was excluded from the abuse rating.

Serious physical abuse was where the 'violent' treatment described above either caused injury or carried a high risk of injury if continued over time or throughout childhood.

Intermediate physical abuse was where 'violent' treatment occurred occasionally but caused no injury, or where other physical treatment/discipline was used regularly over the years and/or led to physical effects such as pain, soreness or marks lasting at least until next day.

Cause for concern was where the injury or potential harm was not immediately serious but where less serious physical treatment/discipline occurred regularly and indicated problems in parenting or the quality of care which could escalate or lead to continued distress for a child.

Physical abuse by parents or carers

The remainder of this chapter describes physical abuse by parents or carers. Results suggested that the family was the primary arena for physical abuse. Physical abuse by other people will be analysed in more detail in a later report.

Serious abuse

Included in the definition of 'serious abuse' are all those who:

- Experienced 'violent' treatment at the hands of their parents or carers if this happened regularly over the years

- Or if it happened less often but led to physical effects (such as bruising, marks, soreness and pain) lasting to the next day or longer on more than half the occasions

- Anyone who received physical injuries as a result of treatment of this nature, regardless of how often they experienced it.

- Anyone shaken by their parents if it happened regularly over the years and was so violent that it caused injury, or physical effects lasting to the next day or longer. Because shaking is only likely to be fatal or disabling with very young children, and many of the sample reported it in later childhood or adolescence, a stricter definition was applied than for other 'violent' treatments.

Although a quarter of the sample reported at least one form of 'violent' treatment, when it is taken into account whether or not these treatments were at the hands of parents or carers and the stricter definitions of serious abuse are applied as described above, the proportion in the serious abuse category falls to 7%. Almost half of these (3%) are included as a result of regularly receiving these forms of treatment from their parents, the remainder as a result of having lasting effects on more than half the occasions that they experienced it or as a result of having been physically injured. The 7% defined as having been seriously physically abused comprises 6% of boys and 8% of girls. There was a strong trend associated with respondents' social grade (4% of ABs, 5% of C1s, 7% of C2s, and 12% of DEs) primarily linked with the greater use of 'violent' treatments towards respondents in grades DE. As pointed out earlier, this is likely to reflect their family of origin to a large extent, but may also indicate adverse experience affecting educational achievement and therefore current status.

Table 23 shows how many of those receiving each of these various forms of violent treatment – from anyone at any time – were rated as subject to serious physical abuse from their parents using the above definitions. Approximately half of those experiencing any individual treatment experienced it from their parents either regularly, or causing injury, or having physical effects lasting to the next day or longer. Those who had been deliberately burned or scalded, though few in number, were particularly likely to be assessed as having been seriously physically abused by their parent/carer. Respondents who had been shaken were least likely to be assessed as having been physically abused by parents or carers, in spite of the stricter definition adopted. One in three of the respondents who said they had been shaken, had experienced this treatment from their parents regularly, and had either been injured as a result or had frequently experienced physical effects lasting until next day or longer.

Table 23 Proportion experiencing violent treatment assessed as having been seriously physically abused by parents/carers

Base: All experiencing violent treatment

Treatment experienced from anyone

	Number	% seriously abused by parents/carers
Burned or scalded on purpose	16	70
Beaten up/hit over and over again	186	57
Hit on bottom with a hard implement	184	53
Hit on another part of the body with a hard implement (not bottom)	182	53
Grabbed round the neck and choked	120	53
Hit with fist/kicked hard	253	52
Thrown/knocked down	269	49
Threatened with a knife or gun	89	49
Shaken	434	31
Any of these	706	29

Intermediate physical abuse by parents/carers

Intermediate/intermittent abuse is where the abuse was less serious than those described above but where it occurred regularly or where serious incidents occurred occasionally but caused no serious injury. It therefore includes:

- 'Violent' treatment that occurred irregularly, caused no injury, and led to physical effects on less than half of the occasions

- Physical treatment/discipline which occurred regularly and led to physical effects lasting at least until the next day, on at least half of the occasions, or which led to physical injury.

By this definition a total of 14% of young people were physically abused to an 'intermediate' degree in their childhood: 12% are included in this intermediate category as a result of receiving occasional 'violent' treatment from their parents that did not lead to physical injury or usually to lasting physical effects, and 2% because they had been slapped, smacked or pinched regularly by parents leading to injury or physical effects lasting at least until next day. There was some gender difference with 15% of boys and 12% of girls in this category, but, unlike the serious abuse, there was no social grade trend.

Cause for concern

This has been defined as including:

- Anyone who received physical treatment/discipline from parents regularly over the years, which led to physical effects lasting until next day on some but less than half of the occasions

- Anyone who received physical treatment/discipline which was not administered regularly but resulted in effects which lasted to the next day on more than half of the occasions

Only 3% of respondents came into this category: 2% included because they were regularly slapped, smacked or pinched, sometimes with physical effects lasting till next day, and less than 1% for physical treatment/discipline which was irregular but more severe. There were slightly more boys (4%) than girls (2%) in this group. Rates were also lower for social grades C1 and C2 (2%) than for the others (4%).

Total levels of physical abuse by parents/carers

Taking all three categories together, 21% of respondents were assessed by the criteria described above as having experienced some degree of physical abuse by parents or carers, with 7% to a serious level. A further 3% experienced aspects of childrearing which could give 'cause for concern'. This represents almost a quarter of the child population whose physical treatment in their families, at least sometimes, breached the standards shown by previous research to be accepted by over 90% of the population.

Other physical treatment/discipline

Apart from those included in the three groups above, an additional 39% of respondents said that they had received less serious physical treatment/discipline in their childhood from their parents irregularly or rarely, and which had rarely or never led to effects lasting until the next day. This was excluded from the calculation of abuse or 'cause for concern' as it represented what appears to be the 'normalised' level of discipline most commonly found in homes where physical punishment is used.

Self-assessment of physical abuse

At the end of the section of the interview concerning physical treatment, the 2,120 respondents who described physical treatment/discipline or violent treatment were asked to assess their own treatment. They were asked firstly whether they thought their treatment had been fair and reasonable or strict and harsh, with answers on a five point scale from 'always fair and reasonable' to 'very much too strict and harsh for a child'. Almost eight out of ten (78%) considered their treatment had been reasonable but 17% said their treatment had been too strict and harsh, with half of them (8% of those physically disciplined) saying it had been very much too strict and harsh. Small numbers said that they didn't know (3%) or did not wish to answer (1%). This represents 13% of the whole sample thinking their treatment had been too strict and harsh. Although men were slightly more likely to report physical discipline (52% were men and 48% women), more of the women said they had been harshly treated (13% of men who were physically disciplined compared to 22% of women). Respondents now in social grades DE were very much more likely to say they had been harshly treated: 26% of DE respondents who had been physically disciplined (16% saying 'very much' too strict and harsh), compared to 9% of AB respondents, 16% of C1s and 14% of C2s.

Secondly, respondents were asked: 'Thinking of the physical treatment you received at home, do you now consider any of this treatment serious enough to be called 'child abuse'? Of the 2001 respondents answering this question, 7% (6% of men and 8% of women) said that they thought their treatment at home was abusive: this represents 5% of the total sample. Again there were social grade differences, with the rate for grades DE twice as high, at 14%, than in the sample as a whole, and compared to 1% for those in AB grades, 6% of C1s and 4% of C2s.

At both ends of the continuum there was a substantial overlap between self assessed abuse and the research rating of abuse by parents/carers, with 48% of those rated as seriously abused by the research measure, considering themselves abused, 10% undecided, 37% thinking they were not abused and 6% unwilling to answer. Of the small group rated by research measure as giving 'cause for concern', only 5% said they were abused, and of those rated as receiving non-abusive physical punishment, less than 1% said they were abused. However of those rated by researchers as experiencing intermediate abuse, very few (7%) considered themselves abused, with 87% answering 'no', 6% undecided, and 3% unwilling to answer. This result is interesting as all of the respondents in this group received treatment which, in the attitudinal section of the questionnaire, was rated as 'never justified' by almost the entire sample. A more detailed exploration of this issue, linking assessments to the specific treatment received and other aspects of the relationships with parents, will be carried out in the next phase of the research.

Summary

- The present study adapted measures from the Conflict Tactics Scale (Straus, 1979) to examine certain kinds of violent experience including being hit with implements such as sticks, being punched, kicked, knocked down, shaken, deliberately burned or scalded, throttled or threatened with a knife or gun. A distinction was made between these more serious experiences, designated as violent, and the physical discipline of slaps, smacks and pinches described in Chapter Two.

- A quarter of the sample had at least one violent experience, with slightly higher levels of men than women doing so. Respondents from social grades D and E were almost 50% more likely to have experienced this level of violence than those from AB grades.

- Most (78%) of the violent experiences happened at home, with mothers (49%) or fathers (40%) being responsible. More than a fifth experienced violence regularly, with young women slightly more likely to report this than young men.

- The violence resulted in effects such as pain, soreness or marks lasting till next day or longer for more than one in ten experiencing it and 12% of the sample reported injuries. This was most often bruising, but small proportions reported other injuries including head injuries, broken bones and burns.

- Using the criteria that there had been violence **regularly over the years**, or violence which **caused physical injury**, or **frequently led to physical effects** lasting at least until next day, 7% of the sample were assessed as **seriously** physically abused by parents.

- Using the criteria that there had been violence which occurred **irregularly and with less frequent lasting physical effects**, or where **other physical discipline** such as slaps, smacks and pinches occurred **regularly and caused injury** or **regularly had lasting physical effects**, 14% of the sample were assessed as experiencing **intermediate abuse** by parents.

- For 3% there was 'cause for concern' about parenting, with them having experienced physical discipline such as slaps, smacks and pinches regularly throughout childhood, or where irregular discipline often had lasting effects.

- Occasional slaps, smacks or pinches which rarely or never had lasting effect were excluded from the assessment of abuse.

- More girls experienced serious physical abuse and more boys intermediate abuse at the hands of their parents or main carer. More respondents from social grades D and E experienced serious abuse but similar trends were not found for intermediate physical abuse or 'cause for concern' categories.

- The association between serious abuse and social grades DE for this sample could be partly reflecting reduced employment prospects caused by abuse. This issue will be explored further in later reports, as will the characteristics of other social grade respondents in serious, intermediate and cause for concern categories.

- Of respondents who had experienced any level of physical discipline or violence, 17% said that their treatment was too strict and harsh for a child and 7% now considered their experience was child abuse. This represented 5% of the total sample. There was a high level of agreement between researcher assessed and self-assessed abuse at the extremes of 'serious abuse' and 'no abuse'.

- Violence by unrelated adults, including professional carers, is rare. Within the family, it is primarily birth parents who mete out the violent treatment, though sibling violence and step-parent violence also occur.

6. PHYSICAL NEGLECT: ABSENCE OF ADEQUATE PARENTAL CARE AND SUPERVISION

Neglect is primarily conceived in terms of the absence of parental care. Although failures to safeguard children by adequate supervision could arise in contexts where other adults have temporary charge of children, the responsibility for nurturing and physical care is attributed to parents or others fulfilling the parental role. We have found only one cross-sectional study which attempts to measure the prevalence of neglect in the general population (Christensen, 1996). Two studies, the National Incidence Studies and the Annual Fifty State Survey, are cited in the US literature as sources of information on reported neglect. The most recent National Incidence Study (NIS -3) gives incidence figures of 5:1000 (harm standard) and 19.9:1000 (endangerment standard) (Sedlak and Broadhurst, 1996). The Annual Fifty State survey gives 20.2:1000 with no distinction between harm and endangerment (Daro and McCurdy, 1992). There is also no agreed definition of neglect by which to measure prevalence although there is considerable agreement among community samples about what is harmful (Dubowitz et al., 1998) and also some consensus amongst professionals (Hallett, 1995). Some class differences have been detected, with working class mothers being more concerned with physical neglect and middle class mothers emphasising the importance of psychological care (Polansky et al., 1983; Dubowitz et al., 1998). Stevenson (1998) points out that:

'Neglect is not a unitary concept but an administrative category covering a range of behaviours which are characterised by the omission of care.' (p.14)

Neglect and poverty

Neglect has been linked in the clinical literature with poverty although the relationship is complex (Stevenson, 1998). Tomison (1995) summarises evidence suggesting that this link leads to the lack of interest in neglect. We do know that during the time that our sample were growing up the number of people living at or below income support level increased from 14% of the population in 1979 to 20% in 1989 and that this included 22% of all children (2,760,000) (Oppenheim, 1993). The position of children living in poverty (defined as living below 50% of average income after housing costs) deteriorated further in the 1990s increasing to a third of the child population. Poverty is not necessarily a cause of neglect, despite correlation between the two. It is however a contributory factor to feelings of helplessness and social distance or exclusion (Gaudin and Polansky, 1986), and susceptibility to physical and mental illness such as depression (Blackburn, 1991). These do characterise carers assessed as neglectful (Stevenson, 1998). Bifulco and Moran (1998) suggest that the relationship between neglect and poverty is found because neglect often follows on structural changes in the family such as the death, departure or illness (in which they include alcoholism) of a parent. This reduces the coping capacity of parents both economically and emotionally, and means that priority sometimes has to be given to getting an income rather than to child care.

A separate but related issue is that where children assume responsibility for the care of their parents or the running of the home, rather than being able to rely on parents caring for them. This may arise in very varied circumstances, ranging from parents' illness or disability to parents with social or emotional problems of their own which take priority in their lives, either temporarily or long term. Bifulco and Moran (1998) describe 'role reversal' in which daughters took over parental responsibilities, often as a result of a parent's death, illness, alcoholism or inability to cope. They identify the overlap between role reversal and neglect, commenting that role reversal 'rarely occurred without parental neglect, and .... between a third and a half of those with neglect were found to have role reversal' (p.37). Dearden and Becker (2000) describe the way in which children matured and acquired practical skills through having carer responsibilities for parents who were sick, disabled, or had drug or alcohol problems, but they also show that these gains were far outweighed by the educational and social deficits which the children experienced. They show that young carers are likely to experience serious poverty, social exclusion and reduced employment opportunities on leaving school. Many families received no or inadequate social care services, or services that were not appropriate, increasing the burden on the young carers. When parents had a severe mental health problem the young carers often reached crisis which led to their departure or removal from the family home.

Bifulco and Moran (1998) report a particularly strong link between neglect in childhood and later isolation and lack of self confidence, with their respondents citing the difficulties in maintaining friendship and social links in childhood when they were embarrassed about their own physical state or the cleanliness and physical state of their home and parents. Some studies indicate that neglected children may be particularly at risk of depression and other mental health problems in adult life, though evidence is contradictory on this point (Kaplan, Pelkowitz and Labruna, 1999).

Varying definitions of neglect

Some of the inconsistencies in tracing long term effects of neglect are likely to be a consequence of the varied definitions used (Zuravin, 1999). All studies include a core of measures concerning adequacy of nutrition, warmth and clothing, basic hygiene and treatment of illness, but beyond this, there is little consensus. Some studies treat neglect as a unitary phenomenon, or focus solely on physical neglect, while others break the concept into varied categories including emotional or psychological neglect, medical or educational neglect. Some include adequacy of supervision of babies and infants at home, while others also include supervision of older children and adolescents outside the home, such as whether they are allowed to stay out late or overnight. There are considerable differences, for example in the treatment of emotional or psychological neglect, with some studies including features such as parental 'unavailability' to the child or antipathy to the child as neglect and others as abuse (Christensen, 1996; Bifulco and Moran, 1998). The USA National Incidence Study, NIS-3, (Sedlak and Broadhurst, 1996), includes expulsion from the home or refusal of custody as neglect whereas other studies regard this as psychological abuse. NIS 3, the largest single study, identifies the primary categories of physical neglect as: refusal of health care; delay of health care; abandonment; expulsion; other custody issues; inadequate supervision and 'other physical neglect'. This final catch-all 'afterthought' category covers the issues which most British definitions regard as central – inadequate nutrition, clothing or hygiene, avoidable hazards in the home – but also includes reckless disregard for the child's safety or welfare such as driving with the child while intoxicated or leaving a young child unattended in a motor vehicle. Separate categories for emotional and educational neglect cover other aspects of the child's development. Stevenson (1998) reports a number of different approaches to assessing neglect which have been developed in social work practice in Britain, each representing a different starting point in terms of the in built assumptions about children's developmental needs, the relationship between physical and emotional needs, and implicit cultural expectations. For example, Minty and Pattinson (1994) assess adequacy of 'food and eating habits', including measures such as whether children appear to be extremely hungry or there is no food in the house, but also whether there is adequate cooking equipment, or adequate seating for children to have meals at table. This builds in cultural assumptions about the way that meals should be managed, as well as about their nutritional adequacy.

One feature on which almost all studies agree is the complex interrelationship between physical, emotional and social wellbeing and development. This is what leads to the variety of approaches to describing and categorising neglect as researchers and practitioners seek to disentangle the relationships from different theoretical and practice standpoints. The differences in definition of neglect used in the research and practice literature made it necessary to review what should be included in a measure of prevalence. It was decided in the present study to attempt measures which separate different aspects of neglect but enable the relationship between them to be explored. This chapter focuses on physical care and supervision. Emotional or psychological care is covered in the next chapter.

The concept of 'physical neglect' adopted in this study includes the two categories of behaviour most commonly found in previous studies: failure to give basic physical care and nurturing over matters such as food, clothing, cleanliness and health care; and failure to safeguard children through supervision appropriate to their age and living situation. There is some evidence of differences in professional views about the importance of these two dimensions (Stone, 1998) and data from the present survey shows some support for the existence of two separate dimensions rather than a single phenomenon. Consequently in this report the data is presented separately for the two categories. Abandonment, which bridges both categories but inevitably leads to inability to nurture and give basic health care, has been included with absence of physical care only to avoid double counting.

Absence of physical care and nurturing

Even with an apparently straightforward category such as this, previous research shows considerable variation on what is considered essential care. While all studies include provision of health care, for example, some include only essential medical treatment for illness, while others include preventive care such as vaccination and dental checks. Hygiene is sometimes included as a health measure, counting as neglectful only potentially hazardous situations such as dirty food storage or unattended human or pet faeces and urine on the premises, while other studies include all socially embarrassing failures in personal or domestic hygiene. There is considerable variation in the treatment of children's involvement in self-care, or in caring for other members of the family. In the present study, a number of questions were asked about all of these areas, to enable exploration of some of the boundaries between common and unusual patterns of care.

Three questions in the questionnaire addressed these issues. All were included in the section of the interview which the respondents completed by themselves, confidentially on the lap top computer. The first question asked: "Parents can have different ideas about when children should be independent and able to look after themselves. When you were a young child (say under 12) did you have any of the following experiences?" Options given included items of varying seriousness in terms of parental care:

- Your parents/carers expected you to do your own laundry

- You had regular dental check-ups

- You went to school in dirty clothes because there were no clean ones available

- You went hungry because no one got your meals ready or there was no food in the house

- You were ill but no one looked after you or took you to the doctor

Respondents were asked to rate the frequency of this happening along a 6 point scale: always; often; sometimes; occasionally; rarely; never. Results show that almost all respondents could take for granted that they would have food, clean clothes, medical and dental care. Only one in a hundred or fewer reported frequently experiencing failures of care on any of these measures. There was little gender difference in the groups reporting frequent absence of care, although men were more likely to report occasional or rare lack of clean clothes or food. There was also little socio-economic difference.

Table 24 Absence of care under the age of 12

Base: All respondents

	Total Ever	Always	Often	Some -times	Occas -ionally	Rarely	Never
Unweighted base	2,869						
Weighted base	2,869						
	%	%	%	%	%	%	%
Expected to do own laundry	21 (20M 23F)	1	2	5	4	10	77
Went to school in dirty clothes because there were no clean ones	11 (15M 7F)	★	★	1	1	8	88
Went hungry because no one got your meals ready or there was no food in the house	7 (8M 5F)	★	1	1	1	4	93
Taken for dental check ups	96 (96M 96F)	72	17	5	2	1	2
Were ill but no one looked after you or took you to the doctor	7 (8M 6F)	1	1	1	1	4	92

The next question asked: "Sometimes because of family circumstances, children find they have adult responsibilities. Did you experience any of the following?" Included in the list were:

■ You often had to look after yourself because your parents had problems of their own e.g. alcohol, drugs etc

■ You regularly had to look after yourself because your parents went away

■ Your parents regularly depended on you for support because they had emotional problems e.g. divorce, separation, death of someone close

■ You regularly had to help care for someone in your family who was ill or disabled

Figures for this were given earlier in Table 8. Numbers reporting absence of care in these individual areas were small: 3% often had to look after themselves due to their parents having problems such as with alcohol or drugs; 2% regularly had to look after themselves because their parents went away; and 4% helped care for someone in the family who was ill or disabled. A higher proportion (8%) had to provide support to emotionally distressed parents. Gender differences were small except that young women were more likely to have supported distressed parents (10% said this compared to 6% of young men). There was a small socio-economic trend, with respondents in social grades D and E being at least twice as likely to report all categories as those in grades A and B. However, the proportion carrying at least one of these responsibilities was rather higher at 14%. In all, 91% of AB respondents said that they carried none of these responsibilities compared to 74% of DE respondents. Again, this will reflect both a greater probability of children in DE grades actually carrying responsibility, together with the likelihood that young people with these responsibilities would have had poorer educational achievement and less access to non-manual employment at the time of the survey.

The third question in this part of the survey concerned ways in which respondents felt they had lacked care. When asked how well they considered they were cared for, 4% said that they were not as well cared for as they might have been or, in a very small number of cases (less than 1%) that they were not cared for at all. The proportion saying they were not well cared for rose to 8% amongst those in social grades D and E. This relatively small group of people were asked in what ways they felt they lacked care.

Options included:

- I was allowed to go into dangerous places or situations

- I was abandoned or deserted

- The physical condition of our home was dangerous

- Our home was unclean

Very few, always less than 1% of the whole sample, said that any of these were the case: only 22 respondents said they were allowed to go into dangerous places, 16 said they were abandoned, 12 that their home was dangerous and 15 that it was unclean.

Assessment of absence of physical care

As in the previous section, absence of care was assessed on three levels, based on the answers to the above questions. It was decided to adopt a stringent approach to the inclusion of these measures. The items concerning 'young carers' providing help for ill or disabled relatives, or emotional support for parents, were excluded from this measure because the wording used did not necessarily mean that the respondents had themselves gone without necessary care. Assignment to categories was hierarchical, with the more serious absence of care having priority so that respondents were only placed in a single group.

Serious absence of care

This was defined as an absence of care which carried a high risk of injury or long term harmful effects. The concept included criteria which were known to carry physical risks, and those which previous research suggested were particularly associated with long term harmful effects such as isolation from other children and lack of self confidence. It included respondents who said that they had any of the following experiences:

- As a young child (under 12) always/often went hungry because no one got their meals ready or there was no food in the house

- As a young child (under 12) always/often were ill but no one took them to the doctor

- As a young child (under 12) always/often gone to school in dirty clothes because there were no clean ones available

- Often had to look after themselves because parents had problems of their own, e.g. alcohol or drugs

- Regularly had to look after themselves because parents went away

- Lacked care because they were allowed to go into dangerous places or situations

- Lacked care because they were abandoned or deserted

- Lacked care because the physical condition of their home was dangerous.

Although very few respondents met the individual criteria, in total, 6% of young adults had experienced serious absence of care in childhood. This comprises 6% of the young men and 7% of the young women. There was an association with the respondents' present socio-economic status: comprising 1% of ABs, 6% of C1s, 6% of C2s, and 10% of DEs.

Table 25 Prevalence of serious absence of care

Base: All respondents

	TOTAL	SEX		SOCIAL GRADE			
		Male	Female	AB	C1	C2	DE
Unweighted base	2,869	1,234	1,635	435	943	627	848
Weighted base	2,869	1,434	1,435	439	969	633	813
	%	%	%	%	%	%	%
Aged under 12 always/ often went hungry because no one got your meals ready or there was no food in the house	★	★	★	★	★	★	2
Aged under 12 always/ often were ill but no one looked after you or took you to the doctor	1	1	★	★	★	★	2
Aged under 12 always/ often went to school in dirty clothes because there were no clean ones available	★	★	★	★	★	★	1
Often had to look after themselves because parents had problems e.g. alcohol or drugs	3	2	4	1	3	3	5
Regularly had to look after themselves because parents went away	2	2	2	★	2	1	3
Lacked care because they were allowed to go into dangerous places or situations	★	★	★	★	★	★	1
Lacked care because they were abandoned or deserted	★	★	★	★	★	★	★
Lacked care because the physical condition of their home was dangerous	★	★	★	★	★	★	1

Intermediate absence of care

This category includes those children for whom the absence of care was less serious but happened regularly, or those who experienced more serious absence of care irregularly or occasionally.

The definition includes those who in response to the questions described above said that they:

■ As a young child (under 12) sometimes, occasionally or rarely went hungry because no one got their meals ready or there was no food in the house

■ As a young child (under 12) sometimes, occasionally or rarely were ill but no one took them to the doctor

■ As a young child (under 12) they were expected to do their own laundry always or often.

Based on these definitions, those indicating intermediate absence of care are shown in Table 26.

Table 26 Prevalence of intermediate absence of care

Base: All respondents

| | TOTAL | SEX | | SOCIAL GRADE | | | |
		Male	Female	AB	C1	C2	DE
Unweighted base	2,869	1,234	1,635	435	943	627	848
Weighted base	2,869	1,434	1,435	439	969	633	813
	%	%	%	%	%	%	%
Aged 12 or under went hungry because no one got your meals ready or there was no food in the house (sometimes/ occasionally/rarely)	6	7	4	3	5	5	9
Aged 12 or under were ill but no one looked after you or took you to the doctor (sometimes/ occasionally/rarely)	6	6	6	4	5	5	8
Aged 12 or under expected to do own laundry (always/often)	3	3	4	2	2	3	5

In total, 9% of respondents experienced intermediate absence of care, based on these definitions. The group comprises 11% of the young men and boys and 7% of the young women. There was a less marked association with social grade, with 8% ABs, 8% C1s, 9% C2s and 11% DEs.

In each case, 6% qualified on the basis of at least sometimes having been hungry or having failed to be taken to a doctor (though in these cases more were 'rare' events than those which happened 'sometimes' or 'occasionally') and 3% were always or often expected to do their own laundry. Respondents in social grades D and E were a little more likely to have had all these experiences and boys were a little more likely to have gone hungry. Girls were a little more likely to report having always or often had to do their own laundry when a young child.

Cause for concern
The third level of absence of care is where what happened was not serious but indicates problems in the quality of basic health care and hygiene which could either escalate or lead to continued distress for a child. These are areas about which there is much disagreement among professionals (Stone,1998), particularly hygiene which contains subjective judgements, but there is evidence that poor home standards can have a very damaging effect on children's social development and friendship patterns (Bifulco and Moran, 1998).

The definition in this case includes those who said that:

■ They lacked care because their home was unclean

■ They sometimes went to school in dirty clothes because there were no clean ones available

■ They never or rarely had dental check ups

Table 27 shows that 2% of respondents gave an answer such that they have been included in the 'cause for concern' subgroup. There were no gender differences or socio-economic trends.

Table 27 Cause for concern about absence of physical care

Base: All respondents

	TOTAL	SEX		SOCIAL GRADE			
		Male	Female	AB	C1	C2	DE
Unweighted base	2,869	1,235	1,634	435	944	627	847
Weighted base	2,869	1,434	1,435	416	1101	594	744
Aged under 12 sometimes went to school in dirty clothes because there were no clean ones available	1	1	1	1	★	★	3
Never/rarely had regular dental check ups	3	3	3	4	2	3	5
Home was unclean	1	★	1	★	1	★	1

In total, 18% of young adults indicated that they had experienced some absence of care in their childhood, 6% indicating serious absence of care, 9% indicating intermediate or intermittent absence of care and a further 2% giving an answer which indicated that there could have been some cause for concern in their childhood care. There was a slightly higher proportion of young men (19%) than young women (16%). The socio-economic trend was also found in this combined group with 11% in social grades AB, 15% C1s, 18% C2s, and 25% DEs

Supervision and safeguarding from harm

Children's need for supervision depends on a variety of factors: their age, the safety of their environment and a judgement of their capacity to take care of themselves. This is an area where there has been public debate and differences of opinion over when, for example, it is safe to leave children alone at home while parents are at work, whether there should be 'curfews' to prevent younger children from being out at night without an adult, or whether teenagers should be employed as 'baby-sitters'. Some of the concerns are about children's safety from accident or assault, others are about the risk of them being drawn into delinquent and other antisocial activity while out unsupervised, or becoming vulnerable to drug pushers, paedophiles and other offenders who might target and exploit the young. Some of the questions concern the length of time for which children are left unsupervised or the specific circumstances in which they may be at risk. The USA 'NIS-3' study, for example, specifies that the child is:

'left unsupervised or inadequately supervised for extended periods of time or allowed to remain away from home overnight without the parent/substitute knowing (or attempting to determine) the child's whereabouts.' (Sedlak and Broadhurst, 1996, 2-17).

The NIS-3 also contains a separate measure of 'reckless disregard for the child's safety' which includes, among other criteria, leaving children in dangerous situations, such as a young child left unattended in a motor vehicle.

Research has shown that parental perspectives on supervision vary between genders, socio-economic groups and according to whether parents see their neighbourhoods as 'high risk' areas. (Newson and Newson, 1978; Wilson, 1980; Riley and Shaw, 1985)

To enable a close examination of perspectives on different aspects of supervision, this category is divided into four levels – the three used before (serious, intermediate and cause for concern) and a fourth level of 'other absence of supervision'. The basis for the assessment incorporates two criteria: whether children were allowed by parents to be unsupervised at home and outside the home, (as distinct from situations where children went out without permission or otherwise illicitly evaded supervision); and the age at which the unsupervised activities began.

The law on the age at which children are regarded as competent to undertake activities and responsibilities in the UK is greatly inconsistent, so that a child for example (at the time of writing) reaches the age of criminal responsibility at ten in England and Wales, eight in Scotland, but must not be left at home with an unguarded fire under the age of 12; can marry at 16, drive a car at 17, but not see certain films or sign a legal contract until 18. Parents can be prosecuted for not sending their children to school, but not for letting them stay out all night, (unless a curfew order is in operation) or for 'reckless disregard of their safety'. It was concluded that the law offered little guidance for the present study in assessing the prevalence of neglect, or what is the expected standard of parental supervision.

Staying at home and going out unsupervised

In the present survey, it was unrealistic to expect respondents to remember absence of supervision when they were babies or 'toddlers', the age at which it could have been most dangerous. Assessment of supervision had to focus on activities which might have involved children capable of significant independent mobility. Questions were asked about the age at which respondents had first been allowed to be in specific situations or carry out various activities without the supervision of an adult or a much older child. The use of the word 'allowed' excluded situations where children might have gone into potentially risky situations without the knowledge or approval of parents. The first question was:

'How old were you when you were first allowed to:

- Stay at home for the evening without an adult to supervise?

- Stay at home overnight without an adult to supervise?

- Go to town centre shops without an adult or much older child?

- Go to school without an adult or much older child?

- Go out in the evening on your own to a friend's/anywhere?

- Stay out overnight without parents knowing where you were?

Respondents were asked to give the age in years, with the option of saying that they had never been allowed these activities unsupervised, (many respondents were still living with their parents). The results have been age grouped for ease of presentation (Table 27). The degree of risk in some of these activities would obviously have been affected by the nature of the environment - whether, for example, the school or the friend was in the same street or across several busy roads, how far or busy was the town centre, or whether there was a known local problem with drug pushers targeting young people.

Very few respondents remembered having unsupervised time at home or outside before the age of five. Between the ages of five and nine only travel to school alone was common, most of these respondents having been aged seven to nine years rather than younger. More independence arises after the age of ten, but the general picture is one of close supervision. For all activities except staying out overnight there is a considerable spread in the ages at which it was permitted, but a clear consensus of the majority that children were not left at home unsupervised or allowed to go far outside unsupervised below the age of ten. For each activity it is possible to identify an age below which more than 80% of parents had not permitted their children to be unsupervised.

There was virtually no socio-economic difference for the first five of these measures, with average ages for each grade very close to the overall average. However the average age for being allowed out overnight (whereabouts unknown) showed a small trend from 16.7 years for social grades AB, decreasing to 15.9 years for grades DE. Gender differences in average age for permitted activities were also small, although there was a consistent trend for male respondents to have been allowed all activities fractionally earlier than female respondents. There was one notable exception: the proportion of women respondents saying that they were 'never allowed' to do each activity without supervision was in each instance at least twice as high as for the men. This was most evident on staying out overnight without parents knowing where you were: 49% of women said they were never allowed this, compared to 22% of the men.

Table 28 Age when unsupervised activity first allowed

Base: All respondents

Age first allowed	Less than 5	5-9 years	10-11 years	12-13 years	14-15 years	16 + years	Never allowed	Average age
Unweighted base 2,869								
Weighted base 2,869								
	%	%	%	%	%	%	%	
Allowed to stay at home in the evening without adult to supervise	★	3	9	24	38	17	3	13.6
Allowed to stay at home overnight without adult to supervise	★	1	2	6	22	25	9	15.8
Allowed to go to town centre shops without an adult or much older child	★	4	17	34	32	10	1	13.0
Allowed to go to school without an adult or much older child	★	30	34	21	6	2	1	10.4
Allowed to go out in the evening on your own to a friend's/anywhere	★	9	16	27	28	13	1	12.8
Allowed to stay out overnight without parents knowing where you were	–	★	1	3	9	43	36	16.3★★

★★Based on the proportion of the sample who gave an age in answer to this question.

Left in charge of younger siblings

The second measure was whether respondents had been left in charge of younger siblings while they were themselves very young. In total, 17% of the sample had been left in charge of younger siblings on at least some occasions when they were themselves under 12. For most of them this had been an occasional or rare event but for 3% it happened 'always' or 'often'. Slightly more women (4%) had regularly cared for younger siblings than men (2%), but there was no socio-economic trend.

As noted earlier, the law gives little or no guidance on the ages at which children can safely be allowed to be unsupervised, but the results showed clear patterns of minimum ages which were adhered to by large numbers of respondents' families. There appeared to be 'staging posts' at ages 10, 12, 14 and 16 for different purposes. Ages 10 and 12 seemed important for decisions on leaving children alone at home. As 16 years is the minimum age at which young people are considered able to live independently, this might be a 'benchmark' age for allowing young people to be out overnight, with whereabouts unknown., but results suggested that more than one in ten young people were allowed out overnight below this age.

Measuring levels of supervision

As with previous measures, neglect and potential neglect resulting from absence of supervision was assessed on three levels: serious, intermediate and 'cause for concern'. Included in the 'serious' and 'intermediate' assessments were circumstances which were likely to create a risk of serious harm: being left at home unsupervised at a young age, being out overnight without parents knowing the child's whereabouts, and being left in charge of younger siblings at a young age. Going unsupervised to the town shops at a young age was included as a 'cause for concern'. Going to school alone or to a friend's house or out in the evening were omitted from the assessment, as for many respondents these activities would have been very close to home and the parents would have known the child's whereabouts.

The analysis of each aspect of supervision therefore incorporated different age levels in an attempt to pinpoint the nature of judgements which were being made, with ages 10, 12, 14 and 16 years incorporated into the measure of supervision.

Table 29 Serious absence of supervision

Base: All respondents

| | TOTAL | SEX | | SOCIAL GRADE | | | |
		Male	Female	AB	C1	C2	DE
Unweighted base	2,869	1,235	1,634	435	944	627	847
Weighted base	2,869	1,434	1,435	416	1101	594	744
	%	%	%	%	%	%	%
Allowed to stay at home overnight without adult to supervise under age 10	1	1	★	★	1	1	1
Allowed to stay out overnight without parents knowing where under age 14	4	5	3	2	3	4	8

Serious absence of supervision

This incorporated measures which were shown to represent exceptionally low levels of supervision for the age groups concerned. It included the following measures:

■ First allowed to stay at home overnight without an adult to supervise under the age of 10 years

■ First allowed to stay out overnight without their parents knowing where they were under the age of 14 years

In total, on this basis, 5% can be said to have experienced serious absence of supervision. Male respondents (6%) and respondents in social grades C2, D and E (7%) were slightly more likely to be assessed in this category. These differences were almost entirely accounted for by differences in staying out overnight.

Included were 1% who had been first left at home overnight under the age of 10 without an adult to supervise, although in individual cases this had occurred very early in childhood. There was little difference in respect of sex or social grade on this. The remaining 4% said that they had stayed out overnight without their parents knowing where they were under the age of 14. In a small number of cases they had been allowed to do this under the age of 10.

Intermediate absence of supervision

Included were three measures which represented less serious levels of risk than the previous category, but which still reflected levels of supervision which would not have been accepted for the large majority of the sample.

■ First allowed to stay at home overnight without adult supervision aged 10 or 11 years

■ First allowed to stay out overnight without parents knowing where they were at age 14 or 15 years

■ When under the age of 12, always or often looked after younger siblings while parents were out

Table 30 Intermediate absence of supervision

Base: All respondents

| | TOTAL | SEX | | SOCIAL GRADE | | | |
		Male	Female	AB	C1	C2	DE
Unweighted base	2,869	1,235	1,634	435	944	627	847
Weighted base	2,869	1,434	1,435	416	1101	594	744
	%	%	%	%	%	%	%
Allowed to stay at home overnight without adult to supervise aged 10 or 11	2	2	2	1	2	2	2
Allowed to stay out overnight without parents knowing where aged 14 or 15	9	11	6	6	7	10	11
Under age 12 always/ often looked after younger brothers and sisters while parents went out	3	2	4	2	3	3	4

On this basis, a total of 12% of respondents were assessed as having experienced intermediate absence of supervision. Males (14%) were more likely to have experienced this than females (10%) and respondents from social grades C2, D and E had greater frequency (14% than those in grades C1 (11%) or AB (9%). Again, gender and social grade differences are largely accounted for by differences in staying out overnight.

Cause for concern about supervision

Respondents were assessed as having experienced a level of supervision causing concern if they were:

- Allowed to stay at home in the evening without adult supervision when under the age of 10

- Allowed to go to the town centre shops without an adult or much older child under the age of 10

Using these criteria, 3% of the sample qualify for inclusion. There were no marked gender or socio-economic differences, though slightly more males and respondents from social grades DE qualified on the basis of going to the town centre unsupervised under the age of 10.

Table 31 Absence of supervision causing concern

Base: All respondents

| | TOTAL | SEX | | SOCIAL GRADE | | | |
		Male	Female	AB	C1	C2	DE
Unweighted base	2,869	1,235	1,634	435	944	627	847
Weighted base	2,869	1,434	1,435	416	1101	594	744
	%	%	%	%	%	%	%
Allowed to stay at home alone in the evening under age 10	3	3	3	3	4	3	4
Allowed to go to town centre shops without an adult or much older child under age 10	4	5	3	4	4	3	5

Other absence of supervision

These were the children in the borderline age range of 11 or 12 years who were allowed to be unsupervised at home or outside the home, and those children under 12 who sometimes, (but not frequently) were left in charge of other children even younger than themselves. Some of these children might have been at risk but the level of risk would be likely to be substantially affected by family and neighbourhood situations, so they were excluded from the three main categories.

Included in this category are 17% of respondents who:

■ Were first allowed to stay at home without an adult in the evening at the age of 10 or 11 (9%)

■ Were allowed to go to the town centre shops without an adult or older child at the age of 10 or 11 (17%)

■ Under the age of 12 sometimes looked after their younger brothers and sisters (3%)

Slightly more of this group were male (18%) than female (16%). The socio-economic pattern contrasted with those earlier in that a higher proportion of respondents were in AB (23%) or C1 (20%) grades, with only 12% in C2 and 13% in DE.

Prevalence of absence of supervision

In total 20% of the sample were assessed as experiencing less than adequate supervision, comprising 5% serious absence of supervision, 12% intermediate absence of supervision and 3% supervision giving cause for concern. A further 17% received a level of supervision which could be seen in some circumstances as problematic, such as being left alone at home in the evening when they were aged 10 or 11 years or being sometimes left in charge of younger siblings while parents were out when they were themselves aged under 12.

This in total represents a substantial proportion of the child population, and raises a number of questions about public perception of the supervision needed in these circumstances, and how closely this accords with professional perceptions. Further analysis will explore the relationship between supervision, other aspects of care, and other demographic factors such as differences between regions or between rural and urban areas.

Self-assessed neglect

At the end of the sections of the interview covering care and supervision, respondents were asked:

'Thinking about the care that was taken of you as a child, does that seem to have been the right amount?'

In response to this, 4% of the sample said that they 'were not as well cared for as they could have been' and just nine respondents, (0.3%) said that they 'were not well cared for at all'. Those giving either of these answers were asked in what ways they lacked care, and whether they considered their treatment serious enough to be called child neglect. The base numbers are small, (127 respondents) but over four in ten (42%) said that they were 'left alone too much', a quarter said they were 'not properly supervised or watched out for', 17% that they were 'allowed to go into dangerous places or situations'. Nineteen respondents (15% of those saying they were not well cared for) said that they were 'not fed properly', 16 respondents (13%) were 'abandoned or deserted', 15 respondents (12%) said that their 'home was unclean' and 12 (9%) that the 'physical condition of our home was dangerous'. Even at this level however, respondents were reluctant to describe themselves as neglected: fewer than half (46%) said that they thought their treatment was serious enough to call neglect, 31% said that it was not, and 22% were unsure. This amounts to just 2% of the whole sample considering themselves neglected. There was a strong overlap with the research assessments of serious absence of care and supervision: 62% of those saying that they were neglected were rated by researchers as having experienced serious absence of physical care, and 60% as having serious absence of supervision.

Summary

- A review of the literature showed the absence of agreed definitions of neglect and of general population surveys of its prevalence. There was evidence that neglect might be particularly damaging in its long term effects, and that it was part of a complex interrelationship with physical, social and psychological well being.

- The present survey focused on the core issues of basic physical nurturing, health care and supervision.

- Answers showed that the majority of respondents had received adequate basic nurturing care, including health care.

- Serious absence of care when they were children was experienced by 6% of the sample. This included: frequently going hungry; frequently having to go to school in dirty clothes; not being taken to the doctor when ill, all when under 12; regularly having to look after themselves because parents went away, or had problems such as with drugs or alcohol; being abandoned or deserted; or living in a home with dangerous physical conditions.

- One or more of the criteria for serious absence of care was experienced by a further 9% of the sample, but with less frequency, and/or they were always or often expected to do their own laundry before the age of 12.

- A further 2% had sometimes had to wear dirty clothes to school, described their homes as 'unclean' and/or had received absence of dental health care, which was regarded as a 'cause for concern'.

- Serious absence of supervision when they were children was experienced by 5% of the sample. This category included children allowed to stay at home overnight without adult supervision under the age of 10, or allowed out overnight without parents knowing their whereabouts, aged under 14.

- Intermediate absence of supervision had affected 12% of the sample. These had experienced one or more of the following: being left unsupervised overnight aged 10-11; allowed out overnight, whereabouts unknown, at the age of 14-15; under the age of 12 frequently left in charge of younger siblings while parents were out.

- A further 3% were allowed to stay at home in the evening without an adult and/or allowed to go to the town centre without an adult or much older child when they were under 10. This was a possible cause for concern.

- There were relatively few distinctions by socio-economic grade, although respondents now in social grades DE were more often assessed as experiencing serious absence of care. There were also some gender differences, most notably with females far less likely than males to have been allowed out overnight with their whereabouts unknown.

- In terms of self assessment, 4% agreed they had not been well cared for and 2% considered their treatment amounted to neglect. This did not include all of those who gave as examples of lack of care that they had not been fed properly, had been abandoned or deserted, had dangerous or unclean homes, had been left alone too much or were not properly supervised or watched out for.

7. EMOTIONAL OR PSYCHOLOGICAL MALTREATMENT

Emotional or psychological maltreatment is a comparatively late addition to officially recognised categories of child maltreatment in the UK. The term 'emotional abuse or neglect' is more common in the UK while American literature more often uses 'psychological abuse or neglect', although the major USA National Incidence Studies use the term 'emotional'. The choice is not purely semantic but reflects a difference in emphasis, with UK literature focusing mainly on the parent-child emotional relationship, while American literature focuses more on the behaviour towards the child, and on specific attacks on the child's personality and self esteem. O'Hagan's (1995) distinction between emotional and psychological health has not been pursued in later studies. In the present report the term 'emotional' will be used except when quoting sources which used alternatives or where there is a specific reason for the choice of 'psychological'.

Emotional abuse was introduced as a criterion for inclusion on child abuse registers in 1980 (Department of Health and Social Security, 1980), including failure to thrive and emotional abuse. The definition was "children under the age of 17 years whose behaviour and emotional development have been severely affected; where medical and social assessments find evidence of either persistent or severe neglect or rejection". From the 1980s, guidance on the assessment and protection of children stressed the child's emotional and developmental needs as much as physical needs (Department of Health, 1988). A series of questions which should be asked in assessment, starting with the areas of concern about the child and his or her upbringing, included the category of emotional abuse, and has been applied throughout the last decade until its recent revision. The 1988 criteria were:

- Rejection
- Lack of praise and encouragement
- Lack of comfort and love
- Lack of attachment
- Lack of proper stimulation (e.g. fun and play)
- Lack of continuity of care (e.g. frequent moves)
- Lack of appropriate handling (e.g. age inappropriate expectations)
- Serious over protectiveness
- Inappropriate non physical punishment (e.g. locking in bedrooms)

In addition to these features a separate category of "exposure to marital or family conflict and/or violence" was identified as a cause for concern. It is notable that most of the items in this list are omissions rather than commissions, and there is little sense that emotional abuse might be deliberate or calculated. All were categorised as 'abuse' and there was no concept of 'emotional neglect'. The importance of the child's emotional and educational development was subsequently embodied in the 1989 Children Act in the "welfare checklist", requiring a court to have regard to the child's "physical, emotional and educational needs". This has been reinforced by the recent *'Framework for the Assessment of Children in Need'* which stresses the importance of emotional development and emotional warmth in child care (Department of Health, 2000).

A familiar story

Although it is the newcomer under categories of abuse, emotional maltreatment is certainly not new in human experience, and our history and literature from all cultures are full of examples showing how early it was identified on an informal level. Biographies of major historical figures commonly identify emotionally abusive or neglected childhoods as having formative influence on the individual and the places they carved for themselves in history. Well-known examples include Lord Shaftesbury, whose campaigning for the welfare of children in mines and factories was said to stem from his wealthy but lonely and emotionally neglected childhood with disinterested parents and his poor treatment at boarding school, and Charles Dickens who used his unhappy childhood as the basis for several of his best known novels. In the world of fiction,

Charlotte Brontë's heroine, Jane Eyre, fainting with terror as a child after being locked in the dark in a room she believed to be haunted, and subsequently denigrated and humiliated at her boarding school, is a classic heroine of English literature. It is of interest that almost all classic English literature which has a child as a central character portrays emotional abuse and neglect, often allied to physical abuse and neglect. In children's literature, the story of Cinderella, an outcast in her family after her mother's death, forced to live in the kitchen, sleep in the garret, and treated as a servant by her stepmother and stepsisters, has enthralled children for centuries. Unlike the 1988 criteria for assessment, literary, fictional and autobiographical examples often include calculated cruelty alongside rejection, insensitivity and disinterest.

There have been no UK general population studies of the prevalence of emotional maltreatment, and few elsewhere. Doyle (1997) found a prevalence level of 29% in a sample of 429 UK undergraduate and mature students. Tomison and Tucci (1997), in a valuable overview of research evidence, summarise the difficulties in assessing prevalence due to the wide variety of definitions adopted, with rates varying from between 0.69 to 25.7%. They consider that, because emotional abuse leaves no physical injuries and rarely precipitates a crisis, it is the 'most hidden and underestimated form of child maltreatment.' In the USA Brassard, Hart and Hardy (1993) developed psychological maltreatment rating scales for children by observing samples of mothers and children, and comparing families where there were substantiated histories of other abuse and those with no known histories. While they found high levels of psychological maltreatment among families with a history of other maltreatment, they also found that 29% of the families with no known history of abuse scored high on psychological maltreatment. Given the extent to which historical and literary tradition focuses on emotional abuse or neglect, it is surprising that the earliest recognition of it in child protection literature generally treated it as less significant or serious than either physical or sexual abuse. Brassard, Hart and Hardy (1993) reviewing the American research on child protection note the serious underestimation of the extent and importance of psychological maltreatment in the past. The authors summarised the evidence that in many ways it is psychological maltreatment which is central to the understanding of all abuse and neglect. This is echoed by Tomison and Tucci (1997) who point to the evidence that even with physical and sexual abuse, it is the associated emotional trauma rather than the physical damage which is most lasting and harmful. This perspective has recently been endorsed in several UK research and practice texts, most notably in the summary of 20 research studies published by the Department of Health (1995) which identified a core problem of families 'low on warmth and high on criticism', creating a risk of additional physical abuse and other adverse childhood experience. This overview report also distinguished emotional neglect from emotional abuse and suggested that neglect was the more common problem of the two.

Difficulties in defining and measuring emotional maltreatment

Nevertheless this is the least studied of all forms of child maltreatment, and the area in which reliable prevalence data is almost non existent. The state of knowledge is considerably less advanced than for physical or sexual abuse and there is a lack of a consensual paradigm within which it has been studied. This is partly to do with the innate difficulties of definition, measurement and proof, which affect both research and practice. Social workers and other professionals feel least confident that they can reach a conclusion and prove a case for abuse when the suffering is emotional than when it is physical or sexual (Cleaver, Wattam and Cawson 1998). Emotional maltreatment is the smallest category officially recorded in child protection statistics in the UK, and this has also been found in the USA and Australia (Tomison and Tucci, 1997). The research which has been carried out has rarely attempted to build on previous evidence or to examine definitions used by professionals, victims or the general public. Studies which have attempted to assess and categorise this form of abuse use various terms: emotional abuse, emotional maltreatment, psychological abuse or maltreatment, psychological attack, emotional or psychological neglect. Each uses different classifications of behaviour considered abusive, and even where some similar categories are used, different behaviour is included under the same category, or similar behaviour in different categories. There is confusion over the boundaries between emotional abuse and neglect, with behaviour such as rejection, unresponsiveness, and violence between carers sometimes being classified as one and sometimes the other. Doyle (1997) notes that 'unlike physical and sexual abuse, where omissions are paramount, and physical neglect, where omissions are pre-eminent, in emotional abuse, omission and commission are inextricably fused' (p.334).

The difficulty of reaching a definitive classification of emotional abuse stems from the very wide range of potential behaviour which could be classified as abusive, together with the possibility of considering omissions as well as commissions. Bifulco and Moran (1998), in a study of the relationship between childhood abuse and neglect and adult mental health, note the 'diversity of perpetrators' techniques and behaviours' which range from casual humiliation to extreme degradation. With physical and sexual abuse there is a relatively limited range of finite behaviours which have been shown in numerous studies to have a consensus that they are abusive. Comprehensive, quantitative measurement of the many ways in which lack of love can be demonstrated, on the other hand, is not easy. Furthermore, it is in the nature of emotional abuse that the goalposts move, because it targets individual vulnerabilities and these will change with the child's development and changing external world - what will isolate, frighten or humiliate a four year old and a fourteen year old is likely to be very different, while increasing links with the world outside the family will both create new vulnerabilities and offer escapes from a punitive or uncaring atmosphere at home (Iwaniec, 1997). (Appendix 2 shows the different categorisations used in different studies.)

The extent to which the child experiences its treatment as abusive may also be far more affected by the context than with physical or sexual abuse. The pain of a physical blow will be dependent on the force of the blow. Hurtful words from a loved adult, however, may be experienced very differently from the same words spoken by one who is disliked, feared, or to whom the child is indifferent (Creighton and Russell, 1995; Iwaniec, 1997; Bifulco and Moran, 1998).

The reality of all human relationships is that people at times say and do things which hurt each other, or fail to notice the other person's needs, intentionally and unintentionally. In a loving or friendly relationship this will not happen continuously and will be overcome. But there is no clarity over the point at which anger or insensitivity shade into abuse, either on a single occasion or over time. How behaviour is perceived may differ according to its recency and what else has happened between the participants, and emotional abuse may be more vulnerable to this than other forms. The few studies which have examined this have shown marked difference between ratings of abusiveness by professionals and those made by victims or the general public (McGee et al., 1995; Friedrich et al., 1997).

Friedrich et al. also showed that ratings of psychological abuse by victims were the most volatile. A random sample of 610 adults from the general population were asked on two occasions about their experience of abuse, at intervals of approximately 20 months apart. Victims of physical and sexual abuse showed respectively 91.8% and 85.6% concordance in their answers on both occasions, whereas for psychological abuse it was 65.4%. In that study the two questionnaires over time were not identically worded, which may have had some effect on the answers, but there is no obvious reason why it should have affected psychological abuse more than other forms. One of the common features of any abusive treatment is that the victims can come to feel that it was their own fault: they were bad or unlovable, or in some other way contributed to or deserved the abuse. Since emotional abuse often deliberately exploits this feature of human nature, it may be harder for victims to maintain a consistent and confident sense that they were badly treated.

In Friedrich et al.'s (1997) research the measurement of psychological abuse included questions on whether respondents had been yelled at, ridiculed or humiliated, embarrassed in front of others and made to feel like a bad person. These are all examples which could have occurred in a range of contexts and to varying levels of seriousness, and illustrate one of the dilemmas of measuring emotional abuse: how to differentiate between unpleasant experiences which most, if not all, people have at one time or another, and experiences which are fundamentally and damagingly abusive. Friedrich et al. suggest that psychological abuse is a more elusive experience than other forms and exists along a continuum. For this reason 'using a dichotomous form to assess it may not be advantageous' (p.171).

Quantitative and qualitative studies

Studies which classify behaviour towards the child as emotionally abusive fall into two groups. Some identify a list of behaviours and rate them as having occurred, with ratings sometimes being dichotomous and sometimes on a measure of frequency of occurrence, or periods of childhood during which they occurred. The behaviours described may be a simple list (or even just one or two items) but are often classified along pre-set dimensions. This approach is used by most studies which attempt quantitative measurement of prevalence or incidence of abuse. Unfortunately no studies use a comprehensive set of behavioural items and no two studies use the same items. While prevalence estimates on individual behavioural measures can give some interesting results, attempts to combine them into a total measure of abuse gives results so diverse as to be virtually meaningless. The studies often fall victim to the problem described above, that they fail to distinguish between common unpleasant experiences and experiences which are known to cause serious, long-term harm.

The most comprehensive and reliable quantitative study is the third USA National Incidence Study (NIS - 3) which uses reports from a nationally representative sample of professionals working with children in social work, health, juvenile justice and education services. It uses four categories of emotional abuse and seven of emotional neglect. Emotional abuse includes tying or binding, other close confinement, verbal or emotional assault (including threats, belittling, scapegoating, overt hostility or rejection) and other punitive, exploitative or abusive treatment. Emotional neglect includes inadequate affection, chronic/extreme spouse abuse, permitted drug/alcohol use or other permitted maladaptive behaviour, refusal or delay in seeking psychological care for emotional or behavioural problems and other emotional neglect such as over protectiveness or age-inappropriate expectations. Because NIS-3 relies on professional judgement to classify examples within a broad framework, it avoids the problems of a limited checklist, but there are still obvious limitations to the survey. It can only identify abuse known to professionals; although great efforts were made to ensure consistency in rating of the data, the known variation in professional perceptions of what constitutes abuse or neglect is likely to have affected what data was submitted to the research team; there are boundary problems over ratings as abuse or neglect, for example between judgement of rejection, rated as abuse, and lack of affection, rated as neglect; items such as 'permitted alcohol use' or 'permitted maladaptive behaviour' shade into more general assessment of parental competence and childrearing standards, and assume that the professionals will know what efforts parents have or have not made to control or guide their children, whereas this is particularly unlikely for professionals whose work does not bring them into close contact with the family.

Nevertheless, the data is still the best and most comprehensive available to date. By applying these measures, Sedlak and Broadhurst estimated that in 1993, 3.0 children per thousand of the USA child population experienced emotional abuse that met the 'harm' standard and 7.9 children per thousand met the 'endangerment' standard. Emotionally neglected children were estimated as 3.2 per 1000 at the harm standard and 8.2 per 1000 at the endangerment standard. Rates of emotional abuse and neglect were considered to have risen greatly from levels recorded in earlier studies, and to have risen at a higher rate than those recorded for other forms of abuse and neglect, but it still has to be demonstrated that this reflected a real increase rather than a change in perception of what should be reported. In most instances perpetrators were parents or parent substitutes. For birth parents, children were approximately equally likely to be abused or neglected by mothers and fathers, but with substitute parents, the abuser was usually male. Gender and race appeared to have little or no effect on rates, but family income had a strong relationship, with children from the poorest families far more likely to be assessed as emotionally abused and neglected to both standards.

The difficulty of comparing rates of abuse across studies is illustrated by comparing NIS-3 figures to those obtained by Christensen (1996), who surveyed Danish 'health nurses' to establish the prevalence of active and passive emotional abuse and neglect among children aged 0–1 years. Active abuse and neglect included confinement, threats, insults to or about the child, hostility, ignoring, isolating and leaving the child to numerous caretakers or to the care of young siblings. Passive abuse and neglect included violence between carers, the child cared for by drunk or otherwise intoxicated adults, unpredictability in family life, unresponsiveness to the child's behaviour or emotional needs, and rejection. By relatively small differences in the categorisations and the use of a narrower range of measures and of professionals, Christensen reached a figure of 2% of Danish babies suffering active and 4% passive emotional abuse and neglect, a considerably higher rate than the American study.

Dimensions of emotional maltreatment

The second approach to measuring emotional abuse and neglect, found in most qualitative studies, develops a conceptual classification of the possible dimensions and then allocates victims' descriptions of their experience to it. This gives a much more meaningful and comprehensive picture of the range of treatment which can be included in the category of emotional abuse, and has also provided a foundation for the development of a research consensus on the meaning of the term. This conceptual approach has also shown a great deal of common ground between the emotional abuse of children and 'domestic violence' or partner abuse, in its focus on the existence and exploitation of power in relationships, and both traditions have been drawn on for the present study.

The most influential work is by Garbarino, Guttman and Seeley (1986) who identified five dimensions of emotional abuse: rejecting; terrorising; ignoring; isolating and corrupting the child. Terrorising includes threats of all kinds and playing upon the child's fears; isolating is keeping the child away from other sources of support, friendship and developmental interaction; corrupting is inducting the child into criminal or other anti-social behaviour, substance misuse or prostitution. These measures allowed both for commission and omission without having to draw hard boundaries between abuse and neglect, but focusing on parental behaviour rather than on how the child was affected by it. However they could not accommodate all relevant behaviour, such as domestic violence, which might affect the child while not targeting the child. Hart, Germain and Brassard (1987) added the dimensions of degrading and denying emotional responsiveness.

In a ground breaking UK study, Bifulco and Moran (1998) examined the link between child abuse and mental illness in three samples of women, one a general population sample, one a sample who were known to have had adverse childhood experience of various kinds and the third a sample of women with a history of depressive illness. Qualitative material from over 800 'history taking' interviews was categorised to describe the women's experience of childhood abuse, and provides a graphic and comprehensive understanding of the complexities of emotional abuse. Bifulco and Moran describe 'psychological abuse', which they assess as domination of the child by use of 'callous actions or words, often premeditated and enjoyed by the perpetrator'. Within this category, behaviour is very similar to that covered in the USA research, although grouped differently: depriving the child of physical and emotional needs to induce submission, including depriving of food, warmth and clothing, locking the child up, destroying something the child loves or values, inflicting pain, terrorising or humiliating, wishing the child dead, threats of abandonment or being sent away, blackmail and threats to loved people, corruption or exploitation. Additional categories which were defined separately and not described by the authors as psychological abuse, but which contain elements classified as such in other studies, were: role reversal, in which children were expected to take on responsibilities beyond their years or give emotional support to fragile or needy parents, and antipathy, defined as critical and rejecting verbal and non verbal behaviour. Bifulco and Moran stress that to assess antipathy it is not enough that the child simply felt unloved; the parents must have exhibited hostile behaviour. Their case examples suggest that hurtful behaviour which is calculated is experienced differently from that which results from poverty, stress or illness of parents. They describe the extraordinary lengths to which abusers would go to distress children: the father who forced his young daughter to watch while he killed, cooked and ate her pet rabbits, the mother who told her children that they were being sent to a 'bad girls' home' and made them sit on stools to wait to be collected by the policeman, while their father was secretly sent out to ring the front door bell as if calling to collect them. The case illustrations demonstrate the extreme difficulty of achieving simple quantitative measures which could encompass the variety of emotional cruelty that humans can inflict on each other.

Similarities between child maltreatment and domestic violence

The qualitative studies, by drawing out dimensions such as terrorising, isolating, domination and calculated cruelty, fundamentally alter the understanding of emotional abuse of children and highlight similarities to other forms of abuse such as domestic violence. Research on spouse and other partner abuse in Britain and the USA has shown the central importance of power relationships, and demonstrated that physical violence is only one of the tactics that abusers use to dominate and control. Isolating victims from friends and relatives, controlling their time and movement, humiliating and denigrating, verbal insults, blackmailing, casting doubt on the victim's stability, sanity or morality, threatening to harm, refusing to speak, are all used in abusive partner relationships alongside physical and sexual violence. Psychological domination and control are the central factors which explain the violence and also explain the difficulty which victims have in escaping from their situation. Quantitative approaches to scaling partner abuse produce very similar results to those used in child abuse (Tolman, 1989; Kasian and Painter, 1992). McGee (2000) in a study of children living with domestic violence shows that the desire to control all aspects of the woman's life was of primary significance in violent relationships between the carers, and that the apparently unpredictable physical violence by fathers or stepfathers toward the mother was often a calculated tactic to increase fear and uncertainty in the victim rather than the result of loss of temper or self-control. McGee shows that children were often subjected to the same patterns of psychological domination as their mothers, even when they were not physically hurt, and that children and mothers were used against each other and as a means of controlling each other through threats of harm to each. This pattern of domination is very similar to that described by Bifulco and Moran in relation to child abuse, where psychological and physical domination, and 'proxy attacks' by destroying the child's possessions or pets, or threats to harm or destroy them, were common forms of abuse. Tutty (1999) in a Canadian study of the intergenerational transmission of partner and child abuse in families where spouse abuse was found, shows the close relationship between abuse of mothers and children by male partners, and that direct emotional abuse of the children (i.e. not simply witnessing the abuse of their mother) had been a feature of all cases of child abuse in his sample.

Defining emotional abuse - the present study

The review of the literature has identified several problems in defining and measuring emotional abuse in a quantitative study of prevalence.

Firstly, there is no 'off the peg' quantitative categorisation which is sufficiently recognised, comprehensive and precise to be used or adapted for the present study. However there is an emerging picture of the nature of emotional abuse which should be built on in developing quantitative measures.

Secondly, some behaviour would legitimately fit into more than one category of abuse. Behaviour towards children can be both physically or sexually and emotionally abusive - or sometimes all three - and also could be both physically and emotionally neglectful. Nevertheless if it is wished to reach an overall estimate of the prevalence of abuse, behaviour has to be allocated to one primary category in order to avoid double counting. Hence, no quantitative study can do more than give an approximation, either of individual types of abuse and neglect or of overlap.

Thirdly, there is no clear boundary between emotional abuse and neglect, although some individual behaviours would clearly be defined as one rather than the other.

Fourthly, the possible range of behaviour towards a child which could be defined as emotionally abusive is far too wide and individually moderated for a quantitative study to give comprehensive, pre-coded coverage of it. The choice has to be made between introducing broad categories for quantification, with consequent loss of detail and the risk that respondents' interpretation of the categories might vary, or using a finite but limited list of abusive behaviour which could exclude much that respondents actually experienced.

Fifthly, in a quantitative study it is difficult to distinguish between negative features of all human behaviour and relationships, and those of regularly or consistently abusive relationships. There is particular difficulty in separating anger and insensitivity which at times everyone displays, from the abusive inducement of fear and distress, and in separating acceptable (even if unfair) criticism from serious attacks on the child's self-esteem and personality.

Finally, in a retrospective study of adults' childhood experience, the research relies on the respondents' accounts of what happened, which will be influenced by their understanding of events at the time. Children may not always have understood the reasons for the behaviour towards them and may have thought they were being targeted when they were not - for example, they may have thought a pet was deliberately destroyed to hurt them when in fact it was ill, or that the parent was hostile to them when in fact the parent had other stresses making them bad tempered. Experience may be re-evaluated by the adult in the light of changing experience and perspectives over time. In a qualitative study these possibilities can be explored but in a quantitative study some assumptions must be made that differences in understanding or interpretation will even out over a large sample.

The questionnaire and the analysis attempt to minimise these disadvantages by building on previous evidence and focusing as precisely as possible on behaviour towards the child, while defining categories sufficiently comprehensive to enable recording of the breadth of emotional abuse. It was concluded that genuinely emotionally abusive treatment represents deep hostility to the child and is most unlikely to have manifested itself in only one kind of behaviour or in a small group of related behaviours, or to have occurred only for a short period. Following Friedrich et al. (1997) it was concluded that a dichotomous assessment of emotional abuse would not be helpful, and that it was better to view emotional abuse as a continuum, taking into account the breadth and continuity of abusive experience over time and assuming disparate forms.

This analysis focuses on abuse by parents/carers, since previous research shows that these are the primary abusers (Sedlak and Broadhurt, 1996; Bifulco and Moran, 1998). Abusive behaviour from others, and the relationship between emotional abuse and bullying will be examined in a later report.

Using concepts primarily taken from Garbarino, Guttman and Seeley (1986), Brassard, Hart and Hardy (1993) and Bifulco and Moran (1998), a number of dimensions for assessing emotional abuse have been developed. These are intended to overcome some of the problems of allocating abusive behaviour found in previous studies and to bring greater conceptual clarity which will aid replication in future studies. In particular the allocation of physical behaviour which may have a multitude of effects - domination, terrorising, humiliating, among others, is problematic and dealt with differently in different studies. Here it is grouped together as having the primary characteristic of the use of physical strength against the child in a way which has psychological rather than physical effects. The analysis focuses on 'maltreatment' to avoid having to make arbitrary distinctions between abuse and neglect, which are especially problematic in relation to lack of affection, rejection or what is sometimes referred to as parental 'unavailability'.

The dimensions are:

1. Psychological control and domination, including attempts to control the child's thinking and isolation from other sources of support and development

2. Psycho/physical control and domination (physical acts which exert control and domination but cause distress rather than pain or injury)

3. Humiliation/degradation - psychological attacks on the person's worth, self-esteem, which could be verbal or non verbal

4. Withdrawal - withholding affection and care, exclusion from the family (including showing preference for siblings, and excluding the child from benefits given to other children in the family)

5. Antipathy - showing marked dislike of the child by word and deed

6. Terrorising - threats to harm the child or someone something the child loves, threatening with fear figures, threats to have the child sent away, making the child do something that frightens them

7. Proxy attacks by harming someone or something the child loves or values. This could include deliberate attacks on the child's possessions or pets, and also includes violence between carers.

The dimension of 'corrupting' the child is also an important aspect of emotional abuse. However it is not included in the calculation of emotional abuse in the present study, as the aspects of the data which represent it, such as showing the child pornography or using the child to make pornography, are included in the assessment of sexual abuse. A thorough examination of this issue would also have needed to venture into aspects of delinquent and antisocial behaviour which would have considerably enlarged the data collection, presented practical problems for the viability of the study, and raised many problems in assessing the corrupting influences of individuals as distinct from local subcultures. The present study did not ask about induction into crime, or about substance use except in relation to its role in obtaining sexual compliance.

Psychological control and domination

The questions used to assess psychological control and domination concerned two aspects of parenting: whether parents offered safe, predictable responses to their children, and the extent to which they attempted to control their children's thoughts, movements and associations.

Research in many contexts has shown that being at the mercy of unpredictable behaviour from someone in a position of power over us is a frightening and paralysing experience. This has been demonstrated as relevant to psychological domination in a range of circumstances including child abuse (Bifulco and Moran, 1998), domestic violence (McGee, 2000), political and religious 'brainwashing' (Sargant, 1963) and bullying in the workplace. McGee (2000) illustrates the way in which inability to predict the father's or stepfather's behaviour, or what would make him angry, affected every aspect of the family's lives, and often made them afraid to do or say anything at all in case it provoked an angry or violent reaction. In Creighton and Russell's (1995) study, 85% had been able to predict their mothers' reactions and 77% their fathers' reactions. This was shown to be strongly linked to the closeness of the relationship with parents.

In the present study it was similarly found that mothers were more predictable than fathers: 88% said that they 'knew where they stood' with mothers and 79% with fathers. The link with closeness of relationship was confirmed, with respondents who said they were close to parents almost twice as likely to find them predictable as were those who were not close. Those who reported that parents were unpredictable were included in the measure for psychological domination.

The 'freedoms' of thought, belief and association included are those guaranteed in the United Nations Convention on the Rights of the Child. The majority of parents seem likely to want to exercise some level of control over the people with whom their children mix - indeed this would normally be thought of as part of good parental supervision. Studies of children's experience show that parents' objections to their children's friends is a common cause of dispute in families (Ghate and Daniels, 1997). Similarly, parents wanting to influence their children's value and belief systems is a normal and essential part of childrearing. When parents themselves have strong religious or political beliefs, or are part of communities with those beliefs, they may be particularly likely to want their children to grow up with the same outlook. But extreme restriction of contact with other sources of support and attempting competely to control values and beliefs have been identified as features of emotional abuse in a number of studies, and are another way in which child abuse and partner abuse have been found to be very similar. Respondents were asked 'during your childhood how much freedom were you allowed in the following things -

- Saying what you thought and having your views considered

- Freedom to meet and mix with other people

- Thinking and believing what you wanted to e.g. politics and religion'

Restrictions on freedom to meet other people, apart from being a controlling technique in itself, also removes the possibility of the child having other sources of emotional support, or the chance to learn that parents' perspectives and values are not the only ones available. Full results from this question are included in Chapter Two (Table 6). The proportions reporting severely restricted freedom were very small and only the most extreme reporting 'no freedom at all' were included in the measure of psychological control and domination.

Table 32 Psychological domination and control

Base: all respondents

	Male	Female	Total
Unweighted base	1,235	1,634	2,869
Weighted base	1,434	1,435	2,869
	%	%	%
Unable to predict mother (stepmother)/reaction varied	10	12	11
Unable to predict father (stepfather)/reaction varied	17	19	18
Unable to predict both parents/reaction varied	6	5	6
No freedom at all to say what you thought and have views considered	1	2	2
No freedom at all to meet and mix with other people	★	1	★
No freedom at all to think and believe what you wanted e.g. politics and religion	1	1	1
Any psychological control/domination	22	26	24

The results on this group of questions suggest that the two aspects of psychological control are quite different, although their effects on the child are not necessarily so. Extreme, direct control of children's freedom of thought, expression or association is clearly not a common feature of parental behaviour in modern family life, but unpredictable parental behaviour is much more common. Although not necessarily classifiable as emotional abuse in itself, its link with problems in relationships with parents clearly marks it as a cause for concern and an indicator of a situation with the potential for abusive or neglectful parenting.

Psycho/physical control and domination

The second dimension differs in that it uses physical control and force, not to cause physical pain or injury but to exercise power and domination. Bifulco and Moran (1998) point out how frequently psychological abuse focused on bodily functions such as eating, sleeping, urination and excretion, using them to cause distress or humiliation, to make the child feel unclean or abnormal. They report their respondents' accounts of being made to wear urine or faeces stained or stinking clothing as a punishment for wetting or soiling, being forced to eat unwanted food or other unpleasant things, and similar exercises of control. Some psycho/physical methods were common punishments in the past. Some were only ended for children in public care when they were prohibited in the regulations governing children's homes introduced in 1974, and are still legal in other contexts including the family home. These punishments included, for example, making children miss meals, keeping them in night clothes during the day or making them wear other inappropriate clothing, often as a means to humiliate them or prevent them leaving the premises, and locking them in a room or closet. Some other psycho/physical treatment, such as putting children to sit 'on the naughty stool', stand in the corner, making them sit with hands on their heads, or physically isolating them were common in schools in the past and some may still be used as parts of behavioural control programmes. The range of possible behaviours in this category is considerable and a judgement has to be made in terms of seriousness and likely damage to children. Only a few could be covered in the present survey, and the criterion applied was whether treatment was known now to be considered generally unacceptable through research or through the prohibition of their use for children in public care, day care or education.

There is no previous comprehensive data on the regularity with which such punishments are used in the family. Creighton and Russell (1995) found that 4% of their sample had been regularly and 21% occasionally or rarely punished by missing a meal or part of a meal. Isolation, which in Creighton and Russell's study included being put in the corner or sent to their room, as well as being locked up, was experienced regularly by 11% and occasionally by 43%. Although Bifulco and Moran (1998) included data on several of these treatments, they do not give frequency data for individual items.

Questions covering psycho/physical control were:

'Did you experience any of these:

- Having your mouth washed out with soap?

- Being made to miss a meal and go hungry?

- Being made to eat something that they knew would make you feel sick?

- Being locked in a room or cupboard?

- Shutting you outside on a cold day without a coat?

- Always having to do the worst jobs in the house

- If you wet the bed you were made to rub your nose in or touch wet sheets'?

Respondents who answered 'yes' were asked who did this to them. Results show that some parents in the UK were still inflicting treatment on their children which would not be considered acceptable for children in other contexts. Although the numbers receiving individual treatments are small, the proportion of respondents experiencing some treatment in this category is substantial. Mothers and fathers seem equally likely to have used these methods.

Table 33 Psycho/physical control

Base: all respondents

	Male	Female	Total
Unweighted base	1,235	1,634	2,869
Weighted base	1,434	1,435	2,869
	%	%	%
Mouth washed out with soap - mother/stepmother	5	4	5
Mouth washed out with soap - father/stepfather	3	3	3
Mouth washed out with soap - both parents	2	1	2
Made to miss a meal - mother/stepmother	5	4	4
Made to miss a meal - father/stepfather	6	2	4
Made to miss a meal - both parents	3	1	2
Made to eat or drink something that would make you sick - mother/stepmother	2	2	2
Made to eat or drink something that would make you sick - father/stepfather	2	2	2
Made to eat or drink something that would make you sick - both parents	2	1	2
Locked in room or cupboard - by mother/stepmother	3	2	3
Locked in room or cupboard - by father/stepfather	4	2	3
Locked in room or cupboard - by both parents	2	1	2
Shut outside on a cold day - by mother/stepmother	1	2	1
Shut outside on a cold day - by father/stepfather	1	1	1
Shut outside on a cold day - by both parents	1	1	1
Always made to do the worst jobs in the house - by mother/stepmother	3	5	4
Always made to do the worst jobs in the house - by father/stepfather	3	2	2
Always made to do the worst jobs in the house - by both parents	2	1	2
Nose rubbed in wet sheets - mother/stepmother	1	1	1
Nose rubbed in wet sheets - father/stepfather	★	★	★
Nose rubbed in wet sheets - both parents	★	★	★
Any psycho/physical control and domination	17	16	17

★ Less than 1%

Humiliation - psychological attack on self-esteem

This is one of the few areas common to almost all of the studies of emotional abuse. Although there is some variation in the items used to measure it there is general agreement that to be constantly 'put down', verbally abused or insulted is damaging to children, and that such treatment from the people who are most expected to show unconditional affection, the parents, can be especially damaging. In the present study, as has been found in previous studies (Creighton and Russell, 1995) most respondents reported that they were sometimes sworn at, shouted or screamed at or otherwise verbally insulted and embarrassed in front of others by parents. In assessing whether psychological attack amounted to emotional abuse a dividing line was drawn in terms of the seriousness and frequency of the verbal attacks.

Respondents were assessed as having experienced humiliation/psychological attack by parents if they reported that 'regularly over the years' they had experienced being:

■ Made to feel embarrassed or humiliated

■ Shouted at or screamed at

■ Sworn at

■ Called stupid or lazy or some similar name

Two other questions were included in this measure, which were assessed as serious enough to count as psychological attack because they were known to be remembered and hurtful much later in life. Respondents were asked:

'Were you ever humiliated in front of other people?

'Did someone ever tell you they wished you were dead or had never been born?'

Those experiencing this treatment by parents or step-parents were counted as having experienced psychological attack.

Creighton and Russell (1995) found that 43% of a general population sample of adults remembered a punishment as a child which had humiliated them, either at home or at school. In the present sample, in the context of a question about physical treatment, 34% said that they had memories of being humiliated in front of other people, and in the context of a question about verbally aggressive treatment 20% said that they had at some time been made to feel embarrassed or humiliated. Most of this humiliation was experienced at the hands of parents, though teachers, siblings and other relatives were also frequently named. Some of the humiliation is likely to have been linked with the psycho/physical treatment described above or with the other verbal treatment included in the 'humiliation/psychological attack' measure. In total, 75% of the present sample reported being shouted or screamed at to some extent, 28% were sworn at and 42% said they had been called stupid or lazy at some time. It was much less common to have experienced verbal insult regularly at the hands of parents, but almost one respondent in five had experienced this, and for a total of 7%, verbal insult had included an expressed wish by one or both parents that the respondent was dead or had never been born.

Table 34 Humiliation/psychological attack

Base: all respondents

	Male	Female	Total
Unweighted base	1,235	1,634	2,869
Weighted base	1,434	1,435	2,869
	%	%	%
Made to feel embarrassed or humiliated by mother/stepmother regularly over the years	3	4	3
Made to feel embarrassed or humiliated by father/stepfather regularly over the years	3	5	4
Made to feel embarrassed or humiliated by both parents regularly over the years	3	3	3
Shouted or screamed at by mother/stepmother regularly over the years	6	6	6
Shouted or screamed at by father/stepfather regularly over the years	7	8	7
Shouted or screamed at by both parents regularly over the years	5	4	4
Sworn at by mother/stepmother regularly over the years	4	4	4
Sworn at by father/stepfather regularly over the years	5	6	5
Sworn at by both parents regularly over the years	4	3	3
Called stupid or lazy or similar by mother/stepmother regularly over the years	5	5	5
Called stupid or lazy or similar by father/stepfather regularly over the years	6	7	6
Called stupid or lazy or similar by both parents regularly over the years	4	3	4
Humiliated in front of others by mother/stepmother	5	10	7
Humiliated in front of others by father/stepfather	6	8	7
Humiliated in front of others by both parents	3	4	4
Told you were wished dead or never born by mother/stepmother	4	7	5
Told you were wished dead or never born by father/stepfather	2	3	2
Told you were wished dead or never born by both parents	1	1	1
Any humiliation/attacks on self-esteem	16	20	18

Withdrawal

The withholding or withdrawal of parental affection is also identified in almost all previous studies, though variously classified as emotional abuse or emotional neglect. Some literature refers to 'rejection' but this term encompasses two qualitatively different behaviours: an absence or omission of affection and an active display of hostile feelings. In the present study the two were separated and 'withdrawal' refers to an absence of usual display of parental affection, which could range from disinterest to coldness, or to non-inclusion of the child in the usual family activities or treats. The last of these is conceptually problematic as it could result from disinterest and insensitivity to the child's needs or be a deliberately punitive or hostile act. Bifulco and Moran (1998, pp.19–32) illustrate graphically the different forms of withdrawal which could be practised, and found that favouring or excluding some children in the family was a commonly reported experience, often in reconstituted families where the children of a previous partner were treated differently. In the absence of qualitative data indicating how individual responses should be classified it was decided to count exclusion from family activities as withdrawal, rather than the alternative of 'antipathy'.

At various points in the interview respondents were asked about relationships with parents/carers and about ways of demonstrating affection. Some of the answers to these questions were used to construct the 'withdrawal' scale.

One question noted that 'families have different ways of showing that they care for each other' and used a list of common means of showing affection and care such as hugging, cuddling and kissing, helping with homework and saying nice things to you. (see above, Chapter Two). Respondents who could not name any ways in which affection was shown to them in their family were included in the 'withdrawal' category.

Separate questions asked 'How often, if at all, when you were growing up, did your mother/stepmother (or father/stepfather) show obvious affection to you such as by a hug or kiss?' Respondents could answer on a scale from 'every day' through to 'never' allowing for families whose demonstrativeness was very frequent or only occasional. Respondents who answered 'never' were included in the 'withdrawal' scale.

Respondents were asked how well they thought they had been cared for as a child, and were able to give a range of responses from 'I was very well cared for' to 'I was not cared for at all.' If they gave the latter answer they were asked for more detailed information on how they lacked care. Respondents who answered 'I was given too little affection' were included in the 'withdrawal' scale.

Finally respondents were asked 'Were you ever left out of a treat that other children were getting?' If this had happened to them at the hands of their parents they were included in the 'withdrawal' scale.

It was rare for respondents to report that they received no affection at all, though responses show wide variations in the demonstrativeness of parents. Only 1% were unable to name any ways in which affection was shown in their families, the same proportion found by Ghate and Daniels (1997) in a survey of children. Although 3% of respondents stated that they were not well cared for because they had received too little affection, most had clearly had at least one parent who sometimes showed affection. It was more common for respondents to have been excluded from family treats, and 8% had had this experience. Overall, one respondent in nine experienced one or more of the treatments classified as withdrawal.

Table 35 Withdrawal

Base: all respondents

	Male	Female	Total
Unweighted base	1,235	1,634	2,869
Weighted base	1,434	1,435	2,869
	%	%	%
No ways of showing affection in the family	1	1	1
Mother/stepmother never showed affection	–	★	★
Father/stepfather never showed affection	3	1	2
Not well cared for because I was given too little affection as a child	2	3	3
I was left out of a treat that other children were getting – by mother/stepmother	6	6	6
I was left out of a treat that other children were getting – by father/stepfather	6	5	5
I was left out of a treat that other children were getting – by both parents	4	3	3
Any withdrawal	12	10	11

Antipathy

Defined by Bifulco and Moran (1998) as 'active loathing and hostility' this is one of the least studied aspects of child abuse. Research on child abuse and child protection rarely addresses the possibility of parental dislike of the child to this level. Studies of runaways, however, identify hostility from the parent as a trigger factor, particularly in adolescence. (Barter, 1996; Rees and Stein, 1999). In the present study antipathy was examined in two ways. Respondents were asked a series of specific questions about adults they knew when they were growing up who had helped them, set them good examples or acted as role models, or had shown hostility towards them ('really seemed to dislike you' or 'seemed to want to hurt you or upset you on purpose'). Secondly those who described treatment rated as abusive or neglectful were asked why they thought the person had behaved to them in that way, with a range of possible answers including the explanation that the perpetrator had disliked or resented them. Those who identified parents or step-parents in either of these categories were included in the 'antipathy' scale.

This measure produced the lowest responses to individual items, although in total one respondent in ten reported antipathy from at least one parent or step-parent and a small number reported it from both.

Table 36 Antipathy

Base: all respondents

	Male	Female	Total
Unweighted base	1,235	1,634	2,869
Weighted base	1,434	1,435	2,869
	%	%	%
Mother/stepmother really seemed to dislike you or have it in for you	2	5	4
Father/stepfather really seemed to dislike you or have it in for you	3	6	5
Both parents really seemed to dislike you or have it in for you	1	1	1
Mother/stepmother seemed to want to hurt or upset you on purpose	2	5	3
Father/stepfather seemed to want to hurt or upset you on purpose	3	6	4
Both parents seemed to want to hurt or upset you on purpose	1	1	1
Neglected because 'parent/carer didn't like me/resented me'	★	1	1
Physically abused because mother/stepmother 'didn't like me/resented me'	1	3	2
Physically abused because father/stepfather ' didn't like me/resented me'	1	3	2
Physically abused because both parents 'didn't like me/resented me'	1	2	1
Emotionally abused because mother/stepmother 'didn't like me/resented me'	★	1	1
Emotionally abused because father/stepfather 'didn't like me/resented me'	1	1	1
Emotionally abused because both parents 'didn't like me/resented me'	★	★	★
Any antipathy	7	14	10

Terrorising

This is also a dimension included in a number of previous studies, but with different criteria for assessment. Some studies include all threats of harm such as threats of physical punishment. Other criteria can include threats of abandonment or being sent away, use of fear figures such as policemen or 'bogeymen', making children do something that frightens them, such as stay in the dark. Some studies include domestic violence in this category, together with threats of violence towards someone the child loves, or a pet, or threats to break or get rid of the child's treasured possessions. In the present study, this broad definition was thought to include some very disparate elements, and a distinction was made between direct threats to the child or exploitation of the child's fears, and harming the child at second hand, through 'proxy attacks' by harming or threatening someone or something the child loves.

Two questions were included as measures of 'terrorising'. In the section of the interview described earlier, respondents were asked about adults that they knew when they were growing up. One of the questions was whether there was someone: 'that you were really afraid of?' The answer that they were really afraid of a parent or step-parent was included in the 'terrorising' scale. Respondents were also asked whether they had been 'threatened with being sent away or thrown out' of their house, or a school or club. Threats with being thrown out or sent away by parents or step-parents were included in the 'terrorising' scale.

Two other questions in the interview which concerned terrorising could not be used in this scale because they were included in other abuse measures. Respondents were asked if they had been threatened with a knife or gun, and this was included in a measure of violent treatment included in the assessment of physical abuse. A question about whether threats or blackmail had ever been used to force respondents to take part in sexual behaviour was included in the sexual abuse measure.

This dimension proved to cover the most common experiences with potential for emotional abuse. A fifth of the respondents reported sometimes being 'really afraid' of their father or stepfather while almost one in five had been threatened with being sent away or thrown out at some time. Sons seem to have been threatened with exclusion slightly more often than daughters.

Table 37 Terrorising

Base: all respondents

	Male	Female	Total
Unweighted base	1,235	1,634	2,869
Weighted base	1,434	1,435	2,869
	%	%	%
Sometimes really afraid of mother/stepmother	7	8	7
Sometimes really afraid of father/stepfather	20	19	20
Sometimes really afraid of both parents	4	3	4
Threatened with being sent away or thrown out by mother/stepmother	17	17	17
Threatened with being sent away or thrown out by father/stepfather	15	13	14
Threatened with being sent away or thrown out by both parents	12	9	11
Any terrorising	33	34	34

Proxy attacks

This was defined to include domestic violence and attacks or threats against the child's pets or possessions. With domestic violence, attacks by one parent against the other are frightening to the child even when the child is not a direct or indirect target, but McGee (2000) has shown that the violent partner will often quite deliberately exploit the mother and children's fears for each other and use threats or violence to both as part of a controlling pattern of aggression. Bifulco and Moran (1998) found that threats or attacks on pets or on treasured possessions had been experienced by a number of their sample. They note that where the attack concerned an object, it often represented a valued relationship or an aspect of the child's identity: examples were the present given to one child by a dead parent, and a photograph of another child's dead parent, each destroyed by step-parents. Ascione (1998), in a small study of a 'safe house' for victims of partner violence, summarises evidence that violence to pets is linked to woman and child abuse, and demonstrates that violent partners' harming or threatening to harm pets is a common feature in families where domestic violence is found. He suggests that it is predictive of child abuse.

Three questions in the interview are used to assess proxy attacks:

- Did physical violence ever take place between those caring for you?

- Did an adult ever deliberately break or throw away one of your treasured possessions?

- Did you experience someone getting rid of your pet or having it put to sleep even though it was quite healthy?

The wording of the question on pets was not as precise as would, in retrospect, have been preferable, and it is possible that this item would include some instances where destruction of pets was not directly targeted to distress the child, but it was decided to leave it in the scale in order to test the possibility that this form of treatment linked with other proxy attacks or abusive behaviour.

Previous research has shown that physical violence between carers is a common experience faced by children. Creighton and Russell (1995) found that 45% of a national sample of adults had witnessed violence between their parents or carers at least once, and that this was equally true across the social spectrum and for all age groups between 18 and 45 years. Although for many of their sample this had been a rare occurrence, 10% had seen it 'constantly' or 'frequently'. Those who had seen violence between carers were also more likely to report having been physically punished and sexually abused, confirming other evidence that it is commonly part of a broader violent, abusive family culture. In the present study respondents could rate the violence between carers on the same scale used by Creighton and Russell, ranging from 'constantly' to 'never'. Including all members of the present sample who had witnessed violence in an emotional abuse scale was problematic as it was not possible to gauge the seriousness of the incidents. Therefore, only those who report 'constant' or 'frequent' violence between carers have been included, since this level of violence is known to be linked with abuse of the child and is also more likely to include patterns of escalation towards serious violence.

In the present study 26% of respondents reported that they had at some time in childhood seen physical violence between their carers, but for most the violence had been rare or occasional. For 5% it had been constant or frequent, a much lower level than in the earlier study. This may reflect a generation difference compared to Creighton and Russell's broader age group, or a change in public and police toleration of domestic violence.

The other two questions required 'yes/no' answers. Nine per cent reported that they had experienced treasured possessions being deliberately broken or thrown away, and 2% had experienced a pet being got rid of or put to sleep. More than one in ten of respondents reported at least one form of proxy attack.

Other negative emotional experiences

The section of the questionnaire which included questions on emotional maltreatment included a number of questions which, while they recorded treatment which was less than sensitive, were not included in the assessment of emotional maltreatment because they were not serious enough to meet the criteria described above. Nevertheless they should perhaps lead us to ask questions about the wisdom of adult approaches to children. For example, 29% of respondents said that they recalled being laughed at when they were really upset about something; and 21% said that an adult had deliberately lied to them about something important. Male respondents were slightly more likely than females to report both experiences. Respondents were also asked about positive emotional experiences such as being made to feel that they were special, or being praised or congratulated for winning prizes or doing well at school. A small proportion could not remember having these positive experiences: 8% had never been praised for doing well at school and 5% had never been congratulated for winning anything, while 11% said that they had not been made to feel special by anyone.

Table 38 Proxy attacks

Base: all respondents

	Male	Female	Total
Unweighted base	1,235	1,634	2,869
Weighted base	1,434	1,435	2,869
	%	%	%
Violence between parents/carers 'constant' or 'frequent'	3	6	5
Treasured possession deliberately broken or thrown away by adult	9	8	9
Healthy pet got rid of or put to sleep by mother/stepmother	1	2	1
Healthy pet got rid of or put to sleep by father/stepfather	1	2	2
Healthy pet got rid of or put to sleep by both parents	★	1	★
Any proxy attacks	12	14	13

The emotional maltreatment measure

Although the design of the original questionnaire incorporated concepts from the research cited, the grouping into the seven dimensions described above is 'post hoc'. It does not give definitive measurement of the seriousness of abuse. It was not possible in this simple quantitative measure to rate the relative seriousness of items against each other: for example whether living with constant or frequent violence between carers is more, less or equally serious compared with being locked in a cupboard, regularly sworn at or insulted for several years, or told that you were wished dead. Instead the seven dimensions were used to assess the experience of the sample across a range of potentially damaging childhood treatment. The measure attempts to determine whether specific examples of potentially abusive treatment were isolated problems in otherwise good or acceptable care, or were part of a general pattern of care which was, at the least, insensitive to the child's needs or distress. The approach took into account as far as possible the nature and seriousness of the experience within each dimension. For some items, answers to specific questions made it possible to rate the seriousness or frequency of what had happened, and for these only the most serious and frequent instances were included. For some items, a dichotomous response was appropriate - the treasured possession, for example, can only be destroyed once. Some items include a simple measure of whether incidents actually occurred, while others required some degree of subjective assessment by respondents on issues such as whether they were given adequate affection or allowed any freedom. Because each dimension had an underlying coherence, it was possible that different items were measuring the same underlying phenomenon. For this reason the items could not be treated cumulatively, but positive scores on several was confirmation that the measure was identifying a real and consistent deficit in parenting experienced by the respondent.

For the purpose of quantification, respondents were given a 'score' on each dimension, indicating how many of the treatments had been experienced: a nil score meant that none of the items were checked, a single item checked scored 1 and two or more items checked scored two. A maximum score of 14 indicated that more than one item was experienced in each dimension, and that the respondent had experienced a wide range of treatment with the potential for abusiveness. To achieve a mid point score of seven, a respondent had to record some treatments on at least four of the seven dimensions. The dimensions are not a comprehensive list of all potentially damaging treatment, and the results should not be seen as a complete account of emotional abuse or neglect in the population, but as an indicator of a generally abusive pattern of emotional maltreatment.

To summarise, items in the measure are:

Psychological control and domination

- Mother unpredictable

- Father unpredictable

- Child allowed freedom of speech- none

- Child allowed freedom to meet and mix with other people - none

- Child allowed freedom of thought/belief - none

Psycho/physical control and domination (physical acts of domination which control and cause distress rather than injury)

- Mouth washed out with soap - by mother/father/stepfather

- Made to miss a meal and go hungry- by mother/father/stepfather

- Made to eat or drink something that would make you sick- by mother/father/step-parent

- Being locked in a room or cupboard - by mother/father/step-parent

- Shut outside on cold day - by mother/father/step-parent

- Always made to do worst jobs in the house - by mother/father/step-parent

- Nose rubbed in wet sheets - by mother/father/step-parent

Humiliation/psychological attack on self esteem

- Made to feel embarrassed, humiliated – by mother/father/step-parent regularly over the years

- Shouted or screamed at – by mother/father/step-parent regularly over the years

- Sworn at – by mother/father/step-parent regularly over the years

- Called stupid or lazy – by mother/father/step-parent regularly over the years

- Humiliated in front of other people – by mother/father/step-parent

- Told he/she was wished dead or never born – by mother/father/step-parent.

Withdrawal

- How did family show they cared about you – None of items from checklist of ways of showing affection, no other ways mentioned

- Did mother/stepmother show affection – never

- Did father/stepfather show affection – never

- Respondent considers he/she was given too little affection as a child

- Left out of treats that other children were getting – by mother/father/step-parent.

Antipathy

- Mother/stepmother really disliked you, had it in for you

- Father/stepfather really disliked you, had it in for you

- Mother/stepmother seemed to want to hurt or upset you on purpose

- Father/stepfather seemed to want to hurt or upset you on purpose

- Respondent neglected 'because carer didn't like me, resented me' (if by mother/father/step-parent)

- Respondent physically abused 'because carer didn't like me, resented me' (if by mother/father/step-parent)

- Respondent experienced emotional treatment 'because (carer) didn't like me, resented me' (if by mother/father/step-parent).

Terrorising

- Sometimes really afraid of – father/mother/step-parent

- Threatened with being sent away or thrown out – by mother/father/step-parent.

Proxy attacks

- Physical violence between those caring for you constantly/frequently

- Adult deliberately broke treasured possession

- Mother/father/step-parent got rid of your pet or had healthy pet put to sleep.

Patterns of emotional maltreatment

The pattern of scores reflected a gradation from 0 to 14. As expected, the most common score was zero, and the number of respondents tailed off as the scores became higher.

It was necessary to determine a point on the scale which could be used as a measure of 'emotional maltreatment' for the purpose of subsequent analysis. The point chosen is inevitably arbitrary but the mid-point score of seven was chosen because it represented that respondents recorded adverse treatment in at least four of the seven dimensions. Results showed that there was a sharp decline at the bottom end of the scale with numbers decreasing substantially from point to point, whereas after the mid-point the tail off became very gradual. In all, 6% of the sample had scores of seven or higher, and these were assessed as experiencing 'emotional maltreatment'. At the lower end of the scale there were no marked gender differences but female respondents were more likely than males to score seven or higher (8% of females and 4% of males). There was no evidence of social class trends. A further 6% had scores of five or six, for which they would have recorded treatment in at least three dimensions of the scale, and these were a 'cause for concern' group.

Table 39: Emotional maltreatment scores

Base: all respondents

Score	Number	%
Unweighted base 2,869		
Weighted base 2,869		
0	1,255	44
1	633	22
2	333	12
3	175	6
4	135	5
5	107	4
6	68	2
7	36	1
8	32	1
9	21	1
10	20	1
11	16	1
12	15	1
13	15	1
14	7	*

Because the measure recorded the extent rather than the seriousness of the various behaviours, respondents with lower scores from 1 - 4, who comprised 45% of the sample, could still have been reporting very serious problems - constant or frequent domestic violence, for example or threats to throw them out of the family home. However they were not being simultaneously attacked in numerous areas of their self-esteem and psychological well being.

Self-assessed emotional maltreatment

It was noted earlier that 3% of respondents said that they were not well cared for because they were given too little affection as a child. The other questions concerning emotional maltreatment were distributed more widely through the questionnaire than with other forms of maltreatment, but there was one central block of questions which covered the issues of attacks on self-esteem, psycho-physical domination, and proxy attacks. After these questions, the 36% of respondents who reported any behaviour included as maltreatment were asked whether they considered their treatment serious enough to be considered child abuse. Of the respondents who recorded such treatment, 8% said that they thought their treatment abusive while 6% were unsure. This represented 3% of the whole sample who thought they had been abused, and 2% unsure.

Hurtful messages to children

This section of the study is the most exploratory, and conclusions are necessarily more tentative than with the other areas of maltreatment, but they do raise a number of serious questions about the insensitive, and sometimes apparently sadistic treatment experienced by many children. Parents who tell their children that they wish the child was dead or had never been born, for example, may be reacting to stress or an immediate family crisis rather than expressing a genuinely held long-term view, but it is hard to imagine a more hurtful thing to say to a child. Even in a generally loving relationship, treatment such as this clearly stays in the mind into adult life, while for some children it formed part of a constant pattern of reminders that they were not loved.

Summary

■ There have been no national population studies of emotional or psychological abuse or neglect in the UK prior to this study on which to base measures, and there is no consensus on its definition. Studies in other countries produce rates varying from less than 1% to more than a quarter of the population, due to the varying definitions used and populations studied. It is described as the most hidden and underestimated form of child maltreatment, and the most difficult to measure or prove.

■ There is an increasing weight of evidence from child protection research and practice suggesting that emotional maltreatment is central to the understanding of all maltreatment. It is an intrinsic part of physical and sexual abuse and neglect, as well as being a primary form of maltreatment in itself. It is often the emotional effects of other forms of abuse and neglect which appear to cause long-term harm long after the physical effects are healed.

■ The literature review suggested that emotional maltreatment should be assessed along a continuum, to take account of the range of abusive experiences. Furthermore emotional maltreatment would appear rarely to operate in just one area of a child's life, and is more likely to feature for prolonged periods.

■ Drawing on previous research (Garbarino, Guttman and Seeley, 1986; Brassard, Hart and Hardy, 1993; Bifulco and Moran, 1998) data were grouped and analysed along seven dimensions. These were:

• **Psychological control and domination**, including attempts to control the child's thinking, and isolation from other sources of support and development;

• **Psycho/physical control and domination** (physical acts which exert control and domination but cause distress rather than pain or injury, such as locking the child up or washing out the mouth with soap)

• **Humiliation/degradation** - psychological attacks on the child's worth or self-esteem, which could be verbal or non verbal

• **Withdrawal** - withholding affection and care, exclusion from the family (including showing preference for siblings, and excluding the child from benefits given to other children in the family)

• **Antipathy** - showing marked dislike of the child by word and deed

• **Terrorising** - threats to harm the child or someone or something the child loves, threatening with fear figures, threats to have the child sent away.

• **Proxy attack** - by harming someone or something the child loves or values. This could include deliberate attacks on the child's possessions or pets, and also includes violence between carers.

■ Findings showed that large minorities of respondents had experience in each category and that most received this from parents or substitute parents. The most common was 'terrorising', reported by over a third of the sample, followed by psychological control and domination recorded by almost a quarter.

■ A measure of emotional maltreatment was constructed by assigning scores for the number of items on each dimension: 6% of respondents had scores of 7 or more indicating adverse experience on at least four of the seven dimensions.

■ When asked whether they thought the way they had been treated was child abuse, 3% said that they had been abused and 2% were unsure.

8. SEXUAL ABUSE

It has been suggested that the history of awareness of sexual abuse in the Western world has been strongly influenced by the development of women's movements (Gordon, 1988). The modern legislation concerning sexual abuse began in this country with the Incest Act in 1906, but it was not until the broadcast of BBC's ChildWatch in 1986 (which had 16.5 million viewers) and the 1987 Cleveland Inquiry (Butler Sloss, 1988) that recognition of the extent and severity of child sexual abuse as a broader category than incest was publicly aired and debated in the UK.

Events in Cleveland precipitated a series of research studies designed to examine the definition of child abuse and the effectiveness of child protection more generally (Department of Health, 1995). This research and other studies carried out in Britain and internationally have raised a number of fundamental questions on the definition and measurement of sexual abuse. These include:

- The boundaries between normal and abusive sexual behaviour

- Boundaries between normal sexual exploration among children and 'peer abuse'

- Whether consensual acts can be abusive, especially in situations of unequal power and status between the parties, or where some groups are culturally inducted into sexual subservience

- How issues of the legality of sexual behaviour should be incorporated into measurement, when this may obscure the reality of what is actually happening.

Some of these issues are encapsulated in one of the twenty studies referred to above, which was directly relevant to the prevalence of child sexual abuse. This was a study conducted by Kelly et al., (1991) with a college based sample of 16–21 year olds. The research found that one in two girls and one in five boys had had an unwanted sexual experience before the age of 18 (such as flashing, sexual suggestions etc.). However, if a narrower definition was used (with a minimum of a five year age difference between the people involved, and narrowing the definition to include penetration or coerced masturbation), the prevalence rate reduced to 4% of girls and 2% of boys.

Unwanted sexual experience and 'normality'

From such research it can be suggested that unwanted sexual experience is normal in that it is experienced by half the female population and indicates the problems of using normality criteria in arriving at definitions of abuse. As Lamb and Coakely (1993) note, 'normal' has at least two meanings: one which describes what is typical in the general population, the other which implies that a behaviour is not detrimental to one's well being. In a study on memories of sexual play, for example, it was found that subjects would call coercive sexual situations 'normal', 'thus supporting the idea of a cultural assumption that force is a 'normal' part of heterosexual relations. Although some respondents believed, looking back, that some harm resulted from the sexual play, they still ranked the play somewhat high on the normality scale. This might suggest that girls are already seeing as 'normal' the lack of choice over what happens to their bodies.' (Lamb and Coakely, 1993, p.524).

Yet, despite theoretical interest in normal childhood sexuality, particularly through the work of Freud, very little research has been directed at examining the topic outside the clinical field. Studies which have been conducted find that experience of sexual play is commonplace (Lamb and Coakely, 1993; Smith and Grocke, 1995), and that children display a wide variety of sexual behaviours (Friedrich et al., 1991). Drawing the line between normal sexual play and what has become known as 'peer abuse' has proved difficult. In a review of the literature, practices and procedures associated with young people who sexually abuse, Calder (1997) maintains that awareness of this problem lags behind that of the US and cites a number of obstacles to recognition, including: viewing sexualised behaviour as experimentation, a fear of labelling and stigmatisation, a mistaken view that peer abuse is less serious or harmful than abuse by adults and the relatively low level of reporting.

Most studies have treated all non consensual acts as abusive, but when apparently consensual sexual behaviour is involved questions arise as to a child's capacity to give informed consent. When, as in the UK, legal ages of consent differ for girls and boys and for homosexual and heterosexual acts, research criteria become complex. The usual solution is to assess the consensual nature of the behaviour together with a judgement on the ages of the participants, in particular when there is an age gap between them which affects the power balance of the relationship. Age differences used to judge 'consensual' acts as abusive have varied from two years to 10 years. Estimates from UK research have suggested that juveniles account for between a quarter (Kelly et al., 1991) and a third of all sexual abuse (Queen's University/Royal Belfast Hospital, 1990; Glasgow et al., 1994). For this reason some researchers argue that the stipulation of a five year age difference in prevalence study definitions is erroneous and likely to prevent accurate estimates of peer abuse. Some now recommend a two year difference (Watkins and Bentovim, 1992). Others go further and suggest no age difference should be imposed (Cermak and Molidor, 1996). Grubin (1999), studying sex offending, points out that most juvenile sex offenders choose victims close in age to themselves, and that it is unusual for them to offend against much younger children. Glasgow et al., (1994) found that relatively minor age differences between the perpetrator and victim in child to child sexual abuse may represent relatively large discrepancies in power. Thus, they suggest that using developmental indices in definitions would provide more accurate data. This has major implications for the judgements to be applied in a quantitative study of the prevalence of abuse.

A feasibility study for a national prevalence study (Ghate and Spencer, 1995) found that definitions of sexual abuse vary according to the:

- Type of activity (usually distinguishing between contact and non-contact)

- Age of victim/survivor (in most studies the top limit is set at 16)

- Age differential between abuser and abused (usually five years, with some studies specifying five years for children under 12, 8-10 years for children over 12, or 5 year differential for total sample but perpetrator over 16). Definitions which set an age differential are attempting to operationalise a distinction between abusive sexual experiences and cases of sexual exploration amongst peers

- Nature of relationship between abuser and abused. In previous studies distinctions have been made between relatives (intra-familial), and people who are not related (extra-familial). Ghate and Spencer suggest that finer gradations are required in relation to extra-familial perpetrators which differentiate between people in a position of trust (peers, family friends, acquaintances and baby sitters, for example) and strangers

- Issue of consent/responsibility/legality. Some studies probe consent, others argue that children do not have the maturity to withhold consent.

Several prevalence studies introduce the topic of sexual abuse to respondents by using a definition based on that provided by Shechter and Roberge (1976):

'The involvement of dependent, developmentally immature children and adolescents in sexual activities that they do not fully comprehend, are unable to give informed consent to, and that violate the social taboos of family roles.'

This definition is widely accepted in professional and clinical practice but is criticised for its restricting focus on intrafamilial abuse (Queen's University/Royal Belfast Hospital, 1990). The first national prevalence study on child sexual abuse as a discrete topic was conducted in this country in the early 1980s (Baker and Duncan, 1985). This study used a broader definition to allow the inclusion of abuse by a sexually mature peer but to exclude peer sexual experimentation:

'A child (anyone under 16 years) is sexually abused when another person, who is sexually mature, involves the child in any activity which the other person expects to lead to their sexual arousal. This might involve intercourse, touching, exposure of the sexual organs, showing pornographic material or talking about sexual things in an erotic way.'

The most recent prevalence study 'Voices from Childhood' (Creighton and Russell, 1995) used the following definition:

'the involvement of dependent children **under the age of 16** in sexual activity which they do not fully understand and to which they are not in a position to give **informed consent** - the activity being intended to gratify or satisfy the needs of **the other** person.'

Legal ages of consent

Some studies have opted for use of legal ages of consent as a measure of abuse. Adopting the criteria of legality would inflate figures as a large minority report sexual experiences, including sexual intercourse, under 16. In their pilots Ghate and Spencer (1995) similarly found that almost half of respondents (43% N=54) reported sexual experiences in which they were willing or indifferent before the age of 16. Consent, rather than legality, is therefore probably a better indicator of abuse if it is accepted that young people under 16 are able to give consent practically rather than legally. This is, however, a contentious area which requires further discussion. Figure 1 summarises some of the arguments for and against accepting consent or legality as criteria

Figure 1 Use of 'consent' rather than legality in prevalence studies

For	Against
Children Act, 1989 principles and Children's Rights perspective (children's feelings and wishes should be taken into account, 'Gillick principle' etc.)	Criminal Law (age of consent is 16)
Peer age experimental sexual relations are not damaging in the same way as adult-child sexual relations (there is insufficient research evidence to either support or refute this)	Young people can be pressurised into peer age sex (Lamb and Coakely, 1993 ; Friedrich et al., 1991) and may not be informed sufficiently to meet the criteria of 'informed consent'.
The general public find it difficult to accept peer age sex as abuse	Perceptions of abuse change across time culture and are subject to awareness raising before certain forms of abuse are recognised. For example, recognition of 'date rape' is a relatively recent phenomenon (Kelly et al., 1991)
Using legal criteria alone to compute prevalence rates will artificially inflate figures	Using consent alone to compute prevalence rates does not take sufficient account of the child/young person's legal position of not being able to give informed consent to sexual relations under 16

There is general agreement by prevalence researchers that the definition employed will affect the rates obtained. In a review of 21 national studies conducted in English and non-English speaking countries across the world, Finkelhor (1994) reports child sexual abuse prevalence rates ranging from 7% to 36% for women and between 3% and 29% for men although fewer studies sought prevalence rates for males. A review in the UK (La Fontaine, 1990) similarly found wide variation in estimates of women sexually abused as children. The most recent prevalence study reported in Britain was the 1995 'Voices from Childhood' study, which found that 16% could be classified as having been sexually abused in some way. Variations in prevalence result from differences in study design and are particularly influenced by the specificity of definition, sampling (college or community, probability or non-probability) and method of administration (mail survey, telephone or face to face interview) (Leventhal, 1998). Including peer abuse can increase prevalence by 9% (Finkelhor, 1986) and including contact and non-contact can raise rates by approximately 16% (Russell, 1984; Kelly et al., 1991). Prevalence rates can also be affected by the inclusion of consent. Bolen and Scannapieco (1999) suggest that the most important issue is the number of detailed questions asked.

More recently, attention has been paid to the utility of providing a definition at all (Kelly et al., 1991) and it is now considered to be better to offer a range of behaviours which offer more than one opportunity for respondents to indicate their experience and which do not make any judgement available to the respondent concerning whether such experiences were abusive or not. Definitions are still required at the stage of analysis in order to compute prevalence levels of sexual abuse. The difficulty is then to decide on which criteria qualify certain interactions or relationships as abusive, although the advantage is that the definition is transparent. For this reason the preferred approach is a *post hoc* rather than *a priori* approach to definition (Ghate and Spencer, 1995).

The US National Incidence Study (NIS-3) (Sedlak and Broadhurst, 1996) breaks sexual abuse down into three components: Intrusion (evidence of penetration), Molestation with genital contact, Other or Unknown (e.g. fondling, exposure, or inadequate supervision of a child's sexual activities). This study is distinctive from all others in that it includes a harm standard in reaching definitions of abuse. No other study defines sexual abuse with harm as a criterion. In the NIS-3 for types one and two harm remains assumed as with other studies and does not have to be shown, however, evidence of harm is required for type three. The incidence figure arrived at using this definition for the US was 3.2:1000.

Conclusions from previous research

In addition to prevalence rates research shows consensus on some general points concerning sexual abuse:

- The majority of studies find that more girls than boys are victims of sexual abuse with a ratio of between one and a half to three times greater for girls

- Children are more likely to be sexually abused by someone known to them than by a family member or a stranger. International studies reveal rates of intra-familial abuse for girls between 14% and 56% and between 0% and 19% for boys (Finkelhor, 1994). In general it appears that girls are more likely to be abused by a family member than boys (Gordon, 1990)

- In relation to incest, estimates indicate that approximately 4%–5% of girls have reported being abused by a father, adoptive father, or stepfather before the age of 18 (Wassil-Grimm, 1995). Data from Williams and Finkelhor (1992) and Russell (1984) indicate that between 1% to 2.8% of girls are abused by a biological father

- Children are more likely to be sexually abused by a man. The highest estimates for female sexual abusers was 20% found in a study of sexual abuse against boys in the US (Finkelhor et al., 1990)

- Approximately one quarter to one third of sexual abusers are themselves juveniles (Glasgow et al., 1994). This highlights the importance of considering the sexual behaviour of peers as well as adults and taking juvenile sex offending seriously, rather than viewing peer sex as natural or experimental on all occasions

- Studies find that sexual abuse, where it does occur, is more often serious than not. For example, Russell (1984) categorised abuse into three levels of severity: very serious (intercourse or oral sex), serious (digital penetration or sexual touching), and least serious (e.g. sexual touching over clothes). The majority of respondents had experienced serious or very serious abuse

- Findings in relation to the prevalence of sexual abuse in all developed countries where studies have been conducted show comparable rates (Halperin et al., 1996). Whilst there is variation depending on the methodology and definitions used, Finkelhor (1994) estimated on the basis of international comparison that a prevalence figure of around 20% for females and 10% for males is realistic

- Despite the prevalence of sexual abuse to children, prevalence studies also show that it is rarely reported to the authorities (Leventhal, 1998).

In a review of the epidemiology of child sexual abuse, Leventhal (1998) proposes that further research is required on:

- Nationally representative samples of males

- Reporting behaviour in young adults who grew up during the 70s and 80s in a period of increased recognition and reporting

- A national probability sample of adults which would be large enough for appropriate sub-analyses (see also Gorey and Leslie, 1997).

Definitions and approach used in the present survey

The review of previous research showed the complexity of possible definitions and their likely effect on results in a prevalence survey. It would clearly not be possible to achieve a definition of sexual abuse which would be universally accepted and which would apply without qualification to all cultures and generations. However the previous research does give pointers to possible measures which would achieve some consensus, and would enable replication and refinement in future studies. Evidence indicated the importance of obtaining descriptions of behaviour experienced, rather than relying solely on respondents' perceptions of abuse. This would make it possible to obtain clearer information on the way in which young adults in the general population would define acceptable and unacceptable sexual behaviour towards children and adolescents, and to compare this with judgements of legality and with professional assessments of potential abuse. Research also indicated the importance of taking account of age, consent, and the relationship between the parties.

The questionnaire therefore asked for information on whether respondents had experienced specific forms of sexual treatment, covering a wide range of possibilities from being shown pornography or exposure of sexual organs to sexual intercourse. To use common terms familiar to respondents was essential, and the questionnaire used the term 'sexual intercourse' to mean heterosexual/vaginal intercourse, and categorised anal intercourse separately. They were asked for some information on the age, gender and relationship of the person(s) treating them in this way. The range of possible experience made it necessary to group the data for follow up, to produce an interview of manageable length. Assessment of abuse took into account the element of consent, the relationship and the age difference between the parties. Age ratings inevitably include arbitrary divisions, and the point is accepted that a child's developmental state may be more important than the chronological age. However in a quantitative study such as this, retrospective judgements of developmental status could not be made, and it has to be assumed that in a large sample, differences would even out. Consent was established by giving respondents a range of options from 'always against my wishes' to 'always with my full consent', allowing for intermediate stages and changes in the consent from one occasion to another.

In the questionnaire, questions relating to sexual activity and abuse were included towards the end of the self-completion section, which was administered on the interviewer's laptop computer. Respondents were reminded again that the survey was confidential and that no one would get into any trouble as a result of the answers they gave. All questions gave respondents the option of saying that they 'did not wish to answer' and questions were phased from the least serious towards the more serious sexual acts, ending with questions about involvement in making pornography and in 'selling' sex in return for money, drugs and favours. Follow up questions established the ages at which under age sexual activity started and stopped, its frequency, the place where it had occurred, whether physical force, blackmail or other threats had ever been used to make the respondent take part in sexual activity, and whether the respondent had told anyone about it at the time.

Respondents' personal experience

Respondents' were asked about their experience of a number of specific sexual activities before they were 16 years old. If the respondent answered 'yes' to any of these, they were asked if this ever happened against their wishes and if the other people involved were five or more years older than themselves. If the answer to either of these questions was 'yes' then they were asked a series of follow up questions, including the age at which this first happened and the relationship of the person to them.

The activities and their groupings were as follows:

NON-CONTACT - Under the age of 16...

- Pornographic photos or videos were taken of you

- You were shown pornographic videos, magazines, computer images or photos

- You were made or encouraged to watch other people having intercourse/performing sex acts or pornographic acts (real people, not pictures)

- Someone exposed their sex organs to you in order to shock you or excite themselves.

CONTACT - Under the age of 16...

- You were hugged or kissed in a sexual way, whether you agreed to it or not

- Someone touched or fondled your sex organs or other private parts of your body

- Someone got you to touch their sex organs or sexually arouse them with your hand

- Someone attempted oral sex on you

- Someone attempted sexual intercourse with you

- Someone attempted anal intercourse with you

- You had full sexual intercourse

- You had anal intercourse

- You had oral sex

- Someone put their finger, tongue or an object into your vagina or anus.

Table 40 shows the sample's experience of sexual behaviour which was against their wishes, and experience with another person five or more years older than them while they were themselves under 16 years. This was the core group from which the 'abused group' was later identified.

For almost all categories girls were more likely than boys to have had unwanted sexual experience. An additional 'consent' category of 'I didn't like it but I put up with it' was recorded by a few respondents for all activities, so it can be assumed that the above figures were for experiences where the respondents were clear about their objections to what happened to them. Girls were also more likely than boys to have experienced sexual attention from someone much older than them, both consensually and against their wishes.

Only eight respondents, less than 1% of the sample, reported that they had 'had sex for money, drugs or favours'. Five were female and three were male. It must be remembered that the sample, being based on domestic postcode addresses, would have excluded some of the groups who might be most vulnerable to selling sex, such as homeless young people, and that some young people involved in prostitution are unaware, or reluctant to face the reality of their situation, but the indications are that this is still a rare experience for young people.

Table 40 Experience of sexual behaviour under 16 against wishes or with a person 5+ years older

Base: All respondents

	Always/sometimes against wishes			The other person was five years or more older		
	M	**F**	**All**	**M**	**F**	**All**
Unweighted base 2,869						
Weighted base 2,869						
	%	%				
Pornographic photos or videos were taken of you	★	★	★	★	★	★
You were shown pornographic videos, magazines, computer images or photos	1	2	1	3	2	3
You were made or encouraged to watch other people having intercourse/performing sex acts or pornographic acts (real people, not pictures)	★	1	★	★	★	★
Someone exposed their sex organs or other private parts of their body to you in order to shock you or excite themselves	3	10	6	4	10	7
You were hugged or kissed in a sexual way, whether you agreed to it or not	2	7	4	3	10	7
Someone touched or fondled your sex organs or other private parts of your body	2	8	5	3	11	7
Someone got you to touch their sex organs or sexually arouse them with your hand	2	5	3	2	8	5
Someone attempted oral sex on you	2	3	2	2	5	3
Someone attempted sexual intercourse with you	2	5	3	2	7	5
Someone attempted anal intercourse with you	2	1	1	1	1	1
You had full sexual intercourse	1	3	2	2	6	4
You had anal intercourse	★	1	★	1	1	1
You had oral sex	1	2	1	2	4	3
Someone put their finger, tongue or an object into your vagina or anus	★	4	2	1	7	4

★ Denotes less than 1%

Who did this behaviour happen with?

To examine this, the 14 sexual behaviours experienced by respondents were grouped into five categories for follow up questions. This was done both to contain the length of the interview within practical limits and because piloting showed that it was necessary to prevent the detailed questioning from becoming distressing and unacceptable to respondents. Follow up was undertaken in all instances where the behaviour had taken place against the respondent's wishes, or if consensual sexual acts had involved another person five or more years older than the respondent. 'Penetrative/oral acts' included sexual intercourse, anal intercourse, oral sex, and insertion of a finger or object into the vagina or anus. Attempts at penetrative/oral acts were categorised separately. 'Touching' included touching or fondling of sexual organs or other private parts of the body, being made to touch the other person similarly, and sexual hugging and kissing. Having pornographic videos or photographs taken of you, being shown pornography, and being made or encouraged to watch other people having intercourse or performing other sex acts were grouped as one 'non-contact' category, and 'deliberate exposure of the sex organs to excite themselves or shock you' was the last category, kept separate because it was more likely than other behaviours to have been a single incident involving a stranger (Creighton and Russell 1995).

Table 41 gives the results on sexual acts involving family members for the present sample, shows the small numbers involved, and shows that a wide range of relatives were involved, almost all males. Brothers or stepbrothers were the relatives most often cited, but the very small base numbers must be borne in mind when considering these results.

Far more of the sample experienced sexual behaviour from non relatives when under 16, which was either against their wishes or from someone much older (five or more years) than themselves. Almost all of this was from someone known to the child. The only exception is 'indecent exposure' but even with this, almost two thirds knew the person cited (Table 42).

Most activity involved boy- or girlfriends, friends of siblings, fellow students or 'someone I recently met' (which would in many instances have been age peers met socially). With actual or attempted penetrative sex, 'boy/girlfriends' is by far the largest group, and 'someone I recently met' the second largest, suggesting that where most intrusive sexual experience is concerned, so called 'date rape' is likely to be the most common sexually abusive experience the respondents faced. This will be explored further in later analysis.

Apart from the indecent exposure, others involved were almost all family friends or neighbours, and very few respondents reported abuse of any kind by professionals (none by priests, religious leaders, social or care workers). It must be remembered that young people living away from home may be under represented in the sample, but the picture is clearly not one of widespread abuse by those charged with responsibility for the care, education and support of the young.

Table 41 Sexual acts within the family

Base: all who reported sexual behaviour with relatives against their wishes, or when they were aged 16 or under with someone 5 years or more older.

Relationship	Penetrative/ oral acts	Attempted penetrative/ oral acts	Touching	Voyeurism/ Pornography	Exposure
Base numbers	30	30	81	24	73
Weighted	33	32	88	23	69
%	100	100	100	100	100
	%	%	%	%	%
Uncle	14	13	19	12	26
Brother/stepbrother	38	43	20	43	29
Stepfather	13	19	16	9	9
Father	23	14	12	21	11
Cousin	8	8	10	4	9
Grandfather	6	1	9	2	17
Sister/stepsister	-	-	6	-	3
Mother	4	6	3	14	2
Stepmother	-	-	1	-	1
Grandmother	-	-	1	-	-
Other Relative	-	-	2	-	2
Don't know	2	-	1	-	1
Do not wish to answer	4	12	6	9	5

Most sexual behaviour was experienced with males, but the picture is affected by the gender of respondents, since the great majority of those reporting sexual activity against their wishes or with someone much older were female (70% – 75% depending on category, and with the exception of voyeurism). For all categories of sexual behaviour, more than 9 out of 10 young women reported that the person/people behaving in this way with them was male, whereas for the young men respondents the picture was more mixed. These results support the previous conclusions from Finkelhor et al., (1990) that abusers of girls are nearly all males, and those studies which have shown a rather more mixed picture for abusers of boys (Dhaliwal et al., 1996).

Respondents were asked where the sexual acts had taken place. The most usual locations for all types of incident were either the respondent's own home or the home of the other person. Other locations mentioned were extremely rare, except for indecent exposure, where 30% of incidents occurred in an open place such as woods or parks, or abandoned buildings.

Table 42 Sexual acts with someone outside the family

Base: all who reported sexual behaviour with non relatives against their wishes, or when they were under 16 with someone 5 years or more older

Person outside the family	Penetrative/ oral acts	Attempted penetrative/ oral acts	Touching	Voyeurism/ Pornography	Exposure
Base numbers	187	204	321	112	207
Weighted	196	212	319	121	211
%	100	100	100	100	100
	%	%	%	%	%
Friend of parents	6	8	10	6	11
Friend of brother or sister	6	5	7	17	9
Boyfriend/girlfriend	70	61	58	34	14
Baby-sitter	2	1	2	2	3
Neighbour	4	6	4	5	11
Teacher	-	1	1	-	2
Priest/Religious Leader	-	-	-	-	-
Care Worker/Social Worker	-	-	-	-	-
Fellow Student/Pupil	10	13	14	39	12
Friends	★	1	2	9	-
Stranger – Man	3	5	5	1	35
Stranger – Woman	4	4	3	1	1
Someone recently met	17	16	17	8	6
Other	2	2	3	4	6
Don't know	-	★	1	-	3
Do not wish to answer	1	★	1	4	2

Respondents were asked whether physical force, threats or blackmail (for example to hurt someone you love or to tell everyone it was your fault) had been used to obtain their compliance. Some respondents reported this for all categories of sexual behaviour, with six in ten (58%) of those reporting unsuccessful attempts to engage them in oral or penetrative sex saying that physical force was used, and 39% reporting blackmail. 40% of those who had experienced full oral or penetrative sex against their wishes or with a much older person reported the use of force, and 31% the use of blackmail.

Table 43 Gender of the person involved in sexual behaviour with respondents

Base: all who reported sexual behaviour against their wishes,
or when they were aged under 16 with someone 5 years or more older.

	Penetrative/ oral acts	Attempted penetrative/ oral acts	Touching	Voyeurism/ pornography	Exposure
Female Respondents					
Number	179	183	296	68	209
Weighted	174	174	285	67	192
	%	%	%	%	%
Male Involved	97	99	95	95	99
Female Involved	2	2	5	33	3
Male Respondents					
Number	43	55	99	66	63
Weighted	58	72	117	71	83
	%	%	%	%	%
Male Involved	30	43	27	78	55
Female Involved	70	67	74	27	45

Respondents were asked at what age the behaviour had started. In previous research (Baker and Duncan, 1985) 61% reported onset at 11 years and older with the mean age of onset for males being 12.03 years and for females 10.74 years. Creighton and Russell (1995) similarly found the average age of onset was 11.5 years. This is a higher age than that found in studies in the US Siegel et al. (1987) found the mean age of onset was 9.5 years, median was 10 years and mode 14 years. Finkelhor et al. (1990) give median age for men as 9.9 and for women as 9.6 years for age at the time of abuse. In a review of recent studies the range of age of onset has been given as 7.7-10.0 years for boys and 7.4-9.6 years for girls (Dhaliwal et al., 1996).

All of these studies give figures in relation to a definition of abuse, whereas the figures in Tables 40-42 refer to sexual acts which include consensual behaviour where the other person was 5 years or more older. However the results of the present study confirmed that most experience of sexual behaviour which is unwanted or which involves a much older person, occurs in adolescence. Approximately three quarters of both male and female respondents who had experienced attempted or actual oral or penetrative sex acts against their wishes or with an older person said that their first experience had been aged 13 - 15 years. Very few reported experience of any kind in the pre-school years. Although this could obviously be affected by unreliable memory of early childhood, this is true of all prevalence studies relying on recall. Experiences become more common as age rises, although most are still much less common at age 12 or less than in adolescence. The most common experience at a younger age was seeing someone deliberately exposing their sex organs or other private parts of the body to excite themselves or shock the child: 70% of men who reported unwelcome experiences of exposure or experiences with an older person had been 12 or less, as had 65% of the women. One third of those who had experienced sexual contact involving touching were aged 12 or less, with no gender difference; 28% of the women and 41% of the men who had experiences involving pornography were 12 or less at the time.

The majority of respondents experiencing unwelcome sexual acts or with an older person had more than one such experience. Only 'exposure' was likely to be 'one-off', with 50% of the women and 40% of the men having only one such experience. Of those experiencing oral or penetrative sex, 51% of the women and 44% of the men had more than one experience with the same person; 20% of the women and 27% of the men had experiences with more than one person. There was no clear pattern to the age at which the sexual activity stopped, although for each activity a number of respondents reported that it had not stopped. Seven in ten men and 47% of the women who had experienced oral or penetrative sex against their wishes or with an older person before they were 16 reported that it had continued after the age of 18, with lower levels for other activities involving contact (43% of men and 33% of women) and the lowest levels of continuance for exposure and pornography.

Respondents were asked why the activities had stopped. Again there was no clear pattern, with small numbers reporting that they had sought help from an adult who had stopped it, or had simply avoided the other person, some having confronted the other person, and some finding that the other person had stopped of their own accord. In a few instances the young person had left home or become pregnant, or the abuser had left the home.

Only just over a quarter (28%) of respondents who had experienced any of these sexual activities had told someone at the time, slightly more women (32%) than men (20%). A further 27% had told someone later, but 31% had never told anyone. Where help was sought, or anyone had been told what was happening, it was usually a family member or friend: 73% of the men and 50% of the women who had told someone had told a friend; 21% of men and 32% of women had told mothers or stepmothers, and smaller proportions had told fathers or siblings. Hardly anyone had told police, social services, teachers, doctors or other professionals. Those who had told no-one (194 respondents) most often said that the reason for this was that 'it was nobody else's business' (28% of men and 27% of women), or that they 'didn't think it was serious or wrong' (31% of men and 18% of women). Smaller numbers 'didn't want parents' (23%) or friends (14%) or the authorities (6%) to find out, were frightened (24%), didn't think they would be believed (13%) or had been threatened by the other person (7%).

Defining sexual abuse

The definition adopted took into account the concerns emerging from the review of previous studies, by building in dimensions for age and informed consent, rather than focusing exclusively on the legal age of consent or on the respondents' own assessment of consent. Because opinions differed over the appropriate age gap for consensual sex, but there was general agreement that no sexual behaviour was acceptable between pre-teen children and those much older or adults, respondents were separated into two groups to assess sexual activities undertaken by consent with an older person.

The sexual behaviour towards the respondent was categorised by the researchers as 'abuse' in the following circumstances:

■ If the other person was a parent or carer (by definition more than five years older)

■ If the relevant behaviour occurred against the respondent's wishes, or

■ If consensual sexual acts involved a person other than a parent who was 5 or more years older when the child was aged 12 or under.

A 'borderline' group was defined where teenagers aged 13–15 had sexual experiences with someone aged five or more years older and stated that this was with their full consent. This is currently illegal when it involves vaginal or anal intercourse. It raises many questions about young people's capacity for informed consent and could be considered exploitative behaviour by the older person, but could also include a wide variety of circumstances in which public opinion might differ on what was acceptable or culpable, and therefore analysis was undertaken separately in order to throw light on the respective prevalence levels.

Consensual activities between age peers were not rated as abuse, although again, some of these would have been illegal.

The definitions are based on research evidence of the likely harmful effects of the abuse, which is known to be affected by the relationship to the abuser and the involvement of physical contact (Finkelhor, 1979; Russell, 1984; Baker and Duncan, 1985).

Abuse involving physical contact is divided into two categories: whether the contact involved touching genital, anal or other normally private areas of the body; and other physical contact such as sexual hugging and kissing. The non-contact category includes exposure of sex organs or other private areas of the body, voyeurism and use in the production of pornography. Abusers were assigned to three groups: parents/carers (including step-parents and parents' partners); other relatives and other known people (including family friends, neighbours, and professionals such as teachers, social workers or youth workers); and strangers or 'someone you had recently met'. This last category enabled separation between non relatives who were longer-standing contacts and casual or chance acquaintances such as people who met for the first time at parties or similar occasions.

Sexual abuse categories

Initially, analysis involved three categories, because there were concerns that 'touching and fondling' might have a very different impact depending on the areas of the body involved. Categories were:

Category A - Abuse involving physical contact with genital, anal or other private areas of the body

- Sexual intercourse or anal intercourse
- Attempted intercourse, or anal intercourse
- Oral sex
- Insertion of finger, tongue or object
- Touching/fondling child's sex organs/private parts or made to touch the abuser.

Category B - Abuse involving physical contact with other parts of the body

- Kissed or hugged in a sexual way (if the only thing that happened)

Category C - Abuse not involving physical contact

- Exposure of sex organs in order to excite themselves or shock the child
- Pornographic videos or photos taken of child
- Child made or encouraged to watch other people having intercourse.

Children may experience both contact and non-contact abuse by the same abuser. In this categorisation, contact and non-contact are mutually exclusive within each relationship type: i.e. if a respondent experienced contact and non-contact abuse from a parent or carer, he or she is only included in the contact abuse category, to avoid double counting. However, if someone experienced contact abuse with more than one category of person – for example, a parent and other relative – then that individual is included in both categories of abuse.

Results showed that very few respondents reported unwelcome sexual contact with non-private parts of the body as their only experience, and for further analysis this behaviour was included in a general category of 'contact abuse'. Table 44 gives the results for sexual abuse involving acts against the respondents' wishes or taking place when they were aged 12 or less. Table 45 gives results for acts involving 13-15 year olds with an adult of five or more years older, to which the respondents consented.

Table 44 Sexual abuse

Base: all respondents

Total abused against wishes or aged 12 or under (unweighted = 435, weighted = 452)

Sexual Abuse Abuser	Contact			Non-contact			Total		
	Male	Female	Total	Male	Female	Total	Male	Female	Total
	%	%	%	%	%	%	%	%	%
Parents/carers	1	1	1	–	★	★	1	1	1
Other relatives	1	3	2	★	1	1	1	4	3
Other known people	5	11	8	3	3	3	8	14	11
Strangers/someone recently met	2	3	2	1	4	2	3	7	5
Total abused by anyone	7	16	11	4	8	6	11	21	16

Previous research has found that sexual abuse was most common from people known to the child, but not family members, with most studies showing approximately a quarter of abusers being in the family (Russell, 1984; Baker and Duncan, 1985; Wyatt, 1985; Siegel et al., 1987; Finkelhor et. al., 1990; Creighton & Russell 1995). However, Finkelhor et al., (1990) found that boys were more at risk from strangers (40% compared to 21% for women). Present results confirm the pattern of abuse primarily by non relatives.

Table 45 'Consensual' activity with an adult

Base: all respondents

Total consensual activity aged 13-15 with an adult aged 5+ years older (unweighted = 164, weighted = 163)

Sexual Abuse Abuser	Contact			Non-contact			Total		
	Male	Female	Total	Male	Female	Total	Male	Female	Total
	%	%	%	%	%	%	%	%	%
Parents/carers	–	★	★	★	–	★	★	★	★
Other relatives	★	★	★	★	–	★	★	★	★
Other known people	2	7	5	1	★	1	4	7	5
Strangers/someone recently met	1	1	1	–	★	★	1	1	1
Total	3	7	5	2	★	1	4	7	6

Sexual abuse by parents/carers

Contact

1% had experienced sexual behaviour involving some form of contact by their parent/carer, this response coming from 1% of males and 1% of females. Most of this small subgroup (17 of 25 respondents – around seven in ten) were female, just eight being male.

Non-contact

A further 4 respondents (less than 1%) had been abused by their parent/carer by either having been involved in pornography or by having been made to watch sex acts. All were female.

'Consensual' activity with parents or carers was rated as abusive regardless of the age of the young person (all were under 16 years.). One respondent reported having been involved in consensual contact and one respondent in consensual non-contact sexual behaviour with their parent/carer when they were aged 13–15. In total 1% of children had been sexually abused by parents/carers. The proportions was so small that further breakdowns amounted to less than 1%. In terms of this small subgroup's profile, it comprises 27% boys and 73% girls.

Sexual abuse by other relatives

Contact

2% said that they had experienced sexual behaviour involving contact by a relative other than their parent/carer against their will, or by an adult relative when they were aged 12 or under. Girls were more likely than boys to have been abused by these relatives – 3% of them, compared with 1% of boys. The gender profile of this group includes 25% boys and 75% girls.

Non-contact

1% had been abused by a relative other than parents, by either having been involved in pornography or by having been made to watch sex acts or seen exposure of sexual or other private parts of the body. Again, girls were more likely to have experienced this, two thirds of this group being girls.

'Consensual' sexual behaviour aged 13-15 years with an adult relative

Four respondents reported having been involved in consensual sexual behaviour with an older relative other than their parent/carer when they were aged 13–15. In two cases, this was with contact and in two without contact. In total, excluding the borderline 'consensual' cases, 3% of children had been sexually abused by relatives other than their parents or carers. These figures break down as follows: 1% of boys and 4% of girls. The profile of this subgroup abused by relatives other than parents and carers is 27% boys and 73% girls.

Sexual abuse by other known people

As in previous research, this proved the largest category for sexual abuse.

Contact
8% had experienced sexual contact against their will or when they were under 12 with an adult known to them but not related. An additional 14 respondents (less than 1%) had agreed to sexual contact of this nature with someone more than five years older than them when they were aged under 12

Taking the two groups together, this gives a total of 8% who were sexually abused involving contact by someone unrelated but known to them. This comprises: 5% of boys and 11% of girls. The profile of this subgroup is as follows: 34% boys and 66% girls.

Non-contact
3% had been abused by an unrelated but known person by either having been involved in pornography or by having been made to watch sex acts (including deliberate exposure) against their will, or when they were aged 12 or younger with someone five or more years older than them. In this instance, there was no difference between the sexes (3% in each case).

'Consensual' sexual behaviour aged 13-15 with a known adult
5% reported having been involved in consensual sexual behaviour with contact when aged 13–15, with someone five or more years older than them. A small number had experienced non contact behaviours when this age but this small group do not affect the total percentage of 5%. The profile of this group is: 36% boys, 64% girls.

In total, excluding the consensual borderline cases, 11% of the sample had been sexually abused by an unrelated known person. This comprises: 8% of boys and 14% of girls. The profile of this group is: 38% boys, 62% girls.

Sexual abuse by a stranger/person just met

Contact
2% of respondents said that they had experienced sexual contact against their will or when they were under 12 with an adult stranger or someone they had just met. The profile of this small group is: 33% boys and 67% girls.

Non–contact
2% had been abused by a stranger/someone they had just met by either having been involved in pornography, having been made to watch sex acts or by witnessing exposure. This breaks down as: 1% of boys and 4% of girls. In terms of profile, the group comprises 22% boys, 78% girls.

'Consensual' sexual activity aged 13 -15 years with an adult stranger or someone just met
1% reported having been involved in consensual sexual behaviour with a stranger aged five or more years older when they were aged 13–15. In all but one case this involved contact: 1% of boys and 1% of girls. The profile of the group is: 52% boys and 48% girls.

In total, excluding the 'consensual' borderline cases, 4% of children had been sexually abused by a stranger or someone they had just met: 3% of boys and 7% of girls. The profile of this group sexually abused by a stranger is: 28% boys and 72% girls.

Experience of abuse with more than one type of person

Previous research produced varying findings over the frequency of incidents. Baker and Duncan (1985) found that 63% of victims reported single abusive experience, 23% were repeatedly abused by the same person and 14% subjected to multiple abuse by more than one person. Siegel et al. (1987) report variations between 39–50% of respondents experiencing two or more abuse episodes in a review of five community-based populations studies, in their own study 46% reported repeated abuse. Creighton and Russell (1995) found that of those who had experienced some form of sexual abuse, for almost half (45%) sexual abuse with physical contact had been involved and they had experienced abuse more than once (this represented 7% of the total sample). As already noted above, at the analysis stage of this survey, if young people had experienced contact and non-contact abuse with the same type of person i.e. parent/carer, other relative, other known person or stranger, they were defined only as having experienced contact abuse. However, if they had experienced abuse from more than one of these types of people, they were included in more than one subgroup.

Experiences of contact abuse with more than one type of person
2% had experienced contact abuse from more than one type of person.

Of the 25 respondents who had experienced contact abuse at the hands of their parents/carers:

Two had also experienced contact abuse at the hands of other relatives

Five had also experienced contact abuse at the hands of other known people

Eight had also been sexually abused involving contact by a stranger or someone they had just met.

Of the 58 respondents who had been abused involving contact by other relatives:

Two had also experienced contact abuse from their parents (as noted above)

Eighteen (a third – 31% of them) had also been abused involving contact by other known people

Two had also been abused by a stranger.

220 respondents reported abuse involving contact by someone known to them and 10% of these people (22 cases) had also been contact abused by a stranger.

Experiences of contact and non-contact abuse with more than one type of person
1% had been abused involving contact by at least one type of person and abused involving non-contact by another.

Of those contact abused by parents/carers, one was non-contact abused by someone known to them and another was non-contact abused by a stranger. Of those contact abused by relatives (excluding parents), one was non-contact abused by parents, two were non-contact abused by other known people and two were non-contact abused by strangers. Of those contact abused by other known people, six (3%) were non-contact abused by relatives excluding parents and 21 (9%) were non-contact abused by strangers.

In total, 37 (11%) people who were contact abused were also non-contact abused by someone other than the contact abuser.

Total prevalence of sexual abuse

In total, using the definition given above, 11% of respondents had been abused involving sexual contact either against their will, by parents/carers or by other people when they were 12 or under and the other person was five or more years older. There was a substantial gender difference, with 7% of boys and 16% of girls, reporting behaviour assessed as definitely abusive. There was a smaller social class difference, with 10% from groups ABC1 reporting this behaviour and 13% from groups C2DE. An additional 6% had been abused not involving contact (4% of boys and 8% of girls, 5% of ABC1s and 7% of C2DEs).

As detailed above, there is some overlap between the contact and non-contact groups. In total 16% were sexually abused as children. This comprises: 11% of boys and 21% of girls; 14% of ABC1s and 18% of C2DEs. The profile of the group is: 34% boys and 66% girls.

5% of these young people said that their abuser behaved similarly with other children in their family and 9% said that he or she did this with other children outside the family.

This figure is pitched at a mid-point between the extremes of the UK studies cited earlier, and is close to the level obtained by Creighton and Russell in 1995, using a national quota sample and including a similar definition of sexual acts taking place before age 16, against the respondent's wishes or with person much older than the respondent.

'Consensual' sexual behaviour aged 13-15 years with an adult

6% of respondents reported having been involved in consensual sexual behaviour when aged 13–15, with someone five or more years older, other than a parent. In almost all cases (5%) this involved contact. In terms of UK law, some of these young people were victims of sexual offences, and all could by some definitions and in some cultures be considered victims of abuse. If this borderline group are defined as 'sexually abused' the total abused would rise to 20%, there being some overlap between the abused and borderline groups.

Self-assessed sexual abuse

Respondents who reported any sexual activity against their wishes, or any consensual activity with a person five or more years older when they were under 16, or who said that they had sex in return for money, drugs or favours, were asked whether they considered themselves to have been sexually abused. Altogether 22% of the sample came into one or other of these categories, of whom over a quarter (28%, comprising 6% of the whole sample) considered themselves to have been abused. Two thirds said that they had not been abused and 7% were unsure. There was a gender difference, with the women more than twice as likely as the men to consider themselves abused (35% of the women and 15% of the men).

Self-assessment of abuse showed marked overlap with research assessments when examining sexual activity within the family: more than two thirds of those assessed as abused by researchers considered themselves to have been abused. Outside the family, the picture was more mixed. Approximately a third of those assessed by researchers as experiencing contact abuse by known people or by strangers, considered themselves to have been abused. Although base numbers are very small, more than half of those rated as experiencing 'non-contact abuse' by known people thought that they had been abused.

Summary

- Estimates of child sexual abuse prevalence from previous research range from 3% to 36% for females and from 3% to 29% for males. There is consensus that females are more likely to be victims of sexual abuse, and that abusers are most likely to be known to the child but not a relative.

- There are considerable differences of opinion on the definition of abuse. Most studies agree that sexual acts occurring against the child's wishes are abusive, but problems arise in deciding when a child is competent to give 'informed consent'. Studies have used age gaps varying from 2 to 10 years in deciding whether apparently consensual activities were abusive, with five years being the one most commonly chosen.

- The present survey asked respondents whether they had experienced specific sexual acts when they were under 16. Those who had done so, were asked further questions about the other person involved, whether they had consented to what happened, and how old they were at the time.

- Respondents who had not consented, and those whose 'consensual' activity had occurred with someone five or more years older, when they themselves were 12 years old or less, were assessed as having been abused. A borderline group was identified who had become involved in consensual sex with an adult of five or more years older when they themselves were aged 13-15 years.

- Abuse was examined separately according to the identity of the abuser, whether a relative, a known but unrelated person, and a stranger or a person just met.

- A distinction was drawn between abuse involving physical contact, (including intercourse, oral sex, touching and fondling, and sexual hugging or kissing), and 'non-contact' abuse, (using the child to make pornographic photographs or videos, showing the child pornography, forcing or encouraging the child to watch live sexual acts, and exposing sex organs to excite themselves or shock the child).

- Using these definitions, 1% of the sample had been abused by parents/carers, almost all of this abuse involving physical contact, and 3% had been abused by other relatives, with 2% contact and 1% non-contact. Abuse by other known people was the most common, and 11% of the sample had this experience, 8% involving physical contact and 3% non-contact. Abuse by strangers or someone just met had affected 4% of the sample, 2% contact and 2% non-contact.

- The borderline group who had consensual sexual activity with an adult other than a parent when they were aged 13 - 15 was primarily involved with known non-relatives: 5% of the sample came into this group.

- 3% reported touching or fondling with relatives which were against their wishes or with a person five or more years older and the same proportion had witnessed relatives exposing themselves. Oral/penetrative acts or attempts and voyeurism/pornography with relatives were reported by 1%.

- Larger numbers had experienced sexual acts by non relatives, predominantly by people known to them and by age peers: boy or girlfriends, friends of brothers or sisters, fellow pupils or students formed most of those involved. Among older people, neighbours and parents' friends were the most common. Very few said that the person involved was a professional.

- The only category which was experienced to any great extent from strangers was indecent exposure: of the 7% of the sample who experienced this, just over a third said that the person concerned was a stranger.

- The majority of those experiencing both contact and non-contact abuse had more than one abusive experience: only indecent exposure was likely to be a single incident.

- Only a quarter of respondents with sexual experience, unwanted or with a person 5 or more years older, had told anyone about it at the time. When they had, their confidant was usually a friend, less often a family member and very rarely the police or other professionals.

- The person involved with the respondent was almost always male and very few respondents of either gender said that the person involving them in sex acts was female. Women respondents were more likely than men to have experienced all forms of abuse.

- 6% of the total sample assessed themselves as having been sexually abused.

9. CONCLUSIONS

Reports of child abuse to child protection agencies have increased in many countries. These increases are in respect of all forms of abuse and neglect. The American Humane Association found a 142% increase in reports between 1976 and 1983 (American Association for the Protection of Children, 1985) and similar increases have been reported in Australia (Thorpe, 1997). An analysis of outcomes over five years in Western Australia revealed consistency in the numbers of children offered service (Thorpe, 1997), and there is very little information by which to assess whether rates of child abuse are increasing or decreasing, or whether service levels have reached a plateau beyond which they cannot offer further resources. A comparison of findings from the National Family Violence Survey in the US suggests that some violence to children may be decreasing (Gelles and Straus, 1987) although their analysis and the claim of decreasing rates has been contested (Knudsen, 1988; Egely, 1991). More recent statistics from the USA show that the rates of children referred for investigation of maltreatment have increased from 39.2 per 1000 in 1990 to 42.0 per 1000 in 1997 (United States Department of Health and Human Services Administration on Children, Youth and Families, 1997).

Trends in the UK are more difficult to track since there is no national co-ordination of statistics on reported cases. Annual returns are made by local authorities of the numbers of children on the Child Protection Register. These refer to children who have been the subject of a case conference which makes decisions about whether a child is at risk of future harm and is in need of child protection intervention. The register statistics show that the numbers of children on the register have declined from 45,300 in 1991 to 31,900 in 1999, (Department of Health, 1999).

Data based on present reporting systems has the disadvantage that it may reflect features of the system or changes in operational practices and does not necessarily reflect the level of actual maltreatment in the population. Still less is known about the nature and extent of child maltreatment in the general population of children and young people. Yet this is the knowledge which is needed if we are to be sure that child protection systems are adequate and that children are not 'falling through holes in the net'.

The need for reliable prevalence data

This new national survey of childrearing and children's experience extends the knowledge base on acceptable and unacceptable ways of treating children and the more extreme forms of child abuse and neglect in the UK. This data can inform the development of appropriate and sensitive children's services and prevention strategies for the future. It can also provide a baseline from which to measure the success of future interventions. The study was also designed to increase understanding of some of the boundary problems in deciding when behaviour towards children becomes abusive or neglectful, and to examine differences of perspective between researchers using accepted professional practice definitions, the general public, and people who had experienced maltreatment.

The sample consisted of 2,869 young adults aged 18-24, obtained by random probability sampling throughout the UK. This comprised 1,235 men and 1,634 women, and the response rate was 69%. The age range was chosen to avoid the ethical and practical problems which would arise from attempting to interview minors about abuse and neglect, while surveying a population whose childhood was recent, minimising the effect of memory loss, and enabling an estimate of the effects of maltreatment relatively uncontaminated by the stresses of later life. Sampling was based on households identified from postcode files, and is correctively weighted using recognised statistical methods so that findings are representative of the total UK population. Interviews were carried out using computer assisted data entry, with the more sensitive information being entered directly by respondents, thus avoiding the need to voice answers to interviewers, and protecting respondents' confidentiality and privacy. Figures below are the weighted figures. Most of the respondents (56%) were still living with parents, but 18% were living with spouses/partners, 8% living alone and the rest with friends, flatmates or other relatives. A minority (15%) had children of their own, most of whom were the young women respondents: 23% of the young women had children compared to 7% of the men.

Prevalence research - the 'art of the possible'

Examination of the previous research literature on the prevalence of abuse and neglect showed very different base lines for the various aspects of child maltreatment. The most frequently researched aspects of child abuse have been sexual abuse and physical abuse, particularly the former. However the varied methods and definitions used produced huge variations in the figures obtained even within a single country, while international rates bore little comparison. It was difficult to tell how far differences in rates reflected the definitions, sampling and interview methods, and how far they represented cultural differences between countries and over time or generations. Nevertheless there was sufficient common ground in the findings to give some understanding of the nature of these forms of abuse, and sufficient evidence on the effect of particular approaches to sampling and definition to guide the present researchers as to the most fruitful and reliable approaches to the problem of measuring prevalence. On physical abuse, there was the great advantage of a replicated approach through use of the Conflict Tactics Scale (Straus, 1979) which makes possible some national and international comparisons. There have also been some quantitative surveys and cohort studies of childrearing which gave valuable insight into the important features of family discipline and relationships in the UK, public attitudes to the treatment of children, and the methodological problems of achieving simple quantitative measures of very complex and varied phenomena (Creighton and Russell, 1995). It was possible both to learn much from previous experience in designing the present survey, and have a base of previous data which could be used for comparison. Results can then be used cumulatively to make an informed assessment of the reliability of the approach to research, and the validity of the findings. Obtaining similar results from replicated measures in different studies increases confidence that the findings are saying something meaningful about childrearing and child maltreatment.

On neglect and emotional or psychological maltreatment, the picture was very different. Virtually no prevalence research had been carried out, and there was no generally accepted paradigm for the study of either. There was not even general agreement on what constituted neglect or abuse, or on when particular treatment was neglect and when it was abuse. Each study used its own definitions and typologies with little reference to previous research or to conceptual frameworks developed by others. There was some evidence of a split between approaches which used a medical or paramedical framework, those which used a social work or social policy approach and those which were primarily psychological in origin. The range of possible behaviours which could be harmful to children was much greater than for physical and sexual abuse, and there was much less evidence of social or professional consensus on acceptable ways to treat children.

Previous research also made it clear that that there was no 'right' definition of any form of maltreatment. Views on the acceptability of the treatment of children vary between national, ethnic and social class cultures and between generations, although there is now some evidence, through the United Nations Declaration on the Rights of the Child, of an international consensus on the more extreme forms of physical and sexual exploitation.

Nor is there evidence that it is practical to aim at achieving a total and absolute figure for the prevalence of maltreatment in general or of specific forms of maltreatment. Evidence from cohort studies of childrearing and from studies of reported maltreatment shows that much happens in early childhood, and will be affected by memory loss later in life. Furthermore there is considerable overlap between the areas of maltreatment, particularly with emotional or psycho-logical maltreatment. Sexual abuse can also involve physical abuse, and all forms of maltreatment are likely to have adverse emotional or psychological effects on children. Hence any division into the areas of maltreatment in a prevalence study will necessarily create arbitrary distinctions, in order to avoid 'double counting', which will have the effect of underestimating the total extent of maltreatment. Figures from the present study inevitably underestimate some of the harmful treatment experienced. The underestimation is also affected by the use of a household base for sampling, since victims of abuse are likely to be overrepresented among the socially excluded - those who are homeless, in prison, hospital or in other institutional care.

What is possible is to establish benchmarks which are meaningful for a particular culture or community at a particular time, and which will be robust for a generation, to enable the planning of services and the monitoring of effects of particular treatment on children. This study attempts to establish those benchmarks, albeit with the necessary limitations and qualifications described above.

Themes arising from the data

Certain themes arise at a number of points in the survey, which challenge us to think about some of the most basic aspects of our society and our approach to childrearing. These concern the family, gender, social class and age peer relationships. Some light has been thrown on all these by the data analysis so far, but all leave questions to be explored further, both from this survey and in new research.

Families

Family life is without question the single most important determinant of a happy childhood and successful transition to adulthood, although 'families' can (and in the present sample did) take many forms. For the majority of the sample, (with figures often reaching 90%) the family was effective in providing a 'warm and loving' background, close relationships with parents, adequate physical care and supervision, emotional and psychological development, and a platform for making successful peer and adult relationships outside the family. Extended family networks were strong, and high proportions of the sample named grandparents, aunts or uncles as people whom they particularly respected, who acted as role models or gave advice or help when needed. Nevertheless, the minorities dissenting from this account of family experience are sometimes worryingly large. Even one in ten of a six year age group saying that their families were not loving or their relationships with parents were not close, for example, means that every full 'double-decker' school bus at the end of the day is likely to be taking home around seven seriously unhappy children. Even within families which are basically loving and supportive to their children, many worries can affect children's well being. Over a third agreeing that there was sometimes 'a lot of stress' in their homes; a third recording ' a lot of worries about the shortage of money'; more than a quarter saying 'there are things in my childhood that I find it hard to talk about' – these are not figures we can, as a society, be comfortable about. Translated into school bus terms, most of the lower deck would at some time in their childhood have been going home to serious worries.

The sources of stress and problems could be many and varied: divorce or separation of parents, illness, bereavement, unemployment, homelessness to name but a few. Previous research (Ghate and Daniels, 1997) has shown the extent to which children carry their parents' worries as their own. Children clearly cannot be completely insulated from the problems which their parents have to live with, indeed there is evidence that to protect them too much from the realities of the world outside can be harmful in leaving them unprepared for adult life. But there are implications for the way in which families and children are to be supported through the trials of life.

There were other problems which were a long way from the usual trials of life. More than one in ten (14%) had regularly to assume adult responsibilities in childhood, because parents were ill, disabled, or had personal problems, including substance abuse, or because they regularly went away leaving their children to fend for themselves. More than a quarter of respondents (26%) had seen violence between their parents at least once and for 5% this was a 'constant' or 'frequent' occurrence. In our crowded school bus, it seems that approximately ten children may be going home to a 'double shift' of cleaning, laundry, shopping, and preparing meals, and two or three will be in fear of violence between their parents while they were out, or of what might happen that evening. These are not situations with which children should have to cope, and there is an urgent need to examine support services to such families.

Yet the greatest concern is that the family is also the arena where children are most likely to experience some forms of maltreatment from adults. These problems affect relatively small proportions of the sample, but 7% were rated by researchers as experiencing serious physical abuse in their families, 6% serious absence of physical care, 6% experienced serious emotional maltreatment, and 5% serious absence of supervision. The rating of maltreatment took into account both the seriousness of what had happened and the frequency with which it happened, so that no respondent was rated as seriously maltreated unless they had either experienced injury, or had been treated quite unacceptably for long periods of their childhood. Larger minorities recorded maltreatment to a less serious level or occurring with less frequency. Although physical maltreatment did occur outside the family, this was rare, and the survey established that in the modern UK this is primarily a family problem. The picture on emotional maltreatment is more complex as many of the forms of bullying and discrimination which children experienced from peers amounted to psychological attack, but when asked who had treated them in this way, parents consistently led the field and emotional maltreatment from other adults was rare. This survey confirms the indications from previous research, that sexual abuse is primarily extra-familial, but 1% of the sample were sexually abused by parents or step-parents and 3% by other relatives.

Gender

Some of the detailed results on the prevalence of specific maltreatment confirm what was thought from previous research on smaller or more selective samples, while other findings contradict or question previous results or common stereotypes concerning abuse and neglect. This will be returned to later in this chapter, but present findings show that the highest risk relationships are with birth parents, and that mothers as well as fathers can be responsible for maltreatment. Indeed, mothers were as likely, and in some instances more likely, to inflict some forms of harm than were fathers. However, the findings also show that relationships with fathers were more likely to be problematic. It must be a matter of concern that, when asked whether there were any adults of whom they had as children been 'sometimes really afraid', almost a fifth of the sample named their father or stepfather, and a tenth their mother or stepmother – with almost all of these being birth parents rather than step-parents. A small number (4%) were really afraid of both parents. Further analysis remains to be done to explore the links between relation-ships and abuse, but the work done so far illustrates the complexity of the situation. The figures show that some young people must be simultaneously reporting that they had loving homes and close relationships, but were afraid of parents, while others were rated by researchers as experi-encing quite marked levels of abuse from the parents reported as loving and close.

The different levels of fear towards parents reflect consistent differences in many areas of the survey. Respondents of both sexes were very much more likely to report close relationships with mothers than with fathers, more likely to see mothers as people they respected, as setting them a good example of adulthood, and as helping them with advice or when in trouble. If abused outside the family, they were more likely to tell mothers than fathers. The difference should not be overestimated: three quarters of the sample still report close relationships with fathers (though far fewer say it was 'very close' than with mothers). But these findings echo those of earlier surveys (Creighton and Russell, 1995; Ghate and Daniels 1997) in showing that there is work to be done to improve the quality of fatherhood for a substantial minority of children.

Gender differences were also found over which children experienced maltreatment. These were usually, but not always in the direction which official child protection statistics and other research would have indicated. More boys are on Child Protection Registers for physical abuse, but in this sample gender differences were quite small. Slightly more male respondents reported ever having received most types of physical treatment/discipline but there were no consistent differences on the more violent treatment such as being burned, knocked down, or kicked. When severity and frequency were taken into account, more females than males were assessed as seriously abused, while more males experienced intermediate abuse.

There were few gender differences on lack of care, but differences in lack of supervision reflect gender differences found in previous research, with males more likely to have experienced being out unsupervised at an early age, especially overnight.

Women respondents more often reported emotional maltreatment, especially in relation to psychological control and domination, humiliation, and antipathy, and they had higher overall maltreatment scores.

Sexual abuse findings support those from official figures and from previous research, with girls far more likely to experience all forms of sexual abuse. Most abusers were male, though a large minority of cases of abuse of boys involved female abusers. Sexual abuse against adults is most often perpetrated by men on women. This is the same for children and young people.

Patterns of childhood maltreatment of female respondents in this sample therefore, in several respects showed similarities to the maltreatment of women in other contexts such as partner abuse and sexual abuse.

Apart from sexual abuse, the similarities between the genders were greater than the differences, but the results on maltreatment highlight some of the particular vulnerabilities of girl children. Together with the material on families and fatherhood, it indicates a number of gender issues of concern. The picture is one of a clear gender imbalance which requires addressing at the most fundamental levels: male socialisation, education and in the national media.

Socio-economic group

This proved important, as it has done in previous research both in the UK and the USA. It was pointed out earlier that social class data from this sample reflect their present position, which for a minority will differ from the social class in which they lived as children. It is also affected by the age group of the sample, with many still students or at an early stage in their employment careers. Nevertheless for most of these respondents their present situation will reflect their childhood socio-economic status. There was a clear relationship between social group and physical discipline and abuse, with absence of care and with the more serious absence of supervision, especially being out all night at a young age. Absence of supervision at the less serious levels however was not particularly linked with socio-economic status and appeared to be an equal issue for all social groups. Sexual abuse and emotional abuse showed little differentiation between socio-economic groups.

However, this study clearly shows that each type of abuse was experienced across social classes to varying degrees. Levels of prevalence in social classes AB shown by this survey are not reflected in official statistics which predominantly include parents in low paid employment or who are unemployed. This confirms that one of the most under reported aspects of child maltreatment is that experienced by upper or middle class children. Much further analysis remains to be done to explore the links between social class and abuse and also with poverty and health problems which may be connected.

Age-peer relationships

This study showed, as have others, that the most common source of distress to children is bullying and discrimination by other young people, suffered by more than 4 out of 10 respondents: most usually verbal but with a substantial amount of physical attack. Much of it was focused on physical or social characteristics over which the children had no control, attacks which would be likely to fundamentally challenge their self-confidence and self-esteem. This was not a study of bullying 'per se'; material on bullying was included in order to complete the picture of possible abuse and enable examination of the relationships between bullying, discrimination and abuse in the family and the community. Nevertheless the findings on levels of bullying are quite similar to those of other recent studies, and as such reinforce previous evidence of the extent to which it a common and miserable experience for so many children and young people. The results represent a serious cause for worry about the development and management of relationships between young people, in settings where they meet in groups, particularly in schools.

A further cause for concern over peer relationships arises from the sexual abuse data, where the typical abuser was likely to be someone close in age to the victim: most commonly someone identified as a boyfriend or girlfriend, but for many a fellow pupil or student, a brother's or sister's friend or 'someone recently met', which would include young people met at parties, 'raves' and other places where the young congregate. Although abuse within the family was rare, when it did occur the most likely abuser was a brother or stepbrother.

These findings raise a number of questions about the way in which we socialise young people in groups, manage their contacts with each other and educate them into expected behaviour with peers. The results illustrate the central importance of 'anti-bullying' strategies to reducing the harm suffered by many children in schools and other youth settings, and of a constructive education programme for the young on sexual relationships.

Stereotypes and reality

The findings challenge some of the stereotypes concerning maltreatment which have become part of popular belief, and in some cases received professional wisdom. Stereotypes can arise from a number of possible sources: media coverage of individual tragedies and scandals; distorted perceptions as the result of imperfect understanding of official figures; or the wealth of literary and fictional tradition featuring wicked stepmothers and other such 'bogeys'. Brodie and Berridge (1996) for example, discuss the belief that stepchildren are particularly vulnerable to being abused, and the way this is affected by researchers' assumptions about family structure, with a wide variety of relationships being classified as 'stepfather'. The selection of stereotypes discussed below is not a particularly scientific or complete one, but reflects some which commonly find expression.

Figure 2 Sexual abuse stereotypes and reality

The Stereotype	This Study
Incestuous relationship between father/stepfather and daughter	True for 0.4%
The most likely relative to abuse within the family is an 'uncle' or grandfather	The most likely relative to abuse within the family is a brother (mentioned in a third (31%) of cases where relatives were involved)
Boyfriend/girlfriend sex is mutual experimentation and relatively minor	Untrue for many. 5% go as far as sexual intercourse or penetration either against their will or with someone 5 or more years older than them when they are under 12. 4% against their wishes, 2% use of force
Stranger danger (rape/indecent assault)	True for approximately 2%
Child sexual abuse is under reported	True for over 90%
Most people experience 'flashing'	Untrue – approximately 15% of children report being exposed to. In 9% of cases this is not the only experience
Most sexual abuse is just a 'one off'	Untrue – the majority had more than one such experience only 'exposure' was likely to be 'one off'
Most child sexual abuse is perpetrated by males on females	True; females were the victims in up to two thirds (66%) of cases; males were most often the perpetrators; boys were more likely than girls to have female perpetrators
Outside the family children are most at risk from adults in a professional capacity such as teachers, doctors, priests or scout leaders	Untrue – this study found evidence of this for 0.3%
Friendly gestures (hugs/kisses/pat on the bottom) are misinterpreted	The majority of incidents involve penetration/oral 'contact' abuse, attempts at these or genital touching. Young people clearly differentiate between what is acceptable and unacceptable sexual behaviour, especially for those under 12.

The challenging of popular stereotypes is particularly notable for sexual abuse. The traditional stereotype of child sexual abuse is that of an incestuous relationship between a father or step-father and his daughter. This prevalence study shows a very different picture. Previous studies have estimated the prevalence of father/daughter incest at between 1% and 5% (Wassil-Grimm, 1995; Williams and Finkelhor, 1992; Russell, 1984). This study gives a figure of 0.3% with attempts at 0.4%. Two conclusions can be drawn from this. Firstly, our attempt to get to a more accurate definition, by defining different types of behaviour rather than accumulating all sexual contact under the heading of sexual abuse, is likely to reflect an accurate estimate of incest preva-lence in the population. Secondly, whilst for this reason it is difficult to compare this figure with other studies, it may reflect a real reduction in incest rates. Given the level of publicity and awareness of sexual abuse over the last decade this may be an anticipated outcome. Figure 2 shows the comparison of some popular stereotypes concerning sexual abuse and the reality shown by the present study.

Sexual violence, however, still remains a significant social problem for children. The large minority of young people who experienced penetrative sex, oral sex or attempts at these against their will by people known to them is still relatively high at approximately 10%. Despite the fact that the majority (over two thirds) of these experiences were perpetrated by someone the respondent referred to as a boyfriend or girlfriend a large number reported the use of force or threat. For example, six in ten (58%) of those reporting unsuccessful attempts to engage them in oral or penetrative sex said that physical force was used, and 39% reported blackmail. 40% of those who had experienced full oral or penetrative sex against their wishes or with a much older person reported the use of force, and 31% the use of blackmail.

Sexual abuse against adults is described as rape and indecent assault. Sexual abuse against children is described as touching, fondling and the like (Kitzinger, 1997). The picture displayed in this study is one which is very similar to adult sexual abuse. Children and young people are raped and indecently assaulted. In a minority of cases this is by members of their own family, in the majority it is (just as it is for adults) by people known to them, most often described as boyfriends and girlfriends.

Stereotypes of physical punishment and physical abuse are also challenged by this survey. Most of these concern gender issues and the relationship between physical punishment and abuse.

The relationship between physical punishment and physical abuse has long been regarded as problematic. Previous research has suggested that physical abuse is more likely to occur in families with a culture of violence, including regular use of physical punishment (Cleaver, Wattam and Cawson 1998). This data endorses that perspective insofar as there is a clear statistical relationship between the greater use of physical punishment for respondents in social grades D and E, and the similarly greater frequency of physical abuse. However other relationships are not so clear cut. In particular there appeared to be a divide between the families where children were hit with implements or often hit to a level which caused lasting pain, bruising or other injury, and those where occasional slaps occurred which rarely or never had lasting effects. There was no substantial bridging group in which smacking was regular but not severe, which we would have expected to find if escalation were a common phenomenon. In general it seems that parents either hit children rarely and lightly, or they do it to cause serious hurt. Newson and Newson (1970) concluded that 'we would tentatively suggest that those mothers who smack most frequently are also likely to smack hardest' (p.448) and this seems as true today as it was thirty years ago. Qualitative studies which describe the process of escalation into more frequent or more serious smacking may give an explanation. Newson and Newson (1970) and Leach (1999) describe the way in which parents became aware that they were coming to use more and more physical punishment which was damaging their relationship with their child, and ineffective in improving the child's behaviour. This may be the point at which parents having fundamentally close relationships with their child call a halt to their own use of physical punishment. It may represent a qualitative difference between parents able to enter into their child's feelings or distress and those who cannot do so, or whose own anger takes precedence over the child's needs.

Figure 3 Stereotypes of physical abuse

The Stereotype	This Study
Most physical abuse is carried out by men, especially fathers or stepfathers	Untrue - 'violent' treatment was more likely to be meted out by mothers(49%) although fathers were responsible for 40%. Step-parents were rarely mentioned
Physical punishment is likely to escalate into abuse	Questionable - data suggested a qualitative difference between the use of occasional slaps and smacks with an open hand (which was experienced by over 70% of the sample), and violent treatment by parents rated as seriously abusive because it caused injury or regularly had lasting physical effects (experienced by 7%). Very few respondents (3%) experienced regular smacking without bruising or other lasting effects, suggesting an abrupt change between the two modes of treatment rather than a 'slide'
Physical abuse is more common in manual workers' families	Probably true - although the socio-economic data available has limitations, there was a markedly greater use of violence towards respondents in social grades D and E, and they were more likely to be rated by researchers and to rate themselves as having been abused
Boys are more often victims of physical abuse than are girls	Untrue - more female respondents (8 %) were rated as seriously abused by parents than were males (6%), though males were more likely to be rated as experiencing intermediate or intermittent abuse (15%) than were females (12%).

Noting this qualitative difference does not undermine the earlier point that there is a continuum along which acceptable and unacceptable treatment of children moves into abuse, and the earlier material on physical punishment and violent treatment shows gradations in seriousness at both ends of the continuum. Nor does it mean that parents using violence do not love their children, are unable to change, or could not use help in modifying their behaviour or developing greater understanding of their children. But it does have implications for the form of help needed to safeguard children in these circumstances.

There appear to be fewer stereotypes of neglect and emotional maltreatment, perhaps due to the relatively low profile of these forms of maltreatment and lack of consensus on their definitions. However those that do exist receive little support from the present data.

Figure 4 Stereotypes of neglect and emotional maltreatment

The Stereotype	This Study
Neglect is a consequence of poverty	No information was available on the family income during respondents' childhoods but since a third of the sample reported money worries in their families while only 6% reported treatment rated as serious lack of care, there was clearly no direct link. Respondents in social grades DE were slightly more likely to be rated as lacking care
Working class children are less well supervised than middle class children	Mixed results. Respondents from social grades DE, especially boys, were more likely to have been allowed out overnight at 14 years old without parents knowing where they were. Children aged 11-12 from social grades AB were more likely to be left at home unsupervised in the evenings and allowed to go to the town centre without an adult than were others
Emotional maltreatment is often from step-parents, especially stepmothers.	Most assessed maltreatment was from birth parents. Verbal and other psychological attacks were equally likely to come from mothers and fathers.

Self-assessed and researcher assessed maltreatment

The results were consistent in showing higher levels of researcher assessed maltreatment than when respondents rated their own treatment. This is also a finding from previous studies which compare the two ratings. Chapter Three pointed out that previous research has found that respondents can experience treatment such as being whipped to the point of laceration and not consider this abusive, because they have been taught that this is the right way to discipline children. Respondents may also excuse or minimise the maltreatment because they love the person responsible, understand the stresses experienced by abusers, or have been taught to take the blame upon themselves because they are 'bad' or provocative. In the present study there was considerable overlap between the self-ratings and researcher ratings on the more serious levels of abuse, but much less agreement on the intermediate levels. However a surprising number of respondents were unsure of whether their own treatment constituted abuse or neglect, even though the section of the interview concerning attitudes showed a clear consensus on what was acceptable treatment for children. This study also found small numbers of respondents who said they were not fed properly but did not consider themselves neglected, who were punched, kicked and even burned, but did not think this was physical abuse, and who were subjected to sexual assault against their will or when they were very young and did not consider this sexual abuse. This is one area of the data where further work remains to be done, but it does indicate the need for a more open and public debate about what it is acceptable to do to children, and what are the normal standards of parental behaviour, with emphasis that some treatment is not excusable, whatever the stress or provocation.

How useful is our present framework for considering maltreatment?

The findings open up some questions about the present UK framework for identifying and tackling maltreatment.

One of those is whether the same child protection strategies can serve for preventing and tackling maltreatment inside and outside the family. This question is most marked in the present study in relation to the differences between sexual abuse, primarily extra-familial, and other forms of maltreatment, which are primarily intra-familial. However it also has broader implications. Barter (1999) in a review of the evidence on protecting children from racial abuse, discusses the limitations of a child protection structure which is family centred, when faced with a problem which is essentially community based. Similar limitations of present routine structures in dealing with 'organised' abuse rings and large scale institutional abuse have become apparent in recent years, and it has become familiar practice to set up special multi-agency investigation and support structures, either on an ad hoc or continuing basis. Studies of abused young people and young victims of crime commonly show that large proportions of victims tell no one, or confide only in friends and relatives, rarely approaching official agencies. The present study, with its very low proportion of the sample seeking official help with sexual abuse, highlights again the importance of strategies and services which are known, available, accessible and acceptable to abused young people, and suggests that the traditional social services, police and health service frameworks may not be sufficient or appropriate for all needs. The relationship between the type and nature of maltreatment and the help sought is one of the issues which will be explored in further analysis of the survey data.

There are also questions about the usefulness of generic terms for 'neglect' and 'emotional abuse', which encompass wider and more disparate ranges of behaviour to children than do physical or sexual abuse. It has sometimes been suggested that the lower rates of registration and legal action for these forms of maltreatment reflect the difficulty of making a case (Cleaver, Wattam and Cawson, 1998) and this may reflect the lack of specificity in the terms used. Should we instead be thinking about breaking these categories down into component parts? This would be relatively simple for physical neglect, which divides clearly into separate issues on supervision and basic physical nurturing care. It would be much harder to do this for emotional abuse, where our understanding is still exploratory, but the data from this study may point the way towards some possible options. We may need to think about the distinction between primary and secondary abuse – which may be more apparent to the observer than to the person on the receiving end. Or perhaps there is a distinction to be made between abuse as psychological attack and abusive exploitation of a relationship of love or trust or dependency, as in for example, using a child excessively for support with a parent's problems while not meeting the child's needs for support. Is emotional abuse targeted as a hostile act to a child qualitatively different from emotional damage caused by gross, hurtful insensitivity or manifest lack of affection, or occurring as a secondary feature of other forms of abuse?

One of the difficulties in assessing neglect, and to some extent sexual abuse, lay in the crucial role played by age in determining when a child is deemed able to cope with self care, be safe without adult supervision, or give informed consent to sexual activity. The legal and child protection frameworks give virtually no help either to researchers, parents or practitioners on this point. Consequently maltreatment is likely to be determined retrospectively in law and practice, by whether disaster has occurred, or someone influential has complained, rather than by what the child or young person has experienced. The data from this survey shows that there are clear majority and minority patterns, but suggests that the level of consensus among families as to what is 'normal' or 'acceptable' is not necessarily the same as that which would be adopted by professionals in child protection services. In general young people appear not to regard it as a problem for them if they had limited supervision at an early age – but then the ones who had fatal accidents, or ended up in prison as a result are not in this sample. The lack of clear guidelines based on public consensus leaves professionals and parents contending with grey areas where an action taken in good faith, of a kind which has seemed normal practice in the local context, is at high risk of later seeming officious or negligent if something goes wrong. A detailed legal framework of age permissions would probably be neither achievable nor enforceable, and any structure would need to allow flexibility to assess children's development. But this emerges as one of the areas in which we need some intelligent review of our expectations of children's competence and independence in relation to the child protection systems.

Next steps

This report is the first in a series of reports and papers on this national study. Further reports will examine in more detail the questions on which it has been possible to touch only briefly so far. These include the ways in which maltreatment in the family is linked to family relationships and other aspects of family life, maltreatment outside the family and the longer term consequences of maltreatment Much more can be learned from this study about the overlap between different forms of abuse and neglect, and the circumstances in which children experience multiple abuse. The relationship between bullying at school and in the community, and abuse at home is also an important issue, as is the connection between early involvement in consensual sexual activity and sexual abuse. The differences between self-assessed abuse and neglect and the ratings made using the measures developed by researchers also needs further exploration in terms of family and other relationships, and respondents' own explanations for the treatment they received. The first stage of analysis has provided a descriptive account of the prevalence of maltreatment in the context of childrearing and normal family life, but detailed exploration which may throw light on its causes and consequences remains for the next stage.

Summary

- The importance of reliable prevalence data for making assessment of service needs is considerable, but its achievement is problematic, due to an absence of consensus over what constitutes the various forms of maltreatment. Different definitions are adopted by different countries, generations, social classes and cultures, although there is some emerging international agreement on the more extreme forms of cruelty and exploitation.

- Some previous prevalence studies of physical and sexual abuse gave a baseline for the development of measures for this study, but there was no accepted paradigm for the study of neglect or emotional maltreatment, so this part of the study is far more exploratory. The different forms of maltreatment are interlinked and overlapping, making it impossible to reach a tidy figure for the total number of maltreated children which is realistic and avoids double counting. Almost all forms of physical or sexual maltreatment simultaneously involve emotional harm.

- The findings challenge us to rethink some fundamental issues about the way we care for children and support families. These include family life, gender, socio-economic status and age-peer relationships.

- The family offers the primary source of nurturing, love and development to children and was effective in doing this for most of the sample. But it was also the source of stress and problems for quite large minorities. Implications of the figures obtained from this random sample are that, in a full double decker-school bus at the end of the day, at least seven children are likely to be going home to families which they do not experience as loving or close; as many as ten may be shouldering a 'double shift' burden of housework and caring for parents who are incapacitated by their own health or social problems; two or three will be going home in fear of the frequent violence between their parents, and two or three will be returning to a life of regular beatings or denigration. These figures are not cumulative and some children will be experiencing several or all of these situations.

- The data on gender raises issues concerning the role of fathers and their relationships with their children. Fathers were consistently less likely to be seen as offering closeness, support and good role models than were mothers, and a fifth of the sample were 'sometimes really afraid' of their fathers.

- There were gender differences in the maltreatment of children, particularly on sexual abuse, where girls were far more at risk, but levels of serious physical abuse and emotional maltreatment were also slightly higher for girls, while boys were less likely to be safeguarded by good supervision. Some of the results suggested similarity between the maltreatment of female children and that of women in abusive partnerships, emphasising once again the common link between domestic violence and child abuse. Abusers, however, could be of either sex. While most sexual abusers were male, women were equally likely to be involved in physical and emotional maltreatment.

- In general there was evidence of a common standard across all social groups which did not find maltreatment of children acceptable either in the expression of attitudes or the reality of respondents' childhood experience, but some maltreatment was found in all social grades.

- There was evidence of a social class pattern, particularly with physical abuse, lack of care and allowing children to be out all night with their whereabouts unknown. Respondents now in social grades DE were more likely to be rated as seriously physically abused, and to rate themselves as abused, than were other groups. This touches on very fundamental questions about the continued existence of social divisions which support potentially abusive, violent cultures for a minority.

■ The levels of bullying, discrimination and sexual violence found between young people in the survey were high, and in some ways these were the most common abusive experience likely to be faced by respondents. These findings emphasise the need for new approaches to working with bullying, to the management of children in group situations, and to educating the young about social and sexual relationships.

■ A number of common stereotypes are challenged by the findings. The relationship between physical punishment and abuse was by no means straightforward, parents dividing into the majority who used physical punishment rarely and lightly, and the minority who used it regularly and severely. Very few respondents were physically, sexually or emotionally abused by step-parents; and very few were sexually abused by strangers or in public places.

■ There were few examples of either sexual or physical abuse by professionals and none of sexual abuse by careworkers or youthworkers. This does not mean that such things never occur – the case files of every child protection agency in the UK could produce real examples – but the findings help to put these situations into perspective, in a way which we hope will enable prevention and protection strategies to address both the common and the rare problems more effectively. It perhaps will also reduce some of the 'moral panic' which may sometimes make parents afraid to give their children the freedoms necessary for childhood development, or to trust their children to the care of others.

■ The findings raise questions about whether a primarily family centred child protection system is able to deal with maltreatment which occurs outside the family, most notably in relation to sexual abuse, or whether we need a fundamentally different approach to dealing with child protection inside and outside the family.

■ There are uncertainties over the usefulness of umbrella terms such as neglect and emotional abuse which represent a range of very different problems, or whether greater precision in terminology might make it easier to identify and tackle damaging behaviour to children.

■ The age at which children are judged competent to deal with self care, the absence of adult supervision, or give informed consent to sexual activity, emerges as a grey area in which neither legal structures nor professional guidelines are adequate. This leaves both parents and professionals in an uncertain and potentially difficult position when making judgements concerning children's safety.

■ Finally, the respondents' attitudinal clarity about what were unacceptable ways to treat children was not always consistent with their ratings of the way they assessed their own treatment. In common with other studies, this research found that young people could experience severe lack of care, physical violence or sexual assault and not rate themselves as abused, or be unsure about whether the treatment was abusive. There is a need for a more informed public debate about acceptable standards for the treatment of children.

Recommendations

The United Kingdom is a signatory to the United Nations Convention on the Rights of the Child. **Article 3** of the Convention requires that 'States Parties undertake to ensure the child such protection and care as is necessary for his or her well-being' and **Article 19** requires 'protection from all forms of maltreatment perpetrated by parents or caretakers'. The present survey shows a number of ways in which we should be improving the protection that we offer to our children. Some require further research to increase knowledge and some could be implemented now on the basis of our existing knowledge.

Recommendation 1:
This study has shown the value of prevalence research, in three ways: by giving a realistic picture of the extent of child maltreatment on which to base policy and service development; by questioning stereotypes and assumptions about maltreatment and opening debate on its nature; and by showing that there are children suffering maltreatment which does not reach the atten-

tion of the child protection authorities. This data needs regular updating if the adequacy of child protection services in the UK is to be monitored and services are to keep abreast of social change.

- **A general population survey of the prevalence of maltreatment should be carried out at regular intervals not exceeding 10 years.**

Recommendation 2:

The Government has indicated in its *'Objectives for Children's Social Services'* (sub-objective 2.2) that it is considering a study of the incidence of child maltreatment, and exploring ways of carrying it out. A national incidence study (similar to that carried out in the USA at regular intervals) monitoring professional knowledge of occurrences of maltreatment, using information from all statutory and voluntary agencies in contact with children, would give performance monitoring information for child protection services. It would complement general population data from prevalence studies and enable assessment of the tasks which services were confronting. In conjunction with prevalence research it would show which aspects of maltreatment were unknown to them.

- **A national incidence study of all known cases of child maltreatment should be developed as part of regular service monitoring, to collate reports from social services, health services, schools, voluntary agencies, the probation service and police.**

Recommendation 3:

Neither prevalence nor incidence studies can cover fatal child maltreatment, since they focus on living children. To understand and prevent such tragedies, and to enable the characteristics and patterns of events to be better monitored, it is necessary to have consolidated information on as many fatalities as possible. A permanent database of all fatal child abuse and neglect cases is needed, accessible for research and for the development of practice initiatives in child protection services.

- **A permanent database of all fatal child abuse and neglect cases should be maintained by Department of Health and the Home Office. This should include all child homicides, and should be available for research and for the preparation of training materials for professionals working with child fatalities.**

Recommendation 4:
Recommendation 5:
Recommendation 6:

The present survey demonstrates, as has other research in this country and elsewhere, that people can suffer extremes of abusive and neglectful treatment in childhood and yet not consider themselves abused or neglected. This often reflects the extent to which they have grown up in a context where violence, abuse and neglect are part of their 'normal' experience. Much clearer understanding is needed of the difference between victims' own and professionals' judgements of maltreatment, in particular why victims often appear to blame themselves for the abuse they have experienced and underplay its importance. This has particular implications for the ways in which victims are dealt with during the investigation of allegations and during court proceedings.

- **Research is needed which examines the basis of differential assessment of child maltreatment by victims and professionals in more detail than hitherto.**

- **Training for those investigating allegations of maltreatment and for judges and other lawyers dealing with the court process should make them aware that, for a variety of reasons, victims may minimise their experience, even when they have suffered considerable harm.**

- **Better, more accessible public information is needed for children and their families on the nature of child maltreatment. This would assist children to recognise when the treatment they or children in their families receive is unacceptable. It would help adults to recognise when children known to them may need protection.**

Recommendation 7:

Criteria for assessment of maltreatment must be founded on social consensus on the acceptable treatment of children, otherwise reporting will not happen and professionals will not feel confident in taking action to protect children. The overview of the state of our present knowledge showed that there is considerable public agreement on unacceptable disciplinary and sexual behaviour towards children, and the present findings endorse that position. We lack equivalent consensual paradigms for neglect and emotional maltreatment, which is a serious deficiency in our ability to protect children. The present research showed this to be a particular issue for the supervision of children, where there are varied expectations of children's competence and independence at different ages, and where legal guidance is largely non existent. For emotional maltreatment, there is now evidence from many sources that in the long term it is the most harmful form and that its potential seriousness is much underestimated, by the public and by professionals. The present research has attempted to provide a framework for future thinking but much is still to be done.

■ **Research, practice and training initiatives are needed to enlarge our knowledge and understanding of neglect and emotional maltreatment, and to establish a consensual base for the development of standards of care, an appropriate legal framework, and measures of 'significant harm'.**

Recommendation 8:

Results suggest a need to reassess some assumptions about sexual abuse both inside and outside the family. The stereotypes of sexual abuse largely concern incest and 'stranger-danger', but research shows that the most common risks are from known but unrelated people. There are some indications that levels of incest may be reducing, but that attention is needed to sibling and step-sibling abuse. As most abuse is extra-familial, we should be considering how far we may need different strategies to deal with these very different situations, particularly in the light of evidence that much sexual abuse comes from age peers and that most goes unreported.

■ **Strategies for dealing with sexual abuse inside and outside the family should be reviewed, to ensure that they address adequately the different characteristics of these situations. Implications for training for the professionals involved are particularly important.**

Recommendation 9:

The evidence that physical, sexual and psychological attack from peers (including siblings and step-siblings) are the most common abusive experiences faced by young people was very clear. Bullying and assaults by young people against each other are often treated as less serious than similar behaviour by adults, but in the present survey many reported that, far from being a trivial or transitory experience, bullying had long term harmful effects. The new elements of the National Curriculum covering Personal, Social and Health Education and Citizenship offer an opportunity for confronting these issues with young people, with their emphasis on teaching young people to value themselves and others.

■ **We should take very seriously the evidence that physical, sexual and psychological attack from peers (including siblings and step-siblings) are the most common abusive experiences faced by young people and address the issues of cultures which promote physical and sexual aggression among young people. Schools and youth services have a major part to play here, but so also does the media, and community initiatives could be particularly valuable where young people experience the streets as unsafe.**

Recommendation 10:

There is reason for great concern in the low level of reporting of abuse, particularly of sexual abuse, and the fact that respondents did not approach professional services. Young people often seemed to have been afraid to approach members of their families and other adults, fearing that they would not be believed or that they would be taken away from home. Under-reporting of sexual offences has been known to be a problem for adults, and strategies have been developed to address this. Similar strategic approaches are needed for children and young people.

- Urgent attention is needed to providing forms of help with sexual abuse which can be easily and confidentially accessed by young people.

Recommendation 11:

The main source of knowledge about under-reporting of violent crime is the British Crime Survey which at present covers only crimes against those aged 16 or over, giving the message that crimes against children 'don't really count' or are less serious than crimes against adults, and the Home Office criminal statistics do not collate and present information on the ages of victims of crimes other than homicide. This is unsatisfactory.

- The British Crime Survey should be expanded to cover crimes against children under 16. Crime statistics should report the ages of victims.

Recommendation 12:

Although trends were found for higher levels of some forms of maltreatment in social grades D and E, differences were relatively small for most issues and some maltreatment was found in all groups. The findings show the need for more attention to maltreatment in middle class families. These are the families least likely to come to the attention of the child protection services, possibly because better material conditions and articulate, well educated parents make problems easier to hide. Again, it is important that services are accessible, both to children and parents.

- Agencies providing child protection services should review their training and management support for identifying and working with maltreatment in middle class families.

Recommendation 13:

This research adds to a growing body of evidence that there is a 'culture of violence' in some families, and highlights the importance of gaining greater understanding of the circumstances in which violence happens. Findings from this and other studies suggest that there is a regular pattern of violence and aggressive psychological domination in some families which gives rise to both physical and emotional abuse, and may often be associated with both domestic violence and child maltreatment. We need to understand much more about what leads to and maintains this culture, and how to help families to escape from it. We must be able to distinguish clearly, and have different strategies for, maltreatment which arises due to parental stress or deficits in parenting skills, and that which arises from a pathological parental need or wish to misuse power in relationships with their children. We also need a better understanding of the contribution of poverty and of beliefs about effective childrearing.

- Research is needed on the dynamics of family violence to assist professionals in identifying the different situations in which violence and emotional maltreatment can arise. Strategies for protecting children will need to be quite different if the problems result from situational pressures such as illness or poverty than if they result from fundamentally pathological, aggressively dominant relationships.

REFERENCES

American Association for Protecting Children. (1988). Highlights of official child neglect and abuse reporting, 1986. Denver, Colorado: American Humane Association.

Arias, I., Samios, M. and O'Leary, K.D. (1987). Prevalence and correlates of physical aggression during courtship. *Journal of Interpersonal Violence, 2 (1)* 82-90.

Arora, C.M.T and Thompson, D.A. (1987). Defining bullying for a secondary school. *Education and Child Psychology, 4 (3),* 110-120.

Ascione, F.R. (1998). Battered women's reports of their partners' and their children's cruelty to animals. *Journal of Emotional Abuse. 1 (1)* 119 - 133.

Badgley, R., Allard, H., McCormock, N., Proudfoot, P., Fortin, D., Rae-Grant, Q., Gelines, P., Pepin, L., Southerland, S. (1984). **Sexual Offences Against Children**. Committee on Sexual Offences Against Children. Ottawa: Canadian Government Publishing Centre.

Baker, A.W. and Duncan, S.P. (1985). Child sexual abuse: a study of prevalence in Great Britain. *Child Abuse and Neglect, 9, (4)* 457-467.

Balding, J. (1998) **Young People in 1997: the health related behaviour questionnaire results for 37,538 pupils between the ages of 9 and 16.** Schools Health Education Unit Exeter:.

Barnett, D., Manly, J.T. and Cicchetti, D. (1993). Defining child maltreatment: the interface between policy and research. In D. Cicchetti and S.L. Toth (Eds.) **Child Abuse, Child Development and Social Policy**. Norwood, New Jersey: Ablex.

Barter C. (1996). **Nowhere to Hide: Giving young runaways a voice**. London: Centrepoint.

Barter C. (1999). **Protecting Children from Racism and Racial Abuse: A Research Review**. London: NSPCC.

Beitchman, J.H., Zucker, K.J., Hood, J.E., DaCosta, G.A., Akman, D. and Cassavia, E. (1992). A review of the long-term effects of child sexual abuse. *Child Abuse and Neglect, 16 (1)* 101-118.

Berger, A.M., Knutson, J.G., Mehm, J.G. and Perkins, K.A. (1988). The self-report of punitive childhood experiences of young adults and adolescents. *Child Abuse and Neglect, 12 (2)* 251-262.

Berrien, F.B., Aprelkov, G., Ivanova, T., Zhmurov, V. and Buzhicheeva, V. (1995). Child abuse prevalence in Russian urban population: a preliminary report. *Child Abuse and Neglect, 19 (2)* 261-264.

Besag, V.E. (1989). **Bullies and Victims in Schools**. Buckingham: Open University Press.

Bifulco, A. and Moran, A. (1998). **Wednesday's Child: Research into Women's Experience of Neglect and Abuse in Childhood, and Adult Depression.** London: Routledge.

Blackburn, C. (1991). **Poverty and Health: Working with Families**. Buckingham: Open University Press.

Bolen, R. and Scannapieco, M. (1999) Prevalence of child sexual abuse: a corrective metanalysis. *Social Services Review (September 1999)* 281-313.

Bower, M.E. and Knutson, J.F. (1996). Attitudes toward physical discipline as a function of disciplinary history and self-labelling as physical abuse. *Child Abuse and Neglect, 20 (8)* 689-699.

Brassard, M.R., Hart, S.N. and Hardy, D.B. (1993). The psychological maltreatment rating scales. *Child Abuse and Neglect, 17 (6)* 715-729.

Briere, J. and Rutz, M. (1988). Multivariate correlates of childhood psychological and physical maltreatment among university women. *Child Abuse and Neglect, 12 (3)* 331-341.

Briere, J.N. and Elliott, D.M. (1994). Immediate and long-term impacts of child sexual abuse. *The Future of Children, 4 (2)* 54-69.

Brodie, I. and Berridge, D. (1996). **Child Abuse and Stepfamilies**. London, The National Stepfamily Association, Fact File 4, July 1996.

Burnett B.R. (1993). The psychological abuse of latency age children: a survey. *Child Abuse and Neglect 17* (4) 441 - 454.

Butler-Sloss, E. (Chairman) (1988). **Report of the Inquiry into Child Abuse in Cleveland**. London: HMSO.

Calder, M. (1997). Young people who sexually abuse: Towards an international consensus. *Social Work in Europe, 4 (1)* 36-39.

CAPCAE (1998). **Moving Towards Effective Child Maltreatment Prevention Strategies in Europe. Report of the Concerted Action on the Prevention of Child Abuse in Europe.** Brussels: European Commission.

Carlin, A.S., Kemper, K., Ward, N.G., Sowell, H., Gustafson, B. and Stevens, N. (1994). The effect of differences in objective and subjective definitions of childhood physical abuse on estimates of its incidence and relationship to psychopathology. *Child Abuse and Neglect, 18 (5)* 393-399.

Central Statistical Office (1994). **Social Focus on Children.** London: HMSO.

Cermak, P. and Molidor, C. (1996). Male victims of child sexual abuse. *Child and Adolescent Social Work Journal, 13,(5)* 385-400.

Christensen, E. (1996). **Definition, Measuring and Prevalence of Child Neglect: A Study of Children Aged 0-1 year.** Copenhagen: The Danish National Institute of Social Research.

Cleaver, H., Wattam, C. and Cawson, P. (1998). **Assessing Risk in Child Protection.** London: NSPCC.

Conte, J. and Schuerman, J.R. (1987). Factors associated with an increased impact of child sexual abuse. *Child Abuse and Neglect, 11 (2)* 201-211.

Conte, J. **Sexual Victimization of Children.** Unpublished manuscript available from the author at the University of Chicago.

Coxell, A., King, M., Mezey, G., and Gordon, D. (1999) Lifetime prevalence, characteristics and associated problems of non consensual sex in men. *British Medical Journal, 318 (7187)* 846-850.

Creighton, S. and Noyes, P. (1989). **Child Abuse Trends in England and Wales, 1983-1987.** London: NSPCC Policy Practice Research Series.

Creighton, S. and Russell, N. (1995). **Voices from Childhood: A Survey of Childhood Experiences and Attitudes to Childrearing Among Adults in the United Kingdom.** London: NSPCC Policy Practice Research Series.

Creighton, S. (2000) Child Protection Statistics. London: NSPCC (Forthcoming).

Daro, D. and McKurdy, K. (1992). **Current Trends in Child Abuse Reporting and Fatalities: The Results of the 1991 Annual Fifty State Survey.** National Center on Child Abuse Prevention Research, National Committee for Prevention of Child Abuse. Chicago: NCPCA.

Davies, P.W. (1996). Threats of corporal punishment as verbal aggression: a naturalistic study. *Child Abuse and Neglect, 20 (4)* 289-304.

Dearden, C. and Becker, S. (2000) **Growing Up Caring: Vulnerability and transition to adulthood - young carers' experiences.** Leicester: Youth Work Press.

Department of Health (1988). **Protecting Children: A Guide for Social Workers undertaking a Comprehensive Assessment.** London: HMSO.

Department of Health (1995). **Child Protection: Messages from Research.** London: HMSO.

Department of Health (1999). **Children and Young People on Child Protection Registers Year Ending 31 March 1999 England.** London: Department of Health.

Department of Health (2000) **A Framework for the Assessment of Children in Need.** London: Department of Health.

Department of Health and Social Security (1980). **Child Abuse: Central Register Systems.** LASSL (80) 4: HN (80) 20. London: Department of Health.

Dhaliwal, G.K., Guazas, L., Antonowicz, D.H. and Ross, R.R. (1996). Adult male survivors of childhood sexual abuse: prevalence, sexual abuse characteristics and long-term effects. *Clinical Psychology Review, 16 (7)* 619-639.

Dingwall, R. (1989). Some problems about predicting child abuse and neglect. In: **O. Stevenson (ed.) Child Abuse: Public Policy and Professional Practice.** Hemel Hempsted: Harvester Wheatsheaf.

Doyle, C. (1997). Emotional abuse of children: issues for intervention.*Child Abuse Review 6 (5)* 330-342.

Dubowitz, H. (ed) (1999) **Neglected Children; Research, Practice and Policy.** London: Sage.

Dubowitz, H., Klockner, A., Starr, R.H. and Black, M. (1998). Community and professional definitions of child neglect. *Child Maltreatment, 3(3)* 235-243.

Egeland, B., Stroufe, L.A. and Erickson, M. (1983). The developmental consequences of different patterns of maltreatment. *Child Abuse and Neglect, 1 (2-4)* 459-469.

Egley, L.C. (1991). What changes the societal prevalence of domestic violence? *Journal of Marriage and the Family, 53 (4)* 885-897.

Elliott, D.M. (1994). The impact of Christian faith on the prevalence and sequelae of sexual abuse. *Journal of Interpersonal Violence, 9 (1)* 95-108.

Enzmann, D., Pfeiffer, C. and Wetzels, P. (1998). **Youth Violence in Germany: A Study of Victimization and Delinquency in Four Major Cities.** Hannover, Germany: Criminological Research Institute of Lower Saxony.

Fergusson, D., Horwood, L. and Woodward, L. (2000) The stability of child abuse reports: a longitudinal study of the reporting behaviour of young adults. *Psychological Medicine 2000 (30)* 529-544.

Finkelhor, D. (1979). **Sexually Victimized Children.** New York: Free Press.

Finkelhor, D. (1986). **Sourcebook on Child Sexual Abuse.** Newbury Park, California: Sage.

Finkelhor, D., Hotaling, G., Lewis, I.S. and Smith, C. (1990). Sexual abuse in a national survey of adult men and women: prevalence, characteristics and risk factors. *Child Abuse and Neglect, 14 (1)* 19-28.

Finkelhor, D. (1994). The international epidemiology of child sexual abuse. *Child Abuse and Neglect, 18 (5)* 409-417.

Finkelhor, D. and Dziuba-Leatherman, J. (1994) Children as victims of violence: a national survey. *Paediatrics, 94 (4)* 413-420.

Finkelhor, D. and Dzuiba-Leatherman, J. (1994). Victimisation of Children. *American Psychologist, 49 (3)* 173-183, 1994.

Fish, V. (1998) The delayed memory controversy in an epidemiological framework. *Child Maltreatment 3 (3)* 204-223.

Foucault, M. (1987). **The History of Sexuality Vol. 2: The Use of Pleasure.** Harmondsworth: Penguin Books.

Friedrich, W., Urguiza, A. and Berlke, R. (1986). Behaviour problems in sexually abused young children. *Journal of Paediatric Psychology, 11*, 47-57.

Friedrich, W.N., Grambsch, P., Broughton, D., Kuiper, J. and Beilke, R. L. (1991). Normative sexual behaviour in children. *Paediatrics, 88 (3)* 456-464.

Friedrich, W.N., Talley, N.J., Panzer, L., Felt, S. and Zinsmeister, A.R. (1997). Concordance of reports of childhood abuse by adults. *Child Maltreatment, 2 (2)* 164-171.

Fritz, G. (1978). A comparison of males and females who were sexually molested as children. *Journal of Sex and Marital Therapy, 7,* 54-59.

Fromuth, M.E. and Burkhart, B.R. (1989). Long-term psychological correlates of childhood sexual abuse in two samples of college men. *Child Abuse and Neglect, 13 (4)* 533-542.

Fromuth, M.E. Burkhart, B.R. and Webb Jones, C. (1991). Hidden child molestation: an investigation of adolescent perpetrators in a nonclinical sample. *Journal of Interpersonal Violence 6 (3)* 376-384.

Garbarino, E., Guttman, J.W., and Seeley, J.W. (1986). **The Psychologically Battered Child: Strategies for Identification, Assessment and Intervention**. San Francisco: Jossey-Bass.

Gaudin, J. and Polansky, N. (1986). Distancing of the neglectful family. *Children and Youth Services Review, 8 (1)* 1-12.

Gelles, R.J. and Straus, M.A. (1987). Is violence toward children increasing? A comparison of 1975 and 1985 National Survey Rates. *Journal of Interpersonal Violence, 2 (2)* 212-222.

Ghate, D. and Spencer, L. (1995). **The Prevalence of Child Sexual Abuse in Britain.** London: HMSO.

Ghate, D. and Daniels, A. (1997). **Talking about My Generation.** London: NSPCC.

Gibbons, J., Conroy, S. and Bell, C. (1994). **Operation of Child Protection Registers.** London: HMSO.

Gibbons, J., Gallagher, B., Bell, C. and Gordon, D. (1995). **Development after Physical Abuse in Early Childhood.** London: HMSO.

Glasgow, D., Horne, L., Calam, R. and Cox, A. (1994). Evidence, incidence, gender and age in sexual abuse of children perpetrated by children. *Child Abuse Review, 3 (3)* 196-210.

Goldman, R. and Goldman, J. The prevalence and nature of child sexual abuse in Australia. *Australian Journal of Sex, Marriage and the Family, 9.*

Gordon, L. (1988). The politics of child sexual abuse: notes from American history. *Feminist Review, 28,* 56-64.

Gordon, M. (1990). Males and females as victims of childhood sexual abuse: an examination of the gender effect. *Journal of Family Violence, 5 (4)* 321-332.

Gorey, K.M. and Leslie, D.R. (1997). The prevalence of child sexual abuse: integrative review and adjustment for potential response and measurement biases. *Child Abuse and Neglect, 21 (4)* 391-398.

Gough, D. (1996). Defining the Problem. *Child Abuse and Neglect, 20 (11)* 993 -1102.

Grayson, J. (ed.) (1993). Defining child abuse: at what level should we intervene? *Virginia Child Protection Newsletter, 39, Spring 1993.*

Groth, A.N. (1979). Sexual trauma in the life histories of rapists and child molesters. *Victimology, 4,* 10-16.

Grubin, D. (1998). **Sex Offending Against Children. Understanding the Risk.** Home Office Police Research Series Paper 99. London: Home Office.

Haapasalo, J. and Altonen, J. (1999). Mother's abusive childhood predicts child abuse. *Child Abuse Review 8 (4)* 231-250.

Hallett, C. (1995) **Inter Agency Coordination in Child Protection**. London: HMSO.

Halperin, D.S., Bouvier, P., Jaffe, P.D., Mounoud, R., Pawlak C.H., Laederach, J., Wicky, H.R., and Astie, F. (1996). Prevalence of child sexual abuse among adolescents in Geneva: results of a cross sectional study. *British Medical Journal*, 312, 1326 - 1329.

Hart S.N. and Brassard M.R. (1993). Psychological maltreatment. *Violence Update, 3 (7)* 3-6.

Hart, S.N., Germain, R.B. and Brassard, M.R. (1987). The challenge: to better understand and combat psychological maltreatment of children and youth. In M.R. Brassard, R. Germain and S.N. Hart (eds.) **Psychological maltreatment of children and youth,** 3-24. New York: Pergamon.

Hawkins, R.M.F. and Briggs, F. (1995). Early childhood experiences of men sexually abused as children. *Children Australia, 20 (2)* 18-23.

Home Office (2000). **Criminal Statistics: England and Wales 1998**. London: The Stationery Office.

Hunter, J.A. (1991). A comparison of the psychosocial maladjustment of adult males and females sexually molested as children. *Journal of Interpersonal Violence, 6 (2)* 205-217.

Iwaniec, D. (1997). An overview of emotional maltreatment and failure-to-thrive. *Child Abuse Review, 6 (5),* 370-388.

Jezl, D.R., Molidor, C.E. and Wright, T.L. (1996). Physical, sexual and psychological abuse in high school dating relationships: prevalence rates and self-esteem issues. *Child and Social Work Journal, 13 (1)* 69-87.

Kaplan, S., Pelkovitz, D. and Labruna, V. (1999). Child and adolescent abuse and neglect research: a review of the past 10 years. Part 1: physical and emotional abuse and neglect. *Journal of the American Academy of Child and Adolescent Psychiatry, 38 (10)* 1214-1222.

Kasian, M. and Painter, S.L. (1992). Frequency and severity of psychological abuse in a dating population. *Journal of Interpersonal Violence, 7(3)* 350-364.

Katz, I (2000) **Poverty, Social Exclusion and Child Abuse.** London: NSPCC. Unpublished paper available from the author.

Kelder, L.R., McNamara, J.R., Carlson, B., and Lynn, S.J. (1991). Perceptions of physical punishment. *Journal of Interpersonal Violence 6(4),* 432-445.

Kelly, L., Regan, L. and Burton, S. (1991). **An Exploratory Study of the Prevalence of Sexual Abuse in a Sample of 16-21 Year Olds.** Polytechnic of North London: Child Abuse Studies Unit.

Kendall-Tackett, K.A. and Simon, A.F. (1992). A comparison of the abuse experiences of male and female adults molested as children. *Journal of Family Violence, 7 (1)* 57-62.

Kendall-Tackett, K.A., Williams, L. M. and Finkelhor, D. (1993). Impact of sexual abuse on children: a review and synthesis of recent empirical studies. *Psychological Bulletin, 113 (1)* 164-180.

Kitamura, T., Kitahara, T., Koizumi, T., Takashi, N., Min Li Chiou and Fujihara, S. (1995). Epidemiology of physical child abuse in Japan. How big is the iceberg? *Journal of Forensic Psychiatry, 6 (2)* 425-431.

Kitzinger, J. (1997). Who are you kidding? Children, power and the struggle against sexual abuse. In: A. James and A. Prout (eds.) **Constructing Childhood, 2nd Edition.** London: Falmer.

Knudsen, D.D. (1988). Child maltreatment over two decades: Change or continuity? *Violence and Victims, 3,(2) 129-144.*

Korbin, J. (1993). Culture, cultural diversity and child maltreatment. *APSAC Advisor, 6 (3)* 23-25.

LaFontaine, J. (1990). **Child Sexual Abuse.** Cambridge: Polity Press.

Lamb, S. and Coakley, M. (1993). "Normal" childhood sexual play and games: differentiating play from abuse. *Child Abuse and Neglect, 17 (4)* 515-526.

Leach, P. (1999). **The Physical Punishment of Children: Some Input from Recent Research.** London: NSPCC Policy Practice Research Series.

Leventhal, J.M. (1998). Epidemiology of sexual abuse of children: old problems, new directions. *Child Abuse and Neglect, 22 (6)* 481-491.

Longo, R.E. (1982). Sexual learning and experience among adolescent sexual offenders. *International Journal of Offender Therapy and Comparative Criminology, 26,* 235-241.

MacLeod, M. and Morris, S. (1996). **Why Me? Children Talking to ChildLine about Bullying.** London: ChildLine.

McCauley, J., Kern, D. Kolodner, K., Schroeder, A., DeChant, H., Ryden, J., Derogatis, L. and Bass, E. (1997) Clinical characteristics of women with a history of childhood abuse: unhealed wounds. *Journal of the American Medical Association 277 (17)* 1362-1368.

McGee, C. (2000). **Childhood Experiences of Domestic Violence**. London: Jessica Kingsley.

McGee, R.A., Wolfe, D.A., Yuen S.A., Wilson, S.K. and Cathochan, J. (1995). The measurement of maltreatment: a comparison of approaches. *Child Abuse and Neglect, 19 (2)* 233-249.

Minty, B. and Pattinson, G.T. (1994) The nature of child neglect. *British Journal of Social Work, 24 (6)* 733-747.

Morgan, J. and Zedner, L. (1992). **Child Victims: Crime, Impact and Criminal Justice.** Oxford: Clarendon.

National Commission of Inquiry into the Prevention of Child Abuse (1996). **Childhood Matters Vol. 1: The Report**. London: The Stationery Office.

Nelson, D.E., Higginson, G.K. and Grant-Worley, J.A. (1995). Physical abuse among high school students. *Archives of Paediatric and Adolescent Medicine, 149 Nov.* 1254 - 1258.

Newson, J. and Newson, E. (1970) **Four Years Old in an Urban Community**. Middlesex: Pelican.

Newson, J. and Newson, E. (1978). **Seven Years Old in the Home Environment**. Middlesex: Pelican.

Newson, J. and Newson, E. (1989). **The Extent of Physical Punishment in the UK.** London: Approach.

Ney, P., Moore, C., McPhee, J. and Trought, P. (1986). Child abuse: A study of the child's perspective. *Child Abuse and Neglect, 10 (4)* 511-518.

Ney, P. (1987). Does verbal abuse leave deeper scars? A study of children and parents. *Canadian Journal of Psychiatry, 32,* 371-378.

Nobes, G. and Smith, M.A. (1997). Physical punishment of children in two-parent families. *Clinical Child Psychology and Psychiatry, 2 (2)* 271-281.

O'Hagan, K. (1995) Emotional and psychological abuse: problems of definition. *Child Abuse and Neglect 19,* 449-461.

Oppenheim, C. (1993). **Poverty: the Facts. 2nd edition.** London: Child Poverty Action Group.

Pilkington, B. and Kremer, J. (1995). A review of the epidemiological research on child sexual abuse: clinical samples. *Child Abuse Review, 4 (3)* 191-205.

Polansky, N.A., Ammons, P. and Weathersby, B. (1983). Is there an American standard of child care? *Social Work, 28 (5)* 341-346.

Portwood, S.G. (1999). Coming to terms with a consensual definition of child maltreatment. *Child Maltreatment,. 4 (1)* 56-68.

Queen's University Belfast/Royal Belfast Hospital (1990). **Child Sexual Abuse in Northern Ireland: A Research Study of Incidence.** Antrim: Greystone Books Ltd.

Rees, G. and Stein, M. (1999). **The Abuse of Adolescents within the Family**. London: NSPCC Policy Practice Research Series.

Riley, D. and Shaw, M. (1985) **Parental Supervision and Juvenile Delinquency**. Home Office Research Study No 83. London: HMSO.

Rose, G. (1985). Sick individuals and sick populations. *International Journal of Epidemiology, 14*, 32-38.

Russell, D.E.H. (1984). **Sexual Exploitation: Rape, Child Sexual Abuse and Workplace Harassment.** Beverly Hills, California: Sage.

Sargant W.W. (1963). **Battle for the Mind: A Physiology of Conversion and Brainwashing.** London, Pan Books.

Schecter, M.D. and Roberge, L. (1976). Sexual exploitation. **In:** R.E. Helfer and C.H. Kempe (eds.) **Child Abuse and Neglect: The Family and the Community.** Cambridge, Massachusetts: Ballinger.

Schellenbach, C.J. and Guerney, L.F. (1987). Identification of adolescent abuse and future intervention prospects. *Journal of Adolescence, 10 (1)* 1-12.

Schultz L.G. and Jones, P. (1983). Sexual abuse of children: issues for social service and health professionals. *Child Welfare, 62 (2)* 99-108.

Sedlak, A.J. and Broadhurst, D.B. (1996). **Third National Incidence Study of Child Abuse and Neglect.** Washington DC: US Government Printing Office.

Sedney, M.A. and Brooks, B. (1984). Factors associated with a history of childhood sexual experience in a nonclinical female population. *Journal of the American Academy of Child Psychiatry, 23.*

Shengold, L. (1989). **Soul Murder**. London: Yale University Press.

Siegel, J.M., Sorenson, S.B., Golding, J.M., Burnam, M.A. and Stein, J.A. (1987). The prevalence of childhood sexual assault: the Los Angeles epidemiologic catchment area project. *American Journal of Epidemiology, 126 (6)* 1141-1153.

Smith, M., Bee, P., Heverin, A. and Nobes, G. (1995). Parental control within the family: the nature and extent of parental violence to children. **In:** Department of Health (1995) **Child Protection: Messages from Research.** London: HMSO.

Smith, M. and Bentovim, A. (1994). Sexual abuse. **In:** M. Rutter, E. Taylor and L. Hersov (eds.) **Child Psychiatry. Modern Approaches.** Oxford: Blackwell.

Smith, M. and Grocke, M. (1995) Normal Family Sexuality and Sexual Knowledge in Children. **In:** Department of Health, **Child Protection: Messages from Research**. London: HMSO.

Smith, P.K. and Sharp, S. (1994). **School Bullying: Insights and Perspectives.** London: Routledge.

Stangler, G.J., Kivlahan, C. and Knipp, M.J. (1991). How can we tell when a child dies from abuse? Missouri's new law will answer that question. *Public Welfare, 49 (4)* 5-11.

Steele, B.F. (1987). Psychodynamic factors in child abuse. **In:** R.E. Helfer and R.S. Kempe (Eds) **The Battered Child. 4th edition.** Chicago: University of Chicago Press.

Stevenson, O. (1998). **Neglected Children: Issues and Dilemmas.** Oxford: Blackwell Science.

Stone, B. (1998). **Child Neglect: Practitioners' Perspectives.** London: NSPCC Policy Practice Research Series.

Straus, M.A. (1979). Measuring intrafamily conflict and violence: the Conflict Tactics (CT) Scales. *Journal of Marriage and the Family, 41* 75-88.

Straus, M.A., Gelles, R.J. and Steinmetz, S.K. (1980). **Behind Closed Doors: Violence In The American Family.** Garden City, New York: Anchor/Doubleday.

Straus, M.A. and Gelles, R.J. (1990). **Physical Violence in American Families: Risk Factors and Adaptations to Violence in 8,145 Families.** New Brunswick, New Jersey: Transaction Publishers.

Straus, M.A., Sugarman, D.B. and Giles-Sims, J. (1997). Spanking by parents and subsequent antisocial behaviour of children. *Archives of Paediatric and Adolescent Medicine, 151, August,* 761-767.

Straus, M.A. and Paschall, M.J. (1998). **Corporal Punishment by Mothers and Child's Cognitive Development: A Longitudinal Study.** New Hampshire: Family Research Laboratory, University of New Hampshire.

Thompson, E.E. (In press). The short and long-term effects of corporal punishment on children: a meta-analytic review. *Psychological Bulletin (forthcoming).*

Thorpe, D. (1997). Review essay: Regulating late modern childrearing in Ireland. *The Economic and Social Review, 28,(1) 1997,* 63-84.

Tolman, R.M. (1989). The development of a measure of psychological maltreatment of women by their male partners. *Violence and Victims, 4 (3)* 159-177.

Tomison, A. (1995) **Spotlight on child neglect.** *Issues in Child Abuse Prevention 4, Winter 1995.* National Child Protection Clearing House Issues Paper. Melbourne: Australian Institute of Family Studies.

Tomison, A.M. and Tucci, J. (1997). **Emotional abuse, the hidden form of maltreatment.** *Issues in Child Abuse Prevention, 8, Spring 1997.* National Child Protection Clearing House Issues Paper. Melbourne: Australian Institute of Family Studies.

Tsai, M., Feldman-Summers, S. and Edgar, M. (1979). Childhood molestation: variables related to differential functioning in adult women. *Journal of Abnormal Psychology, 88,* 407-417.

Tutty, L.M. (1999) Considering emotional abuse in the link between spouse and child abuse: a review and exploratory study. *Journal of Emotional Abuse 1 (4)* 53-79.

United States Department of Health and Human Services Administration on Children, Youth and Families. (1997) **Child Maltreatment 1997: Reports from the States to the National Child Abuse and Neglect Data System.** Washington DC: US Government Printing Office.

Vissing, Y., Straus, M., Gelles, R. and Harrop, J. (1991). Verbal aggression by parents and psychosocial problems of children. *Child Abuse and Neglect, 15 (3)* 223-238.

Wassil-Grimm, C. (1995). **Diagnosis for Disaster: The Devastating Truth About False Memory Syndrome and its Impact on Accusers and Families.** Woodstock, New York: Overlook Press.

Waterhouse, L., Pitcairn, T., McGhee, J., Secker, J. and Sullivan, C. (1995). Evaluating parenting in child physical abuse. **In:** Department of Health (1995) **Child Protection: Messages from Research.** London: HMSO.

Watkins, B. and Bentovim, A. (1992). The sexual abuse of male children and adolescents: a review of current research. *Journal of Child Psychology and Psychiatry and Allied Disciplines, 33 (1)* 197-248.

Wattam, C. and Woodward, C. (1996). "And Do I Abuse My Children?...No!" **In: Childhood Matters: Report of the National Commission of Inquiry into the Prevention of Child Abuse. Vol. 2: Background Papers.** London: The Stationery Office.

Wattam, C. (1996). Can filtering processes be rationalised? **In:** N. Parton (ed.) **Child Protection and Family Support: Tensions, Contradictions and Possibilities.** London: Routledge.

Williams and Finkelhor, D. (1992). The characteristics of incestuous fathers. **In:** N.H. Durham. **Report for the National Center for Child Abuse and Neglect**. New Hampshire: Family Research Laboratory, University of New Hampshire.

Willow, C. and Hyder, T. (1998). **It Hurts You Inside: Children Talking About Smacking.** National Children's Bureau and Save the Children. London: National Children's Bureau Enterprises.

Wilson, H. (1980). Parental supervision: a neglected aspect of delinquency. *British Journal of Criminology, 20 (3)* 203 - 235.

Wyatt, G.E. (1985). The sexual abuse of Afro-American and white American women in childhood. *Child Abuse and Neglect, 9 (4)* 507-519.

Wyatt, G., Loeb, T., Solis, B. and Carmona, J (1999) The prevalence and circumstances of child sexual abuse: changes across a decade. *Child Abuse and Neglect 23 (1)* 45-50

Zuravin, S. (1999) Child neglect: a review of definitions and measurement research. **In:** Dubowitz, H. (ed.) **Neglected Children; Research, Practice and Policy.** London: Sage.

APPENDIX 1

Sample design

For practical and ethical reasons, it would have been inappropriate to interview children in this survey. It was therefore decided to interview very young adults aged 18 – 24 years. This subgroup was selected on the grounds that their experience of childhood was sufficiently recent and their recall of the details would therefore be relatively accurate. Additionally, they were considered to be less likely than older adults to have experienced other major events in their lives which would affect their views and make it more difficult for them to isolate the impact of any childhood experiences on their lives. It was recognised that few adults have very detailed memories of their lives before the age of five years old, and it is known that more serious child abuse is likely to be experienced by younger children. However, this was not a major concern as it was considered unlikely that those having abusive experiences before the age of five would cease to have them afterwards.

A random probability sampling technique was employed, using the Postcode Address File as the basic sampling frame. 633 postcode sectors throughout the United Kingdom were selected with probability proportional to the population of 18–24 year olds after stratification by ACORN (A Classification of Residential Neighbourhoods, which is based on Census data). Within each postcode sector one address was selected at random and then every fourth address subsequently, with a total of 90 addresses being selected in each postcode sector – a total of 56,970 addresses being sampled throughout the United Kingdom.

Where successful contact was made, details of any 18–24 year olds in the household were taken. Where two or more 18–24 year olds were present, a random selection process was used to select one of them. An attempt was made to take the full interview with the selected individual.

A total of 2,869 interviews were achieved. In order to be eligible for interview, all 18–24 year olds had to have spent the majority of their childhood (a minimum of 10 years) in the United Kingdom.

Fieldwork

Fieldwork took place between 7th September, 1998 and 8th February, 1999. All fieldwork was carried out by fully trained and experienced interviewers who were members of BMRB's face to face fieldforce. Interviewers were all personally briefed and also received comprehensive written instructions.

Each interviewer received 90 paper contact sheets for the postcode sector to which s/he had been assigned. These detailed the addresses selected for the sample and interviews for the main sample could only be carried out at these addresses. Interviewers were also provided with letters about the survey, one from BMRB to state that the survey was taking place, and the other from the NSPCC thanking those who had taken part.

The vast majority of fieldwork took place during the hours of 1.30pm and 9.00pm or during the day at the weekend. Interviewers made at least six attempts to achieve a contact at each address they had been given. Calls were made on a variety of days and times of day, with at least three calls being made in the evenings after 7.00pm or at weekends. Interviewers kept a full record of all the calls made and the final outcome.

In those instances where the address covered more than one occupied household unit (more common amongst this age group than amongst any other, due to many being in student accommodation), interviewers were instructed to select one dwelling unit, following written instructions to ensure random selection.

If the contact at the issued address said that that a neighbouring household contained a young person from an ethnic minority background, then an additional contact sheet was initiated for this neighbouring household. Interviewers then followed the same rules about making contact with that household, calling at various times of the day and on different days of the week, until a final outcome for that address was achieved.

Response

Full details of the outcome at each address issued are shown below. (The figures are provisional as a small number of contact sheets still remain to be counted).

	Number	%
Addresses issued:	56,970	100
Not located/demolished	1,475	3
Unoccupied /other deadwood	2,680	5
Non residential	1,078	2
Total valid residential addresses	51,737	91

Presence of 18-24 year old residents

	Number	% (n =)
Valid residential addresses issued	51,737	100
Details not established:		
Refused household details	188	*
No contact after 6+ calls	1,542	3
Other unsuccessful	493	1
Valid addresses, details unknown	2,223	4
Valid addresses, details known	49,514	96
18-24 year olds found	3,999	8

If we assume that the same proportion of households at which we failed to make successful contact (8%) as those at which we did make contact contained an 18–24 year old, the response breakdown looks like this:

Assume 8% of valid addresses for which details unknown also have 18–24 year olds
= 2223 x 8% = 178

178 + 3999 = 4177

Response rate (interviews as a % of known/assumed in scope)

	Number	% (n =)
Total addresses known/ assumed to contain 18-24 yr olds	4,177	100
18-24 year old refused	676	16
No contact with 18-24 year old selected	251	6
Broken appointment	200	5
Other unsuccessful	178	4
Partial interview	37	1
Full interview	2,835	68
Total interviews	2,872	69

Sample loss and bias

In addition to sample loss from non response, the use of the postcode address file excluded homeless people, and a decision was also made to exclude any addresses which were institutions rather than private households. Therefore people living in hostels, hotels, boarding houses, hospitals, colleges, religious and penal institutions at the time of the fieldwork were excluded, though it of course entirely possible that respondents now living in private households would have had earlier experience of these settings. The decision to exclude institutions was taken on the pragmatic grounds that negotiating access directly with respondents would be difficult or impossible in many of these situations where 'gatekeepers' would operate, and interviewers on the ground could not be expected to undertake this, or judge when it was necessary. Apart from

Young Offenders Institutions and larger young people's hostels, none of these populations would have been expected to have high numbers in the relevant age range. However some populations, particularly the homeless, and those in custody or in psychiatric hospitals and hostels, are known to have been particularly vulnerable to childhood maltreatment. The low chance of sampling such an address randomly, together with the decision to take only one eligible person from each address, means that very few respondents would have been expected to be recruited had the institutions been retained in the sampling frame. Levels of childhood maltreatment among these especially vulnerable populations are already among the best documented in research. However some at least of these populations are lost to the present sample.

The decision to sample only one eligible person from each address also potentially creates a source of bias in that it excludes siblings where two or more young people still at the same address were within the age range, and may therefore underestimate situations where more than one child in a family was maltreated. This decision was taken for pragmatic reasons because many young people in this age range were expected to be living in shared flats and houses, and maintaining confidentiality of the interview questions would be difficult if time elapsed between interviews of residents in the same household. This would be equally true in households with siblings. Corrective weighting was applied to the data to deal with sample loss from this source (see below).

Finally, the sample has also lost any of this age cohort who died prematurely, including those who died in childhood as the result of abuse and neglect. There are approximately 80 - 100 homicides of children under 16 years in the UK each year, and an unknown number of other children to whose deaths maltreatment could have contributed but which are not recorded as homicides. Approximately seven in ten of these children would have been killed by someone in their family, usually a parent (Creighton, 2000) The numbers would have given a loss of over 2000 members of the age group who could potentially have been sampled. The loss in terms of numbers for the sample is small but it should be noted that it is not possible in a study of this kind to include the prevalence of the most serious and dangerous forms of child maltreatment.

All sources of bias in the sample loss would be expected to reduce the probability of reporting of maltreatment. Prevalence measures quoted in this report would therefore be more likely to underestimate than overestimate the true levels of maltreatment.

Weighting

Corrective weighting was applied to the data to deal with the higher levels of non response from men than from women, with regional variations in response, and with the selection of one respondent from households where more than one person would have been eligible.

Interviewing

All the interviews were carried out using CAPI (Computer Assisted Personal Interviewing). The average interview length was 47 minutes. The first part of the interview, involving questions about current living situation, family structure and opinions on the acceptable treatment of children, and some aspects of childhood experience, was carried out by the interviewer asking the questions and entering the answers. Any possibly sensitive questions were asked using show cards for which the respondent had only to read out a code. Then respondents were shown how to use the computer and given a few moments for practice questions and answers. The section of the interview concerning possible experience of maltreatment was entered directly on to computer by respondents, meaning that they did not have to speak aloud or discuss their experiences, and could complete the interview in complete confidentiality, even if other members of the household were in hearing. At the end of the interview the interviewer collected and entered basic demographic data.

Interviewers were briefed that they could clarify any questions or points concerning the interview or questionnaire but should not get into discussion of respondents' childhood. They were briefed on appropriate responses if anyone became distressed during interview. Respondents, at the start of the self completion section, were given the option of stopping interviews, continuing at another time or in another place if they wished, or having a different interviewer, for example, of a different gender. All respondents were given contact telephone numbers and addresses at BMRB and the NSPCC, plus details of the NSPCC Child Protection Helpline and other helpline services should they wish to discuss anything arising from the research or the interviews.

Interviewers noted whether the respondents' parents were present during any part of the interview, and whether they thought that the interview environment had affected the respondents. Although 56% of respondents were still living with parents, parents were present at any time in only 14% of interviews. Interviewers noted that aspects of the interview environment seemed to affect 11% of interviews, with 4% affected 'a lot' and 7% 'a little'. The effects could have come from many sources – interruptions from other members of the household or from outside, for example. Further analysis will explore how, if at all, parental presence and interview environment related to answers.

Memory issues

The primary memory issue for this study is that of recall of events in early childhood. It is known from several prospective and contemporaneous studies of childrearing that physical punishment is primarily used in the pre-school years, with the peak ages being 3-4 years. From then it begins to tail off, declining sharply after age seven and being unusual after age 11 (Creighton and Russell 1995, Smith et al. 1995; Leach, 1999). It is possible that respondents have forgotten or underestimated experiences of physical punishment in early childhood, although this seems less likely if the punishment was frequent or severe. Long-term studies also suggest that parents who believe strongly in physical punishment are likely to continue using it.

The peak ages for registration of children suffering or at risk of significant harm from physical abuse and neglect are also of young children. The largest group of registrations are aged five to nine years, and the highest rate per 1000 of registrations is for children under one year old. It is not possible for any study of prevalence which relies on adult recall to eliminate the possibility that respondents suffered abuse in early childhood which they cannot remember. Long term follow up studies of children on child protection registers suggest that approximately 20% will suffer further abuse or neglect, (with those who have experienced more than one form of maltreatment most vulnerable) and many others suffer poor care resulting from continuing problems in their families (Gibbons et al., 1995).It is inevitable that some experiences of maltreatment will have been underestimated in the present study but likely that most respondents who experienced maltreatment in early childhood continued to have poor care at an age which they can remember.

Some studies suggest a full account of abusive experience will only be obtained if more than one interview is held (Ghate and Spencer 1995, Fergusson et al. 2000). Fergusson et al. found that recall of physical punishment and sexual abuse differed at ages 18 and 21 in a general population cohort. Their analysis indicates that reports at the two ages were complementary, not contradictory, with both cumulatively giving a truer picture than the separate age studies gave singly. However Friedrich et al (1997) found reports of physical and sexual abuse stable over time, although psychological abuse was less so. Bolen and Scannapieco (1999), in a review and reanalysis of all (22) American random probability prevalence studies of sexual abuse, suggest that many methodological differences between studies may have had less effect on prevalence rates than previously thought, and that problems could largely be overcome by the inclusion of a larger number of questions screening for abuse. The importance of including multiple probes for abuse was accepted and incorporated into the design of the present study for all types of maltreatment.

The second issue is the possibility that traumatic memories of abuse in childhood may have been suppressed, or that memories of abuse may be false. Research evidence is contradictory on the question of recovered memories of abuse but the balance of evidence is that false negatives (i.e. forgotten abuse) is more likely than false positives (or so called 'false memory')(Fish, 1998). Most research on memories of abuse has concerned sexual abuse and very little attention has been paid to memories of physical or emotional abuse or neglect.

As with response bias, the most likely effect of memory problems is to increase the probability that figures for maltreatment are underestimates rather than overestimates.

Methodological issues from previous research evidence on sexual abuse

Response Rates: Response rates to prevalence studies on child sexual abuse vary between 50%–69% (Finkelhor, 1986). These have been found to be affected by a number of methodological issues.

Sampling: Most prevalence studies have focused on the prevalence of child sexual abuse. Early studies are characterised by the use of non-probability or convenience samples, such as college students, which impose limitations on the extent of generalisation that can be drawn from findings. During the 80s methodologies became more refined and some general population samples were included. There are now a large number of studies which have utilised these samples. The most well known are those by Russell (1984) in the US and Badgley et al (1984) in Canada. However, there have been few national samples in the US which covers both males and females and only two in the UK (Baker and Duncan, 1985; Creighton and Russell, 1995) one of which was carried out over 15 years ago and neither of which use random probability sampling methods. Ghate and Spencer (1995) note that:

'In order to provide prevalence estimates of optimum reliability, to allow for the relatively low base rate for child sexual abuse in the general population, to examine the circumstances and effects of child sexual abuse and to permit a comparative analysis of different sub-groups, a much larger random sample would be required than has hitherto been attempted.' p.14.

Age of Sample: Controversy surrounds the issue of whether to reduce age limits of participation to include children and young people themselves. Recent population studies on young people and victimisation through crime which generally incorporate questions on sexual victimisation have included young people without difficulty (Enzmann, Pfeiffer and Wetzels, 1996; Finkelhor and Dzuiba-Leatherman, 1994d; 1994e). Indeed such studies have led to arguments towards encouraging greater participation and further research concerning pre-adolescent children. Alternatively, Ghate and Spencer (1995) suggest that involving young people under 18 in a study about child sexual abuse has a number of ethical and methodological difficulties. Parents can act as gatekeepers to the young person's participation thereby biasing response rates, particularly where their consent is required. Secondly, young people who have not had extensive sexual experience may find such a survey distressing. Thirdly, young people tend to live with their parents and those who have been sexually abused may still be living with a perpetrator. Ghate and Spencer conclude that the emotional and physical wellbeing of 'the most vulnerable' would be seriously compromised and thereby rule out their inclusion. Furthermore, they state that from the pilot research that they conducted it was found that some of these problems continue to be relevant for 18 year olds, since of respondents aged 25 and under more were living in the home than not. This leads them to propose an increase in the lower age limit to 20, or even 25.

There is some indication that the age of the sample has an effect on the prevalence rate of sexual abuse which is obtained. Baker and Duncan found an overall prevalence rate of 10% in a sample ranging from 15 to 65+. They note that US prevalence studies generally obtain higher prevalence rates with younger populations and computed that the prevalence rate for 15–24 year olds in their study was higher, at 13%. They suggest that this may reflect more openness amongst the younger population with regard to sexual matters.

Approach: There are inevitable sensitivities involved in conducting a study on experiences of child sexual abuse, these relate to:

■ The topic of child sexual abuse itself which has negative and potentially distressing connotations

■ The fact that a minority of respondents will have experience of child sexual abuse with the implication that a study may evoke painful memories, force respondents to reframe previous child experience as abuse, ask people to give information on subjects they would rather not give information about, rekindle or initiate fears about disclosure, discovery and consequences

Ghate and Spencer consider some of these issues in relation to prevalence studies on sexual abuse, considering the advantages and disadvantages of oblique or direct approaches in the research. An oblique approach which did not give any forewarning of abuse content has two disadvantages:

- If sexual abuse is presented as only part of the agenda it is ethically and technically only possible to ask a few questions, thereby limiting the amount of knowledge that can usefully be gained

- Ethical issues arise from the potential of evoking painful memories without forewarning.

Some more indirect approaches to child sexual abuse prevalence refer to childhood or sexual experiences in general. This contexts the study in these broad areas. For example 'child maltreatment' (Ghate and Spencer, 1995), the 'sexual experience of women' (Russell, 1984) or 'family, sexuality and violence' (Kelly et al., 1991). Ghate and Spencer concluded that, because of a lack of consensus over definition, their selected 'direct' approach would be:

'learning about sex: adults' memories of their own childhood, growing up and what they learned about sexual development and sex, and their views about their own childhood experiences.'

Prevalence of Physical Abuse: Summary Table of Studies Reviewed

Authors	Date	Country	Respondents	Age of Children	Definition/Focus	Sampling	Total N	Response Rate	Prevalence Rate	Incidence
Straus & Gelles	1975	USA	Parents	3–17	CTS	RP	2,143	65%		36:1000
Straus & Gelles	1985	USA	Parents	3–17	CTS	Random Digit Dial	4,032	84%		19:1000
Sedlak	1986	USA	Sentinels	0–18	Harm Standard	Agency	N/A	N/A		4.9:1000
Berger et al.	1988	USA	16–67 (mean 18)	As a child	PPScale	College Students	4, 695	N/A	9%	
Daro & McCurdy	1991	USA	Agency	0–18		Agency reports		N/A		10.5:1000
Nelson et al.	1993	USA	Adolescents	Adolescents	Broad	Schools	1957	82%	31.50%	16.3%
Sedlak & Broadhurst	1993	USA	Sentinels	0–18	Harm Standard	Agency	N/A	N/A		5.7:1000
Finkelhor et al.	1994	USA	10–16 & caretakers	0–16	Complete family assault	Random Digit Dial	2000	82%	7.5%	5.2%
Berrien et al.	1995	Russia	11–16	0–16	Serious injury potential	Gifted children	412	N/A	28.9%	
Kitamura et al.	1995	Japan	Over 18	0–16	Punching Hitting Burning	Geographical Region	508	45%	18%★	
Smith et al.	1995	UK	Parents & children	1–11	Punishment	Child Health Registers	403	N/K	15% (Severe punishment)	
Enzmann et al.	1997	Germany	13–24 (mean 15)	13–24	CTS	Schools	9,775	90%		15.9%
Enzmann et al.	1997	Germany	13–24 (mean 15)	>12	CTS	Schools	9,775	90%	26.9%	
Christensen	1996	Denmark	1031 Health Nurses	0–1yr	Harm/ Potential Harm	National – all Health Nurses	78,625 children (90% of age group)	83% (Health nurses)	1% active (abuse)	

^ CTS = Conflict Tactics Scale (Straus, 1979), Harm Standard = Child has suffered demonstrable harm (Sedlak and Broadhurst, 1996), PPScale = Physical Punishment Scale (see Berger et al., 1988)
• Figures computed from presentation of results in Kitamura et al., 1995.

Prevalence of Neglect

Authors	Date	Country	Respondents	Age of Children	Definition/Focus	Sampling	Total N	Response Rate	
Christensen	1996	Denmark	1031 Heath Nurses	0–1	Harm/Potential Harm	National – all Health Nurses	78,625 children (90% of age group)	83% (Health nurses)	4% passive (neglect)

Definitions: left without supervision 1–2 hours or more; repeated non collection from day centre; abandoned several days; malnourished; lack of medical care – preventive and treatment for illness; extrordinarily tired or atonic; untidy or dirty; dressed inapropriately for weather.

Incidence of Neglect

Category	NIS-3 1993 Number of Children	Rate per 1000	NIS-2 1986 Number of Children	Rate per 1000	NIS-1 1980 Number of Children	Rate per 1000
All Neglect	879,000	13.1	474,800	7.5	315,400	4.9
Physical Neglect	338,900	5.0	167,800	2.7	103,600	1.6
Emotional Neglect	212,800	3.2	49,200	0.8	56,900	0.9
Educational Neglect	397,300	5.9	284,800	4.5	174,000	2.7

Source: National Incidence Study (NIS-3) Sedlak and Broadhurst, 1996

Definitions :
Physical Neglect: Refusal of health care; delay in health care; abandonment; expulsion; other custody issues; inadequate supervision; other physical neglect (avoidable hazards in home; inadequate nutrition; clothing or hygiene, reckless disregard for child's welfare).
Educational Neglect: Permitted chronic truancy; failure to enrol/other truancy; inattention to special educational need.
Emotional Neglect: Inadequate nurturance/affection; chronic/extreme spouse abuse; permitted drug/alcohol abuse; permitted other maladaptive behaviour; refusal of psychological care; delay in psychological care; inattention to child's developmental emotional needs.

Definitions/components of emotional abuse in recent studies

Behaviour/concept*	Garbarino, Guttman & Seeley, 1986, USA	Hart, Bingelli & Brassard, 1998, USA	Sedlak & Broadhurst, 1996, USA	Christensen, 1993, Denmark	Bifulco & Moran, 1998, UK	Friedrich et al, 1995, USA	Burnett, 1993, USA	Doyle, 1997, UK
Refusal/failure to show affection	Rejecting	Denying emotional responsiveness	Emotional neglect – Inadequate nurturance/affection	Passive emotional neglect			Not providing a loving home	Rejecting
Abandonment/leaving home	Rejecting				Psychological abuse			
Excluding child from family activities/treats	Rejecting	Spurning			Antipathy		Cinderella syndrome	Ignoring
Refusing approaches or affection from a child	Rejecting	Denying emotional responsiveness	Emotional neglect – Inadequate nurturance/affection	Passive emotional neglect				
Belittling child's achievements	Rejecting	Spurning	Emotional abuse – Verbal/emotional assault		Antipathy			Degrading
Insulting e.g. calling demeaning names such as 'dummy' 'stupid' 'monster' 'making you feel like a bad person'	Rejecting	Spurning		Active emotional abuse	Antipathy	Psychological maltreatment	Severe verbal abuse	Degrading
Scapegoating, favouring siblings	Rejecting	Spurning	Emotional abuse – Verbal/emotional assault		Antipathy		Cinderella syndrome	Inappropriate roles
Humiliating	Rejecting	Spurning	Emotional abuse – Verbal/emotional assault		Psychological abuse	Psychological maltreatment	Public humiliation	Degrading

Behaviour/concept*	Garbarino, Guttman & Seeley, 1986, USA	Hart, Bingelli & Brassard, 1998, USA	Sedlak & Broadhurst, 1996, USA	Christensen, 1993, Denmark	Bifulco & Moran, 1998, UK	Friedrich et al., 1995, USA	Burnett, 1993, USA	Doyle, 1997, UK
Excessive criticism	Rejecting	Spurning	Emotional abuse – Verbal/ emotional assault		Antipathy		Severe verbal abuse	Rejecting
Infantilising (treating as younger than age)	Rejecting	Exploiting/ corrupting	Emotional neglect – other					
Expelling from family	Rejecting							
Threatening with extreme punishments	Terrorising	Terrorising	Emotional abuse–Verbal/ emotional assault	Active emotional abuse		Psychological maltreatment	Severe verbal abuse	Fear-inducing
Creating climate of unpredictable threat	Terrorising	Terrorising	Emotional abuse–Verbal/ emotional assault	Passive emotional neglect	Psychological abuse			
Creating unmeetable expectations/ punishing when not met	Terrorising	Terrorising	Emotional neglect – other		Antipathy			
Teasing, scaring threats of 'monsters', 'bogeys'	Terrorising	Terrorising	Emotional abuse–Verbal/ emotional assault		Psychological abuse			Tormenting
Inconsistent demands, double binds	Terrorising				Psychological abuse			
Frequent raging at child	Terrorising	Terrorising	Emotional abuse–Verbal/ emotional assault	Active emotional abuse	Psychological maltreatment			
Threats of public humiliation, ridicule	Terrorising	Terrorising			Psychological abuse			

Behaviour/concept*	Garbarino, Guttman & Seeley, 1986, USA	Hart, Bingelli & Brassard, 1998, USA	Sedlak & Broadhurst, 1996, USA	Christensen, 1993, Denmark	Bifulco & Moran, 1998, UK	Friedrich et al., 1995, USA	Burnett, 1993, USA	Doyle, 1997, UK
Threats of loss of love	Terrorising	Terrorising		Active emotional abuse				
Psychologically unavailable to child	Ignoring	Denying emotional responsiveness		Passive emotional neglect	Neglect			
Not responding to child	Ignoring	Denying emotional responsiveness	Emotional neglect – Inadequate nurturance/affection	Passive emotional neglect	Neglect		Not providing a loving home	
Coolness and lack of affect	Ignoring	Denying emotional responsiveness	Emotional neglect – Inadequate nurturance/affection	Passive emotional neglect			Not providing a loving home	Rejecting
Not speaking to child	Ignoring	Denying emotional responsiveness	Emotional neglect – Inadequate nurturance/affection	Passive emotional neglect				
Not protecting child e.g. from siblings, bullying	Ignoring				Neglect		Not providing a loving home	
No interest in child's progress e.g. at school, adolescent activities	Ignoring		Emotional neglect – Inadequate nurturance/affection		Neglect			
Prevent child's social relations	Isolating	Isolating		Active emotional abuse	Psychological abuse		Not allowing social/emotional growth	Isolating

Behaviour/concept*	Garbarino, Guttman & Seeley, 1986, USA	Hart, Bingelli & Brassard, 1998, USA	Sedlak & Broadhurst, 1996, USA	Christensen, 1993, Denmark	Bifulco & Moran, 1998, UK	Friedrich et al., 1995, USA	Burnett, 1993, USA	Doyle, 1997, UK
Leaving unattended for several hours	Isolating							
Denying others access to the child	Isolating	Isolating						
Punishing child's approaches to others	Isolating						Not allowing social/ emotional growth	
Prohibits play or contact with other children	Isolating	Isolating		Active emotional abuse	Psychological abuse		Not allowing social/ emotional growth	Isolating
Prohibits joining clubs, after school activities	Isolating	Isolating			Psychological abuse		Not allowing social/ emotional growth	
Withdrawing child from school e.g. to work in the house	Isolating				Role reversal			
Encouraging antisocial and deviant behaviour e.g. stealing	Corrupting	Exploiting/ corrupting	Emotional neglect – permitted other maladaptive behaviour		Psychological abuse		Coercing into delinquency	Corrupting
Encouraging aggression	Corrupting	Exploiting/ corrupting	Emotional neglect – permitted other maladaptive behaviour					

Behaviour/concept*	Garbarino, Guttman & Seeley, 1986, USA	Hart, Bingelli & Brassard, 1998, USA	Sedlak & Broadhurst, 1996, USA	Christensen, 1993, Denmark	Bifulco & Moran, 1998, UK	Friedrich et al., 1995, USA	Burnett, 1993, USA	Doyle, 1997, UK
Encouraging sexual precocity/exposing to pornography	Corrupting	Exploiting/corrupting	Emotional neglect – permitted other maladaptive behaviour		Psychological abuse		Coercing into delinquency	
Inducting into prostitution	Corrupting	Exploiting/corrupting	Emotional neglect – permitted other maladaptive behaviour		Psychological abuse		Coercing into delinquency	
Encouraging drug and alcohol use/sale	Corrupting	Exploiting/corrupting	Emotional neglect – permitted drug/alcohol abuse				Coercing into delinquency	Corrupting
Tying or binding			Emotional abuse – Close confinement					
Confining to enclosed area (e.g. a cupboard)		Isolating	Emotional abuse – Close confinement				Confinement	Isolating
Attempted or potential physical/sexual abuse			Emotional abuse – Other/unknown					
Withholding food, shelter, sleep, other necessities as punishment			Emotional abuse – Other/unknown		Psychological abuse			Isolating
Chronic/extreme spouse abuse or other domestic violence in child's presence			Emotional neglect – Chronic/extreme spouse abuse	Passive emotional neglect				

Behaviour/concept*	Garbarino, Guttman & Seeley, 1986, USA	Hart, Bingelli & Brassard, 1998, USA	Sedlak & Broadhurst, 1996, USA	Christensen, 1993, Denmark	Bifulco & Moran, 1998, UK	Friedrich et al., 1995, USA	Burnett, 1993, USA	Doyle, 1997, UK
Refusal to allow treatment for emotional/behaviour problems		Mental health, medical and educational neglect	Emotional neglect – Refusal of psychological care				Refusal of psychiatric treatment	
Failure to seek treatment for emotional/behaviour problems		Mental health, medical and educational neglect	Emotional neglect – Delay in psychological care					
Role reversal – child takes over parents' responsibilities		Exploiting/ corrupting			Role reversal			Inappropriate roles
Role reversal – child supports parents					Role reversal			Inappropriate roles
Domination of child					Psychological abuse			
Harm/threats to pets, treasured objects		Terrorising			Psychological abuse			
Economic exploitation			Emotional abuse – Other/ unknown					
Left in care of drunk, otherwise intoxicated adults				Passive emotional neglect				
Constantly changing carers				Active emotional abuse				Terrorising
Mostly left in care of older children				Active emotional abuse				

* Several studies include some of these behaviours in ratings of physical or sexual abuse or physical neglect

Prevalence of Sexual Abuse: Summary Table of Recent Studies*

Authors	Date	Country	Respondents	Age of Children	Definition/ Focus	Sampling	Total N	Response Rate	Prevalence Rate	Incidence
Kelly, Regan and Burton	1991	UK	Students	0–18	Unwanted and abusive experience	F.E. colleges in representative areas	1,244	3% refusal rate	46%, total (59% F, 27% M)	
Ghate & Spencer	1995	UK	General population aged 18–60	0–16	Consensual and non consensual experience	RP	127 (feasibility study)	56–71%	36/127	
Creighton and Russell	1995	UK	General population aged 18–45	0–16	Non consensual, 'with a much older person'	Quota	1,032	N/A	16% total (24%F, 9% M)	
Sedlak and Broadhurst	1996	USA	Sentinels	0–16	Harm standard	Agency	N/A	N/A		3.2:1000
McCauley et al.	1997	USA	Women attending primary care medical practices	0–18	'Sexual abuse'	4 community based medical practices	1,931	N/K	15.7%	
Coxell et al.	1999	UK	Men attending GP's surgery	0–16 and adult	Non consensual experience plus consensual childhood with person 5+ years older	18 General Practices	2,474	79%	(childhood) 5.35% non consensual, 7.69% consensual with person 5 or more years older	
Wyatt et al.	1999	USA	General population in one county - women	0–18	Contact abuse - non consensual or with person 5 or more years older	African American and European American women – stratified samples	338	71%	34%	

*International studies from 21 countries prior to 1994 are reviewed in Finkelhor, 1994. Bolen and Scannapieco (1999) reanalyse 22 random probability studies from the USA.

APPENDIX 3

BMRB International Ltd, Hadley House, 79–81 Uxbridge Road, Ealing, London W5 5SU.

CHILDHOOD: QUESTIONNAIRE

Is this a main sample interview or an ethnic boost interview?

Main sample

Ethnic boost

SHOW CARD A

1. First of all, can you tell me which of the following applies to you?
Please do not include children.

I am living with my parents (one or both)

I am living with brother(s) and/or sister(s)

I am living with other relatives (not parents/immediate family)

I am living with my partner/husband/wife

I am living with friends/flatmates etc.

I am living alone

Other

Don't know

Refused

2. Do you have children of your own?

Yes

No

Don't know

Refused

IF YES, ASK

3. How many?

1

2

3

4

5

6

Don't know

Refused

4. How old were you when he or she/the first one was born?
TYPE IN AGE

5. Does that child/Do they live with you?
By live with, we mean full time or part time such as at weekends.

Yes – full time

Yes – part time

No

Don't know

Refused

6. Do you work with children, or have you done so in the past?
By work, I mean paid employment, including full and part time.

Yes – currently

Yes – previously

No

Don't know

Refused

ASK ALL

SHOW CARD B
7. When you were a child, did you ever experience any of these situations?

Living with grandparents or other relatives (not parent(s))

Living in residential care (e.g. children's home)

Living with foster parents

Being adopted by new parents (INTERVIEWER NOTE:
Adoption does not include legal adoption by long term step-parents)

Having a long stay in hospital (i.e. more than 1 week)

Attending a boarding school

Having a childminder or nanny

None of these

Don't know

Refused

IF ANY EXCEPT NONE, ASK
8. Was this/Were any of these while you were aged up to 11, or aged 12 plus?

Up to 11

12+

Both

Don't know

Refused

**9. Do you regard yourself as having a disability, or long term
illness which limits you in any way?**

Yes

No

Don't know

Refused

....

IF YES, ASK

SHOW CARD C

10. Which of these best describes your disability or illness?

Mobility

Sight

Hearing

Communication/speech

Learning difficulty

Other

Don't know

Refused

....

11. Have you had a disability or illness from birth?

Yes

No

Don't know

Refused

....

IF NOT FROM BIRTH

12. From what age?

TYPE IN AGE

....

ASK ALL

PINK SHUFFLE PACK

On these cards are printed some things which people have said to us. Please look at the cards and show me how much you agree or disagree with each statement, by placing it on this board.

13. Please read out the numbers of the cards you strongly agreed with.

It is easy to give children a healthy diet, even on a low income

A home can be happy for children even if it is not clean

If children say they are ill, they should always be taken seriously

Children don't have as much freedom these days

Parents should talk openly about sex to their children right from the start

None of them

....

14. And now please read out the numbers of those you slightly agreed with.

....

15. And those you neither agreed nor disagreed with.

It is easy to give children a healthy diet, even on a low income

A home can be happy for children even if it is not clean

If children say they are ill, they should always be taken seriously

Children don't have as much freedom these days

Parents should talk openly about sex to their children right from the start

None of them

....

16. And those you slightly disagreed with.

It is easy to give children a healthy diet, even on a low income

A home can be happy for children even if it is not clean

If children say they are ill, they should always be taken seriously

Children don't have as much freedom these days

Parents should talk openly about sex to their children right from the start

None of them

....

17. And those you strongly disagreed with.

It is easy to give children a healthy diet, even on a low income

A home can be happy for children even if it is not clean

If children say they are ill, they should always be taken seriously

Children don't have as much freedom these days

Parents should talk openly about sex to their children right from the start

None of them

....

18. Any you don't know about.

It is easy to give children a healthy diet, even on a low income

A home can be happy for children even if it is not clean

If children say they are ill, they should always be taken seriously

Children don't have as much freedom these days

Parents should talk openly about sex to their children right from the start

None of them

....

19. Any you do not wish to place in a category.

It is easy to give children a healthy diet, even on a low income

A home can be happy for children even if it is not clean

If children say they are ill, they should always be taken seriously

Children don't have as much freedom these days

Parents should talk openly about sex to their children right from the start

None of them

....

20. At what age do you think the average child learns the facts of life?

Up to

5 - 10

11 - 14

15+

Gradually over a long period of time

Don't know

Refused

21. The current legal age of consent for sexual intercourse between a male and a female is 16.
In your opinion, what age do you think the legal age of consent should be?

22 or older

21

20

19

18

17

16

15

14

13 or under

Shouldn't be any law

Don't know

Refused

22. Now thinking of sexual relations between people of the same sex, in other words between 2 men or 2 women. In your opinion, what should be the legal age of consent for people in same sex relationships?

22 or older

21

20

19

18

17

16

15

14

13 or under

Same as heterosexuals

Shouldn't be any law

Shouldn't be allowed

Don't know

Refused

23. Now thinking of heterosexual intercourse (male/female) between a young person and an older person who has responsibility for them, such as a teacher, social worker etc. Do you think the age of consent should be higher in this case than for other couples, or the same?

Same

Higher

Lower

Shouldn't be any law

Shouldn't be allowed

Don't know

Refused

24. And what about same sex relationships between a young person and an older person who has responsibility for them. Should the age of consent be higher in this case than for other couples?

Same

Higher

Lower

Shouldn't be any law

Shouldn't be allowed

Don't know

Refused

BLUE SHUFFLE

I'd like you to tell me how you feel about certain ways of treating children IN GENERAL. On each of these cards is a description and I would like you to consider each one and place it on the board to show whether this treatment is ever justified.
25. Please read out the numbers of the cards you think are often justified.

Discussion and explanation of how to behave

Withdrawal of privileges

Grounding

Imposing (additional) chores or tasks

Slapping with an open hand

Isolation (locking child in a room, sending child to their room or to stand in the corner)

Verbal threats of beating or similar (not acted upon)

Embarrassing or humiliating a child

Silence (not speaking to the child)

Warning about fear figures, e.g. bogey man

Making the child miss a meal/part of a meal

Slapping with a soft implement, eg. belt

Slapping with a hard implement, eg. stick

Hitting with a closed fist

None of them

26. And now please read out the numbers of those you think are occasionally justified.

Discussion and explanation of how to behave

Withdrawal of privileges

Grounding

Imposing (additional) chores or tasks

Slapping with an open hand

Isolation (locking child in a room, sending child to their room or to stand in the corner)

Verbal threats of beating or similar (not acted upon)

Embarrassing or humiliating a child

Silence (not speaking to the child)

Warning about fear figures, e.g. bogey man

Making the child miss a meal/part of a meal

Slapping with a soft implement, eg. belt

Slapping with a hard implement, eg. stick

Hitting with a closed fist

None of them

27. And those you think are never justified

Discussion and explanation of how to behave

Withdrawal of privileges

Grounding

Imposing (additional) chores or tasks

Slapping with an open hand

Isolation (locking child in a room, sending child to their room or to stand in the corner)

Verbal threats of beating or similar (not acted upon)

Embarrassing or humiliating a child

Silence (not speaking to the child)

Warning about fear figures, e.g. bogey man

Making the child miss a meal/part of a meal

Slapping with a soft implement, eg. belt

Slapping with a hard implement, eg. stick

Hitting with a closed fist

None of them

28. Any you don't know about.

Discussion and explanation of how to behave

Withdrawal of privileges

Grounding

Imposing (additional) chores or tasks

Slapping with an open hand

Isolation (locking child in a room, sending child to their room or to stand in the corner)

Verbal threats of beating or similar (not acted upon)

Embarrassing or humiliating a child

Silence (not speaking to the child)

Warning about fear figures, e.g. bogey man

Making the child miss a meal/part of a meal

Slapping with a soft implement, e.g. belt

Slapping with a hard implement, e.g. stick

Hitting with a closed fist

None of them

29. Any you do not wish to place in a category.

Discussion and explanation of how to behave

Withdrawal of privileges

Grounding

Imposing (additional) chores or tasks

Slapping with an open hand

Isolation (locking child in a room, sending child to their room or to stand in the corner)

Verbal threats of beating or similar (not acted upon)

Embarrassing or humiliating a child

Silence (not speaking to the child)

Warning about fear figures, e.g. bogey man

Making the child miss a meal/part of a meal

Slapping with a soft implement, e.g. belt

Slapping with a hard implement, e.g. stick

Hitting with a closed fist

None of them

GREEN SHUFFLE PACK

On these cards are some reasons for parents not giving children attention. Do you think any of the following situations would be harmful to children, and if so, how harmful?
30. Please read out the numbers of the cards you think are very harmful.

Parents leaving them at home without an adult, even though they know there should be an adult there

Not taking them to the doctor when they need it

Letting young children watch 18 rated (X) videos or films to keep them quiet

Not going to their school on parents' open evening

Parents being so caught up in their own problems for a while, that they are not able to give them affection

Not making sure there is food in the house for them

Parents being so drunk or high on drugs sometimes that they couldn't take care of them

None of them

31. And now please read out the numbers of those you think are quite harmful.

Parents leaving them at home without an adult, even though they know there should be an adult there

Not taking them to the doctor when they need it

Letting young children watch 18 rated (X) videos or films to keep them quiet

Not going to their school on parents' open evening

Parents being so caught up in their own problems for a while, that they are not able to give them affection

Not making sure there is food in the house for them

Parents being so drunk or high on drugs sometimes that they couldn't take care of them

None of them

---

32. And those you think are a little harmful?

Parents leaving them at home without an adult, even though they know there should be an adult there

Not taking them to the doctor when they need it

Letting young children watch 18 rated (X) videos or films to keep them quiet

Not going to their school on parents' open evening

Parents being so caught up in their own problems for a while, that they are not able to give them affection

Not making sure there is food in the house for them

Parents being so drunk or high on drugs sometimes that they couldn't take care of them

None of them

---

33. And those you think are not harmful.

Parents leaving them at home without an adult, even though they know there should be an adult there

Not taking them to the doctor when they need it

Letting young children watch 18 rated (X) videos or films to keep them quiet

Not going to their school on parents' open evening

Parents being so caught up in their own problems for a while, that they are not able to give them affection

Not making sure there is food in the house for them

Parents being so drunk or high on drugs sometimes that they couldn't take care of them

None of them

---

34. Any you don't know about.

Parents leaving them at home without an adult, even though they know there should be an adult there

Not taking them to the doctor when they need it

Letting young children watch 18 rated (X) videos or films to keep them quiet

Not going to their school on parents' open evening

Parents being so caught up in their own problems for a while, that they are not able to give them affection

Not making sure there is food in the house for them

Parents being so drunk or high on drugs sometimes that they couldn't take care of them

None of them

35. Any you do not wish to place in a category.

Parents leaving them at home without an adult, even though they know there should be an adult there

Not taking them to the doctor when they need it

Letting young children watch 18 rated (X) videos or films to keep them quiet

Not going to their school on parents' open evening

Parents being so caught up in their own problems for a while, that they are not able to give them affection

Not making sure there is food in the house for them

Parents being so drunk or high on drugs sometimes that they couldn't take care of them

None of them

The next few questions are about the way you have been feeling over the last few weeks.

SHOW CARD D

36. How much of the time during the past 4 weeks have you been a very nervous person?

37. How much of the time during the past 4 weeks have you felt so down in the dumps that nothing could cheer you up?

38. How much of the time during the past 4 weeks have you felt calm and peaceful?

39. How much of the time during the past 4 weeks have you felt downhearted and low?

40. How much of the time during the past 4 weeks have you been a happy person?

All of the time

Most of the time

A good bit of the time

Some of the time

A little of the time

None of the time

Don't know

Refused

Childhood circumstances/childrearing

We now want you to think about how you were brought up and whether you think children should be brought up in the same way or differently in the future.

SHOW CARD E

41. Many children experience changes in the adults that live with them and look after them. Which of these did you ever live with?

Natural mother & natural father together

Natural mother only

Natural mother and stepfather(s)

Natural father only

Natural father and stepmother(s)

With other relative(s) (without parents)

With foster parent(s)

With adoptive parent(s)

Other arrangements (TYPE IN)

Don't know

Refused

SHOW CARD E

42. Which of these best describes how you were brought up for most of your childhood?

Natural mother & natural father together

Natural mother only

Natural mother and stepfather(s)

Natural father only

Natural father and stepmother(s)

With other relative(s) (without parents)

With foster parent(s)

With adoptive parent(s)

Other arrangements (TYPE IN)

Don't know

Refused

IF WITH NATURAL MOTHER/NATURAL FATHER (NOT BOTH)

43. Which of these best describes why you were brought up the way you were?

Natural mother/father did not live together – separated/divorced

Natural father/mother died

Other (TYPE IN)

Don't know

Refused

IF LIVED WITH MOTHER (NATURAL/STEP/FOSTER OR ADOPTIVE PARENTS)

44. During your early childhood - say up to the age of 11, did your (step) mother work part-time, full-time or not at all?

P/T

F/T

In & out of work from week to week/seasonal

Not at all PA

Don't know

Not applicable

Refused

45. During your early childhood - say up to the age of 11, did your (step) father work part-time, full-time or not at all?

P/T

F/T

In & out of work from week to week/seasonal

Not at all PA

Don't know

Not applicable

Refused

46. When did your (step) mother finish full-time education?

15 or younger

16 – 18

19 – 21 (university /college)

After 21

Other

Don't know

Not applicable

Refused

47. What was the highest qualification that she achieved?

No qualifications

GCSE (O level/O grade/CSE etc.)

Up to A level etc.

Up to Degree/Postgraduate

Apprenticeships

Professional qualification e.g. Nursing

Other (TYPE IN)

Don't know

Refused

48. When did your (step) father finish full time education?

15 or younger

16 – 18

19 – 21 (university /college)

After 21

Other

Don't know

Not applicable

Refused

49. What was the highest qualification that he achieved?

No qualifications

GCSE (O level/O grade/CSE etc.)

Up to A level etc.

Up to Degree/Postgraduate

Apprenticeships

Professional qualification e.g. Nursing

Other (TYPE IN)

Don't know

The following cards contain descriptions of childhood. Please read the statement and tell me how much each one applies to you by reading out the number next to the answer you wish to give.

SHOW CARD F

50. There was a lot of stress in the family home.

51. There are things that happened in my childhood that I find it hard to talk about.

52. There were always a lot of worries about the shortage of money.

53. I was a happy child.

54. Most other children had things which my family could not afford.

55. I had a warm and loving family background.

56. I often had problems making friends.

Strongly agree

Slightly agree

Neither

Slightly disagree

Strongly disagree

Don't know

Refused

57. Now I'd like to talk about the different ways that families do things, because every family is different. For example, families have different ways of showing that they care for each other. In your family, did people do any of the things on this card, to show that they cared about you? Just tell me the number next to the description.

Praise you or tell you that you did something well

Give you money/extra pocket money

Hug you/cuddle you/kiss you

Give you sweets or nice things to eat

Say nice things to you, or tell you they cared about you

Buy you presents or special treats

Help you do things, e.g. homework

Take you out on trips to places you liked

Something else (TYPE IN)

None of these things

Don't know

Refused

58. How often, if at all, when you were growing up, did your mother show obvious affection to you such as by a hug or kiss?

Every day

Most days

At least once a week

Sometimes, not every week

Rarely

Never

Don't know

Not applicable

Refused

59. How often, if at all, when you were growing up, did your father show obvious affection to you such as by a hug or kiss?

Every day

Most days

At least once a week

Sometimes, not every week

Rarely

Never

Don't know

Not applicable

Refused

IF LIVED WITH MOTHER (NATURAL/STEP/FOSTER OR ADOPTIVE PARENTS) AT 42
SHOW CARD O

60. When you were growing up, how would you describe the relationship you had with your (step) mother? Please just read out the number beside your answer.

Very close

Fairly close

Not very close

Not close at all

Not applicable

Don't know

Refused

IF LIVED WITH FATHER (NATURAL/STEP/FOSTER OR ADOPTIVE PARENTS) AT 42
SHOW CARD O

61. When you were growing up, how would you describe the relationship you had with your (step) father? Please just read out the number beside your answer.

Very close

Fairly close

Not very close

Not close at all

Not applicable

Don't know

Refused

ASK ALL WITH MOTHER/STEP MOTHER AT 43
SHOW CARD P

62. Please read the question on this card and read out the number next to the answer you wish to give.
IF SOMETIMES COULD PREDICT, SOMETIMES COULD NOT, CODE AS 2 (VARIED)
When you were growing up did you feel you knew how your mother would react to something you did or said or were you unable to predict?

Knew where you stood

Unable to predict/reaction varied

Not applicable

Don't know

Refused

ASK ALL WITH FATHER/STEP FATHER AT 43.
SHOW CARD Q

63. Please read the question on this card and read out the number next to the answer you wish to give.
IF SOMETIMES COULD PREDICT, SOMETIMES COULD NOT, CODE AS 2 (VARIED)
When you were growing up did you feel you knew how your father would react to something you did or said or were you unable to predict?

Knew where you stood

Unable to predict/reaction varied

Not applicable

Don't know

Refused

....

SHOW CARD R

Thinking now about the adults you knew when you were growing up, were there any from this list that:

64. **You particularly respected or looked up to (when you were growing up)?**

65. **Who really seemed to dislike you and have it in for you (when you were growing up)?**

66. **Who set you a particularly good example of the sort of adult you wanted to be (when you were growing up)?**

67. **That you were sometimes really afraid of (when you were growing up)?**

68. **Who helped you especially with advice when you needed it (when you were growing up)?**

69. **Who seemed to want to hurt or upset you on purpose (when you were growing up)?**

70. **Who gave you a helping hand when you were in trouble or things were going wrong for you?**

A teacher

Your father

Your stepfather

Your mother

Your stepmother

Your older brother/sister

Your doctor

Your grandmother

Your grandfather

A social worker/care worker

An aunt

An uncle

A priest or other religious leader

A youth club/scout/guides leader or someone like that

A neighbour

Other

None of these

Don't know

Refused

The next section of the interview asks you some more questions about your own child-hood. Please read the questions on the screen and enter your answers directly onto the computer. The NSPCC thinks it is very important to respect people's privacy, so the reason that we are asking you to complete this section yourself, is that nobody will know what you have answered. Over 3,000 other people are also completing this survey, and your answers will be recorded only with a serial number, not your name. Because it is entirely confidential nobody can get into any trouble, regardless of what you say. Please try to be as honest as possible as this is an important and serious study.

If at any time you want to stop, or finish the interview elsewhere, or at another time, or with another interviewer (say a man or a woman), just say so and we will sort it out. To show you how to use the computer, I'll do the first few questions with you. Please read the question on the screen.

NOW HAND COMPUTER OVER TO RESPONDENT

(3 practice questions – age, yesterday's activities, favourite film – not analysed)

So firstly, how old were you when you were first allowed to:

PRESS RETURN WHEN READY

71. Stay at home for the evening without an adult to supervise?

72. Stay at home overnight without an adult to supervise?

73. Go to the town centre shops without an adult or much older child?

74. Go to school without an adult or much older child?

75. Go out in the evening on your own to a friend's/anywhere?

76. Stay out overnight without parents knowing where you were?

1 year old
2 years old
3 years old
4 years old
5 years old
6 years old
7 years old
8 years old
9 years old
10 years old
11 years old
12 years old
13 years old
14 years old

15 years old

16 years old

17 years old

18 or older

Never allowed

Don't know

Can't remember

Not applicable

Do not wish to answer

During your childhood, how much freedom were you allowed in the following things:

77. Saying what you thought and having your views considered?

78. Freedom to meet and mix with other people?

79. Thinking and believing what you wanted to e.g. politics and religion?

Complete freedom

Quite a lot of freedom

A little freedom

Very little freedom

No freedom at all

Don't know

Do not wish to answer

Parents can have different ideas about when a child should be independent and able to look after themselves. When you were a young child (say under 12) did you have any of the following experiences?

80. Your parents/carers expected you to do your own laundry (under the age of 12).

81. You had regular dental check ups.

82. You went to school in dirty clothes because there were no clean ones available.

83. You went hungry because no one got your meals ready or there was no food in the house.

84. You looked after younger brothers or sisters while your parents were out.

85. You were ill but no one looked after you or took you to the doctor.

Always

Often

Sometimes

Occasionally

Rarely

Never

Don't know

Can't remember

Not applicable

Do not wish to answer

86. Sometimes because of family circumstances, children find that they have adult responsibilities. Did you experience any of the following?

You regularly had to help care for somebody in your family who was ill or disabled (mentally or physically)

You often had to look after yourself because your parents had problems of their own e.g. alcohol, drugs etc

Your parents regularly depended on you for support, because they had emotional problems e.g. divorce, separation, death of someone close

You regularly had to look after yourself, because your parents went away

None of the above

Don't know

Do not wish to answer

87. Thinking about the independence and responsibility you had, does it seem now to have been the right amount?

Far too much responsibility

A bit too much responsibility

About right

Not quite enough responsibility

Far too little responsibility

Don't know

Do not wish to answer

88. And thinking about the care that was taken of you by adults, does that seem to have been the right amount?

Yes, I was very well cared for

I was reasonably well cared for

I wasn't as well cared for as I could have been

I was not cared for at all

Don't know

Do not wish to answer

FOR THOSE WHO SAY THEY WERE NOT WELL CARED FOR:
89. What were the ways in which you feel you lacked care?

I was abandoned or deserted

I was left alone too much

I was not fed properly

I was given too little affection

I was not properly supervised or watched out for

I was allowed to go into dangerous places or situations

I wasn't encouraged or helped to go to school

The physical condition of our home was dangerous

Our home was unclean

Other (PLEASE SPECIFY)

Don't know

Do not wish to answer

90. Do you now consider any of the treatment you experienced to be serious enough to call child neglect?

Yes

No

Not sure

Do not wish to answer

IF INDICATORS OF NEGLECT, ASK

91. Were the problems you had due, partly or wholly, to any of these factors?

Carer had money worries

Carer had other worries/stress

Carer had mental health problems

Carer being physically ill/disabled

Carer having problems with alcohol

Carer having problems with drugs

Carers had problems in own relationship

Carer's own relationship was violent

Carer didn't like me/resented me

I was not an easy child to look after

Other (PLEASE DESCRIBE)

None of these

Don't know

Do not wish to answer

IF OTHER WORRIES/STRESS

92. What was the cause of that worry/stress?

(CODE AND TYPE IN)

Don't know

Do not wish to answer

ASK ALL

93. Did physical violence ever take place between those caring for you?

Constantly

Frequently

Occasionally

Rarely

Never

Don't know

Do not wish to answer

These next few questions are about ways in which children can be treated. Some of the things mentioned are unusual, but we want to compare the situation in Britain with the results of surveys elsewhere in the world, so it is very important for us to know about them.

Thinking of the ways you personally were treated as a child, did you ever experience any of the following ways of being treated, in your family, at school or anywhere else?

(23 STATEMENTS IN 4 BATCHES:)

94. It was explained to me why I was wrong.
95. I was given something to distract me from what I was doing which was wrong.
96. Grounded/stopped from going out or privileges stopped.
97. Sent to room.

(VERBAL TREATMENT)

98. Made to feel embarrassed or humiliated?
99. Shouted at or screamed at?
100. Threatened with smacking, though not actually smacked?
101. Sworn at?
102. Called stupid or lazy or some similar name?
103. Threatened with being sent away or thrown out of the house/school/club?

(PHYSICAL TREATMENT)

104. Smacked on the bottom with a bare hand?
105. Slapped on the leg or arm or hand with a bare hand?
106. Pinched?
107. Slapped on the face, head or ears?

(VIOLENT TREATMENT)

108. Hit on the bottom with a hard implement, e.g. stick?
109. Hit on another part of the body with a hard implement, e.g. stick?
110. Shaken?
111. Hit with a fist or kicked hard?
112. Thrown or knocked down?
113. Beaten up, being hit over and over again?
114. Grabbed around the neck and choked?
115. Burned or scalded on purpose?
116. Threatened with a knife or gun?

Yes

No

Don't know

Do not wish to answer

IF YES TO ANY VERBAL TREATMENT

You say you were:
Made to feel embarrassed or humiliated
Shouted at or screamed at
Threatened with smacking, though not actually smacked
Sworn at
Called stupid or lazy or some similar name
Threatened with being sent away or thrown out of the house/school/club

117a. Where did this/these things happen?

At home

At club/church/social group

At school

In a public place, e.g. park, shops, street

Friend's/relative's house

Other

Don't know

Do not wish to answer

117b. Who did that/these things?

Mother

Stepmother

Father

Stepfather

Brother

Sister

Grandparent

Other relative

Teacher

Police

Care worker

Other authority figure, e.g. church/club leader

Other young person

Other adult

Don't know

Do not wish to answer

117c. How old were you when it/these things first happened?

1 or under

2

3

4

5

6

7

8

9

10

11

12

13

14

15

16

17

18 or over

Don't know

Do not wish to answer

117d. Did this/these things happen regularly?

Regularly over years

Regularly for a certain period

On and off over time

Not regularly

Don't know

Do not wish to answer

117e. How old were you when it/these things stopped happening?

1 or under

2

3

4

5

6

7

8

9

10

11

12

13

14

15

16

17

18 or over

Continues/has not stopped

Don't know

Do not wish to answer

IF YES TO ANY PHYSICAL TREATMENT

You say you were:

Smacked on the bottom with a bare hand

Slapped on the leg or arm or hand with a bare hand

Pinched

Slapped on the face, head or ears

118a. Where did this/these things happen?

At home

At club/church/social group

At school

In a public place, e.g. park, shops, street

Friend's/relative's house

Other

Don't know

Do not wish to answer

118b. Who did that/these things?

Mother

Stepmother

Father

Stepfather

Brother

Sister

Grandparent

Other relative

Teacher

Police

Care worker

Other authority figure, e.g. church/club leader

Other young person

Other adult

Don't know

Do not wish to answer

118c. How old where you when it/these things first happened?

1 or under

2

3

4

5

6

7

8

9

10

11

12

13

14

15

16

17

18 or over

Don't know

Do not wish to answer

118d. Did this/these things happen regularly?

Regularly over years

Regularly for a certain period

On and off over time

Not regularly

Don't know

Do not wish to answer

118e. How old were you when it/these things stopped happening?

1 or under

2

3

4

5

6

7

8

9

10

11

12

13

14

15

16

17

18 or over

Continues/has not stopped

Don't know

Do not wish to answer

IF YES TO ANY VIOLENT TREATMENT
You say you were:
Hit on the bottom with a hard implement, e.g. stick
Hit on another part of the body with a hard implement, e.g. stick
Shaken
Hit with a fist or kicked hard
Thrown or knocked down
Beaten up, being hit over and over again
Grabbed around the neck and choked
Burned or scalded on purpose
Threatened with a knife or gun

119a. Where did this/these things happen?

At home

At club/church/social group

At school

In a public place, e.g. park, shops, street

Friend's/relative's house

Other

Don't know

Do not wish to answer

119b. Who did that/these things?

Mother

Stepmother

Father

Stepfather

Brother

Sister

Grandparent

Other relative

Teacher

Police

Care worker

Other authority figure, e.g. church/club leader

Other young person

Other adult

Don't know

Do not wish to answer

119c. How old were you when it/these things first happened?

1 or under

2

3

4

5

6

7

8

9

10

11

12

13

14

15

16

17

18 or over

Don't know

Do not wish to answer

119d. Did this/these things happen regularly?

Regularly over years

Regularly for a certain period

On and off over time

Not regularly

Don't know

Do not wish to answer

119e. How old were you when it/these things stopped happening?

1 or under

2

3

4

5

6

7

8

9

10

11

12

13

14

15

16

17

18 or over

Continues/has not stopped

Don't know

Do not wish to answer

....

IF EXPERIENCED CODES 104-116
120. Thinking of when you were treated this way, how often, if ever, did you suffer effects which lasted to the next day or longer (e.g. bruising, marking or pain and soreness)?

Every time

On most occasions

About half of the occasions

Sometimes, but less than half of occasions

Rarely

Never

Don't know

Not applicable

Do not wish to answer

....

ALL EXCEPT 'NEVER' AT 120
121. As a result of being treated this way, did you ever experience any physical injuries?

Broken bones

Head injuries

Bites

Genital/anal area injuries

Poisoning

Internal injuries

Burns

Bruising

Other physical injuries

No physical injuries

Don't know

Do not wish to answer

....

IF EXPERIENCED CODES 98-116
122. To what extent, if at all, do you feel that you suffered any EMOTIONAL effects as a result of treatment you received as a child?

No effects felt

Was upset at time but no long term effects

Had long term effects on me

Don't know

Do not wish to answer

123. Do you think that the treatment you received was:

Always fair and reasonable

Mostly fair and reasonable

About right

A bit too strict and harsh for a child

Very much too strict and harsh for a child

Don't know

Do not wish to answer

IF AT HOME AT 119a.

124. Thinking of the physical treatment you received at home. Do you now consider any of this treatment serious enough to be called "child abuse"?
FOR AT HOME, AT SCHOOL AND ELSEWHERE

Yes

No

Don't know

Do not wish to answer

IF AT HOME AT 119a.

125. Do you think the way you were treated at home was due, partly or wholly, to any of these factors? FOR AT HOME, AT SCHOOL AND ELSEWHERE - DIFFERENT ANSWER TEXT FOR EACH

Carer had money worries

Carer had other worries/stress

Carer had mental health problems

Carer being physically ill/disabled

Carer having problems with alcohol

Carer having problems with drugs

None of these

Don't know

Do not wish to answer

126. And was it due, partly or wholly, to any of these factors?

Carer had problems in own relationship

Carer had a violent relationship

Carer didn't like me/resented me

I was not an easy child to look after

They enjoyed doing it

Other (PLEASE DESCRIBE)

None of these

Don't know

Do not wish to answer

IF WORRIES/STRESS 125
127. What was the cause of that worry/stress?

(CODE AND TYPE IN)

Don't know

Do not wish to answer

BULLYING AND DISCRIMINATION

128. Thinking now about your relationships with other children, either at home, school, or elsewhere were you ever bullied, discriminated against or made to feel different, like an outsider?

Yes – bullied

Yes – discriminated against

Yes – made to feel different, like an outsider

No – none of these things

Don't know

Do not wish to answer

IF YES AT 128.
129. Did that happen at home, at school or somewhere else?

At home

At club/church/social group

At school

In a public place, e.g. park, shops, street

Friend's/relative's house

Somewhere else (PLEASE SPECIFY)

Don't know

Do not wish to answer

---

130. Why do you think it happened?

Race

Gender

Disability

'Class' (money, how you spoke, clothes etc.)

Intelligence

Size

Religion

The place you lived

Sexuality

Interests/hobbies

Other (PLEASE SPECIFY)

Don't know

Do not wish to answer

131. What form did that treatment take?

Name calling/insults/verbal abuse

Telling lies/spreading rumours about you

Embarrassing/humiliating you deliberately

Ignoring you/not speaking to you

Physical bullying, e.g. pinching, punching, hitting etc

Threatening violence but not actually attacking you

Damaging your things

Stealing or demanding things from you, e.g. money, sweets

Getting you into trouble with parents, teachers, older children etc.

Didn't treat me fairly

Other (TYPE IN)

Don't know

Do not wish to answer

132. How old were you when it first happened?

1 or under

2

3

4

5

6

7

8

9

10

11

12

13

14

15

16

17

18 or over

Don't know

Do not wish to answer

133. Did this happen regularly? IF APPROPRIATE, USE MORE THAN ONE CODE

Regularly over years

Regularly for a certain period

On and off over time

Not regularly

Don't know

Do not wish to answer

134. To what extent, if at all, do you feel that you suffered any EMOTIONAL effects as a result of this treatment?

No effects felt

Was upset at time but no long term effects

Had long term effects on me

Don't know

Do not wish to answer

135. Now thinking of adults who you knew when you were a child. I don't mean parents, but other relatives, neighbours, teachers, church/sports/club leaders and so on. Were you ever bullied, discriminated against or made to feel different or like an outsider, by these sort of adults?

Yes – bullied

Yes – discriminated against

Yes – made to feel different, like an outsider

No – none of these things

Don't know

Do not wish to answer

IF YES AT 135.

136. Did that happen at home, at school or somewhere else?

At home

At club/church/social group

At school

In a public place, e.g. park, shops, street

Friend's/relative's house

Somewhere else (PLEASE SPECIFY)

Don't know

Do not wish to answer

137. Why do you think it happened?

Race

Gender

Disability

'Class' (money, how you spoke, clothes etc.)

Intelligence

Size

Religion

The place you lived

Sexuality

Interests/hobbies

Other (PLEASE SPECIFY)

Don't know

Do not wish to answer

....

138. What form did that treatment take?

Name calling insults/verbal abuse

Telling lies/spreading rumours about you

Embarrassing/humiliating you deliberately

Ignoring you/not speaking to you

Physical bullying, e.g. pinching, punching, hitting etc.

Threatening violence but not actually attacking you

Damaging your things

Stealing or demanding things from you, e.g. money, sweets

Getting you into trouble with parents, teachers, older children etc

Didn't treat me fairly

Other (TYPE IN)

Don't know

Do not wish to answer

....

139. How old were you when it first happened?

1 or under

2

3

4

5

6

7

8

9

10

11

12

13

14

15

16

17

18 or over

Don't know

Do not wish to answer

....

140. Did this happen regularly? IF APPROPRIATE, USE MORE THAN ONE CODE

Regularly over years

Regularly for a certain period

On and off over time

Not regularly

Don't know

Do not wish to answer

141. To what extent, if at all, do you feel that you suffered any EMOTIONAL effects as a result of this treatment?

No effects felt

Was upset at time but no long term effects

Had long term effects on me

Don't know

Do not wish to answer

142. Do you think any of this treatment was serious enough to be considered child abuse?

Yes

No

Don't know

Do not wish to answer

143. Do you think the way you were treated was due, partly or wholly, to any of these factors?

The person who did it had money worries

The person who did it had other worries/stress

The person who did it had mental health problems

The person who did it being physically ill/disabled

The person who did it having problems with alcohol

The person who did it having problems with drugs

None of these

Don't know

Do not wish to answer

144. And do you think it was due, partly or wholly, to any of these factors?

The person who did it had problems in own relationship

The person who did it had a violent relationship

The person who did it didn't like me/resented me

I was not an easy child to look after

They enjoyed doing it

Other (PLEASE DESCRIBE)

None of these

Don't know

Do not wish to answer

....

The way that people are treated as children can have an effect on how good they feel about themselves then and later in life. Please tell us if you had any of the following experiences.

145. Did you ever get the blame for things that other children did wrong?

146. Were you ever laughed at when you were really upset about something?

147. Were you ever humiliated in front of other people?

148. Did you ever get congratulated for winning a prize or competition?

149. Did an adult ever deliberately break or throw away one of your treasured possessions?

150. Did someone ever tell you they wished you were dead or never been born?

151. Did you ever get praise or a treat for doing well at school?

152. Were you ever left out of a treat that other children were getting?

153. Did an adult ever deliberately lie to you about something important?

154. Were you ever made to feel you were special?

Yes

No

Don't know

Do not wish to answer

....

IF YES AT STATEMENTS 147, 150, 152, AND 153

155. Who did this or was responsible for it happening?

A teacher

Your father

Your stepfather

Your foster father

Your mother

Your stepmother

Your foster mother

Your doctor

Your grandmother

Your grandfather

Older brother

Older sister

Childminder

A care worker

A religious leader

A club leader

A neighbour

Other (PLEASE SPECIFY)

Don't know

Do not wish to answer

156. There are other ways of treating children. Did you ever experience any of these?

Having your mouth washed out with soap

Being made to miss a meal and go hungry

Being made to eat or drink something that they knew would make you feel sick

Being locked in a room or cupboard

Shutting you outside on a cold day without a coat

None of these

Don't know

Do not wish to answer

157. Did you experience any of these.

Someone getting rid of your pet or having it put to sleep even though it was quite healthy

Having to stand or sit in the corner

Always having to do the worst jobs in the house

Having to sit with your hands on your head

If you wet the bed you were made to rub your nose in or touch wet sheets

None of these

Don't know

Do not wish to answer

IF EXPERIENCED ANY AT 156 OR 157

158. Who was MOST OFTEN responsible for this/these things?

A teacher

Your father

Your stepfather

Your mother

Your stepmother

Your doctor

Your grandmother

Your grandfather

A social worker/care worker

An aunt

An uncle

A priest or other religious leader

A youth club/scout/guides leader or someone like that

A neighbour

Other

Don't know

Do not wish to answer

159. Do you think any of this treatment was serious enough to be considered child abuse?

Yes

No

Don't know

Do not wish to answer

IF YES
160. Do you think the way you were treated was due, partly or wholly, to any of these factors?

The person who did it had money worries

The person who did it had other worries/stress

The person who did it had mental health problems

The person who did it being physically ill/disabled

The person who did it having problems with alcohol

The person who did it having problems with drugs

None of these

Don't know

Do not wish to answer

161. And do you think it was due, partly or wholly, to any of these factors?

The person who did it had problems in own relationship

The person who did it had a violent relationship

The person who did it didn't like me/resented me

I was not an easy child to look after

Other (PLEASE DESCRIBE)

None of these

Don't know

Do not wish to answer

IF OTHER WORRIES/STRESS
162. What was the cause of that worry/ stress?

(CODE AND TYPE IN)

Don't know

Do not wish to answer

In the past many people found it too embarrassing to talk about sex to young people. This sometimes made it difficult for young people to get the help and advice they needed with relationships, or if someone was putting pressure on them to have sex.

163. How easy did you find it to talk to your parent(s) about sex?

Very easy

Quite easy

Neither easy nor difficult

Quite difficult

Very difficult

Don't know

Do not wish to answer

Please look at these descriptions of sexual activity at different ages, and tell me whether, in general, you think this is acceptable. Please highlight each one that you think is acceptable between a male and a female.

164. Sexual activity between an adult (18+) and a young person of 13-15.

165. Sexual activity between an adult (18+) and a young person aged 12 or under.

166. Sexual activity between young people both aged 13-15.

167. Sexual activity between young people both aged 12 or under.

Nothing acceptable

Kissing & cuddling

Touching & fondling under the clothes

Full intercourse or oral sex

Don't know

Do not wish to answer

Please remember that this is entirely confidential and nothing you say can get anyone into any trouble.
So, before you were 16, did you experience any of the following?

168a. Did a person ever deliberately expose their sex organs or other private parts of their body to you, in order to excite themselves or shock you?

Yes

No

Don't know

Do not wish to answer

IF YES

168b. Did this/these things ever happen against your wishes? Please pick the code that is nearest to what happened.

Yes, always against my wishes

Sometimes against my wishes/sometimes with my consent

I didn't like it but I put up with it

No, it only happened with my full consent

Don't know

Do not wish to answer

168c. Was this person 5 or more years older than you? (If more than 1 person, you should use more than 1 answer if needed)

Yes

No

Don't know/ can't say

Do not wish to answer

IF DIDN'T WANT TO HAPPEN OR OLDER PERSON
IF EXPOSURE

168d. How often did this/these things happen?

Once only

Two or more times but always with the same person

Two or more times and with different people

Don't know

Do not wish to answer

168e. About what age were you when this/these things first happened?

1 or under

2

3

4

5

6

7

8

9

10

11

12

13

14

15

Can't remember/don't know

Do not wish to answer

IF MORE THAN ONCE AT 168d

168f. About what age were you when it/these things stopped?
If these experiences stopped at different ages, you can use more than one answer.

1 or under

2

3

4

5

6

7

8

9

10

11

12

13

14

15

16

17

18+

Has not stopped

Don't know/can't remember

Do not wish to answer

168g. Were the people/Was the person male or female? You can code both answers.

Male

Female

Don't know

Do not wish to answer

168h. And were any of these people/Was the person related to you or not?

All related

Some related and some not related

All not related

Don't know

Do not wish to answer

IF RELATED

168i. And of those that were related to you, what was their relationship to you?

Father

Mother

Stepfather

Stepmother

Brother/stepbrother

Sister/stepsister

Grandfather

Grandmother

Uncle

Aunt

Cousin

Other relation (TYPE IN)

Don't know

Do not wish to answer

IF NOT RELATED

168j. Of those that weren't related to you, what was their relationship to you?

Friend of parents

Friend of brother/sister

Boyfriend/girlfriend

Baby-sitter

Neighbour

Teacher

Priest or other religious leader

Care worker/social worker

Fellow school or college student

Stranger – man

Stranger – woman

Someone I had recently met

Other person (TYPE IN)

Don't know

Do not wish to answer

Thinking only of the sexual experience you have described, which you did not want to happen:

168k. Where did this/these things take place?

In your own home

In the home of the other person

Club/Youth club/Sports club

In a hotel/guest house

In school

In a car

In a park/an abandoned building/field/woods etc.

Other place (TYPE IN)

Don't know

Do not wish to answer

168l. Was physical force ever used to make you take part?

Yes

No

Don't know

Do not wish to answer

168m. Were threats or blackmail (by blackmail we mean for example to hurt someone you love or to tell everyone it was your fault) ever used to make you take part?

Yes

No

Don't know

Do not wish to answer

168n. How or why did the activity stop, if it stopped?

It hasn't stopped/it continued after the age of 16

I confronted and stopped the person myself without involving anybody else

We stopped seeing each other

I avoided the person

I told an older person who got it stopped

He/she just stopped themselves

I left home

I became pregnant

I went to the police

I went to a social worker/advice centre

The other person moved on to do this with another person

Other reason (TYPE IN)

Don't know

Do not wish to answer

REPEAT QUESTIONS 168 b and c FOR THE 3 STATEMENTS BELOW
Before you were 16:
169. Were you hugged, or kissed in a sexual way, whether you agreed to it or not?

170. Did someone touch or fondle your sex organs or other private parts of your body?

171. Did someone get you to touch THEIR sex organs or sexually arouse them with your hands?

IF TOUCHING AT 169 – 171
172.Now thinking of the following sexual experiences that happened to you before you were 16:

When you were hugged, or kissed in a sexual way, whether you agreed to it or not.

When someone touched or fondled your sex organs or other private parts of your body.

When someone got you to touch THEIR sex organs or sexually arouse them with your hands.

IF DIDN'T WANT TO HAPPEN OR OLDER PERSON REPEAT QUESTIONS 168d TO 168n
REPEAT QUESTIONS b and c FOR THE 3 STATEMENTS BELOW
Before you were 16:
173. Did someone attempt oral sex on you?

174. Did someone attempt sexual intercourse with you?

175. Did someone attempt anal intercourse with you?

IF ATTEMPTS AT 173 – 175

176. Now thinking of the following sexual experiences that happened to you before you were 16:

when someone attempted oral sex on you

when someone attempted sexual intercourse with you

when someone attempted anal intercourse with you

IF DIDN'T WANT TO HAPPEN OR OLDER PERSON REPEAT QUESTIONS d TO n
REPEAT QUESTIONS b and c FOR THE 4 STATEMENTS BELOW
Before you were 16:

177. Did you have full sexual intercourse?

178. Did you have anal intercourse?

179. Did you have oral sex?

180. Did someone put their finger, tongue or an object into your vagina or anus?

IF ORAL AND PENETRATION AT 177 – 180

181. Now thinking of the following sexual experiences that happened to you before you were 16:

When you had full sexual intercourse.

When you had anal intercourse.

When you had oral sex.

When someone put their finger, tongue or an object into your vagina or anus.

IF DIDN'T WANT TO HAPPEN OR OLDER PERSON REPEAT QUESTIONS d TO n
REPEAT QUESTIONS b and c FOR THE 3 STATEMENTS BELOW
Before you were sixteen:

182. Did you have pornographic photos or videos taken of you?

183. Were you shown pornographic videos, magazines, computer images or photos?

184. Were you made or encouraged to watch other people having intercourse/ performing sex acts or pornographic acts (real people, not pictures)?

IF PORNOGRAPHY AT 182 – 184

185. Now thinking of the following sexual experiences that happened to you before you were 16:

When you had pornographic photos or videos taken of you.

When you were shown pornographic videos, magazines, computer images or photos.

When you were made or encouraged to watch other people having intercourse/performing sex acts or pornographic acts (real people, not pictures).

IF DIDN'T WANT TO HAPPEN OR OLDER PERSON REPEAT QUESTIONS d TO n
186. Before you were 16 did you ever have sex for money or drugs or favours, such as somewhere to stay?

Yes

No

Don't know

Do not wish to answer

IF YES AT 186
187. What age did this start?

8 or under

9

10

11

12

13

14

15

Don't know

Do not wish to answer

---

188. What age did this stop?

8 or under

9

10

11

12

13

14

15

16

17

18 or older

Has not stopped

Don't know

Do not wish to answer

IF AT LEAST ONE ACTIVITY NOT CONSENTED OR PERSON OLDER, OR HAVE WORKED AS A PROSTITUTE OR RENT BOY
Thinking now about those sexual experiences before you were 16 and that you did not want to happen/ those sexual experiences before you were 16 and with a person 5 or more years older than you/ when you had sex for money, drugs or favours:

189. Did you tell anyone about any of these sexual experiences that you did not want to happen/with a person 5 or more years older than you when you had sex for money, drugs or favours, at the time or at a later date?

Yes – told someone at the time

Yes – told someone at a later date

No – didn't tell anyone

Don't know

Do not wish to answer

IF TOLD NOBODY

190. Why did you not tell anybody?

I was frightened

I was threatened by the other person

I didn't think it was serious/wrong

I didn't want friends to find out

I didn't want parents to find out

I didn't want the authorities to find out

It was nobody else's business

I didn't think they would believe me

I promised not to

Other (PLEASE DESCRIBE)

Don't know

Do not wish to answer

IF TOLD SOMEBODY

191. Who did you tell?

Mother/step mother

Father/step father

Sister/step sister/brother/step brother

Other relative

Social worker

Priest/religious figure

Doctor/health worker

Police

Teacher

Friend

Boyfriend/girlfriend

Childline/Helpline

Other adult

Other (TYPE IN)

Don't know

Do not wish to answer

192. Having told what happened to you, did you feel you got help and support from those you told, or did you feel let down by them?

I got help and support

I felt let down

I got help and support at first, but was later let down

Don't know

Do not wish to answer

193. Did they take your experiences seriously?

Yes

No

Don't know

Do not wish to answer

Thinking now about those sexual experiences before you were 16 and that you did not want to happen/those sexual experiences before you were 16 and with a person 5 or more years older than you/when you had sex for money, drugs or favours:

194. Did this person/any of these people do it with other children?

Yes, other child(ren) in my family

Yes, other child(ren) outside my family

No

Don't know

Do not wish to answer

195. Were your actions or your judgement affected by alcohol or drugs at any time during these sex acts?

Yes, by alcohol

Yes, by drugs

Yes, by both

No

Don't know

Do not wish to answer

196. Do you now consider what happened to you to be sexual abuse?

Yes

No

Don't know

Do not wish to answer

197. Do you think that the actions of the other person/people were due, partly or wholly, to any of these factors?

Just for their own pleasure or satisfaction

To punish me/threaten me

The person who did it had money worries

The person who did it had other worries/stress

The person who did it had mental health problems

The person who did it was physically ill/disabled

The person who did it had problems with alcohol

The person who did it had problems with drugs

None of these

Don't know

Do not wish to answer

198. And do you think that they were due, partly or wholly, to any of these factors?

The person who did it was lonely

The person who did it had problems in own relationship

The person who did it had a violent relationship

They didn't like me/resented me

I was not an easy child to look after

Other (PLEASE DESCRIBE)

None of these

Don't know

Do not wish to answer

IF OTHER WORRIES/STRESS

199. What was the cause of that worry/stress?

(CODE AND TYPE IN)

Don't know

Do not wish to answer

IF CONSIDERED THEY HAVE BEEN HARSHLY TREATED, ABUSED OR NEGLECTED IN ANY WAY

200. Thinking over everything you have told us about the treatment you received as a child, to what extent, if at all, do you feel that you have suffered any LONG-TERM effects as a result of what happened to you?

It has had no real effect on me at all

It was upsetting at the time, but I got over it quite quickly

It affected me for quite a long time, but I have got over it since

It had a lasting and harmful effect

Don't know

Do not wish to answer

201. What sort of effect has it had?

Physical health problems

Mental health/psychological problems

Personal/social problems

Family problems

I have trouble with authority

Other (PLEASE DESCRIBE)

Don't know

Do not wish to answer

People who have experiences like yours can find that they have problems, but others say it has make them stronger. Which of these describes you?

202. I can take whatever life throws at me

Describes me a lot

Describes me a little

Does not describe me at all

Don't know

Do not wish to answer

203. I have low self-confidence.

Describes me a lot

Describes me a little

Does not describe me at all

Don't know

Do not wish to answer

204. I'm more streetwise than other people of my age.

Describes me a lot

Describes me a little

Does not describe me at all

Don't know

Do not wish to answer

205. I tend not to trust certain types of people.

Describes me a lot

Describes me a little

Does not describe me at all

Don't know

Do not wish to answer

206. During your childhood, did you, or anybody else, ever make a formal complaint or attempt or make a formal complaint, to the authorities about any sort of maltreatment you had received?

Yes, just once

Yes, 2 or more times

No

Don't know

Do not wish to answer

IF YES

Please answer the next few questions about the main or most recent complaint only.

207. What did you, or anybody else, report/make a complaint about?

(CODE AND TYPE IN)

Don't know

Do not wish to answer

208. Who was the complaint made to?

Social services (e.g. a social worker)

Child Line, or other telephone helpline

A teacher or someone else affiliated to your school

A doctor, nurse or medical professional

A youth club leader (e.g. Scoutmaster)

Police

Other (PLEASE TYPE IN)

Don't know

Do not wish to answer

209. What was the outcome of the complaint?

I was ignored/not believed

I was believed, but no action was taken

Action was taken but the problem continued

Action was taken and the problem stopped

Other (PLEASE TYPE IN)

Don't know

Do not wish to answer

210. How did you feel about the outcome of the complaint?

It was what I needed/wanted

Helpful in some ways, but not in others

Not what I wanted at all

Don't know/can't remember

Do not wish to answer

211. Is there any other form of abuse or neglect you have experienced which has not been covered elsewhere?

Yes (PLEASE DESCRIBE)

No

Don't know

Do not wish to answer

Thank you. That is the end of the self completion section of this interview.
Please hand the laptop computer back to the interviewer, who will now ask you just a few more questions.

212. What do you think is the best way for children to be protected from abuse and neglect?

CODE AND TYPE IN

Don't know

Refused

213. The NSPCC may be conducting further research on this subject. Would you be prepared to help again?

Yes

No

Depends

Don't know

Refused

RC1. Can you tell me what the best address to contact you at would be?
NOW ENTER THE FULL ADDRESS STARTING WITH THE NUMBER AND STREET NAME ONLY ON THIS SCREEN.

NOW ENTER THE TOWN

NOW ENTER THE COUNTY

NOW ENTER THE FULL POSTCODE

RC2. And can you tell me the best telephone number to ring you on?

NOW ENTER TELEPHONE NUMBER STARTING WITH THE EXCHANGE NUMBER

I would now like to collect a few details about you and the people you live with.
REASSURE RESPONDENT OF CONFIDENTIALITY AND THAT NAME AND ADDRESS ARE USED ONLY FOR QUALITY CONTROL.

C1. NOW COLLECT CLASSIFICATION

First, could you tell me your name please?

C2. NOW ENTER RESPONDENT'S FULL ADDRESS STARTING WITH THE STREET NUMBER AND NAME ONLY ON THIS SCREEN

YOU MAY ENTER 'SAME AS ABOVE' IF ALREADY PREVIOUSLY ENTERED

NOW ENTER THE TOWN

NOW ENTER THE COUNTY

NOW ENTER THE FULL POSTCODE

(e.g. W5 5SU)

C3. REMEMBER TO ENTER THE WORD PRACTICE UNLESS THIS IS A REAL INTERVIEW

NOW ENTER RESPONDENT'S (MAIN) HOME TELEPHONE NUMBER STARTING WITH THE EXCHANGE NUMBER

C4. SEX OF RESPONDENT

Male

Female

C5a. What was your age last birthday?

IF RESPONDENT REFUSES TO GIVE HIS/HER AGE TYPE <ESC> D

BASE: AGE NOT GIVEN

C5b. Can you tell me in which of these age groups you are? Stop me when I mention the correct one.

READ OUT

18-20

21-24

Refused

C6. SHOW CARD S

Which of these on this card describes your marital status

Single/never married

Married/Living as couple

Widowed/Divorced/Separated

Refused .

C7. At what age did you finish your full time education?

14 or under

15

16

17

18

19

20

21-23

24 or more

Still studying

Not stated

C8. Does your household own this accommodation or rent it?

PROBE FOR DETAILS

Owned/being bought on mortgage/loan

Rented from council

Rented from housing association

Rented (unfurnished) from private landlord

Rented (furnished) from private landlord

Tied to job

Other – TYPE IN

Don't know

Refused

SHOW CARD T

C9. What is your current situation? Please choose your answer from this card,

PROBE FOR CURRENT SITUATION

At school/full time student

Working in a paid job (30+ hours)

Working in a paid job (less than 30 hours)

Self-employed

Government training scheme

Unemployed/seeking work

Unable to work – disability

Looking after home/family

Retired from paid employment

Other (TYPE IN)

Refused/Don't know

IF NOT IN WORK NOW

C10. Can I just check have you ever had PERMANENT full- or part-time work?

Yes

No

ESTABLISH CHIEF INCOME EARNER

C11. Which member of your household would you say is the Chief Income Earner, that is the person with the largest income whether from employment, pensions, state benefits, investments or other incomes?

N.B. IF EQUAL INCOME IS CLAIMED FOR 2 PERSONS, YOU SHOULD CLASSIFY THE ELDER AS THE CHIEF INCOME EARNER

Respondent

Someone else

COLLECT OCCUPATION DETAILS OF RESPONDENT

C12a. What type of firm or organisation do you work for?

DESCRIBE TYPE OF FIRM INCLUDING WHAT THE FIRM OR ORGANISATION MAKES OR DOES

....

C12b. What job do you do?

....

C12c. Are you an employee or self-employed?

Self-employed

Employee

....

C12c. Do you have any position, rank or grade in the organisation (i.e. responsible for the work of other people)?

PROMPT AS APPROPRIATE: Foreman, Sergeant, Office Manager, Executive Officer etc.

Yes – TYPE IN DETAILS

None

....

C12d. Roughly, how many people work at your work place, including yourself?

C12e. For how many people are you responsible?

C12f. Do you have any qualifications?

PROMPT AS APPROPRIATE: Apprenticeship, professional qualifications, university degrees, diplomas etc

....

NOW CHECK EMPLOYMENT STATUS OF CHIEF INCOME EARNER

IF NECESSARY ASK

C12g. Does Chief Income Earner have a paid job full- or part-time?

Yes

No

Don't know

Refused

....

SHOW CARD U

C12h. Looking at this card please tell me which of these describe ...(CHIEF INCOME EARNER). Just read out the letter.

A

B

C

D

E

F

G

H

I

J

Don't know/Refused

BASE: CHIEF INCOME EARNER IS NOT RESPONDENT AND IS FULL-TIME STUDENT

C12i. Is the Chief Income Earner studying at school, at sixth-form college or at university or college of further education?

School

Sixth-form college

University/college/higher education

Don't know

Refused

C12j. NOW COLLECT DETAILS OF JOB

What type of firm or organisation does this person work for?

DESCRIBE TYPE OF FIRM INCLUDING WHAT THE FIRM OR ORGANISATION MAKES OR DOES

C12k. What job does this person do?

C12l. Is this person an employee or self-employed?

Self-employed

Employee

C12m. Does this person have any position, rank or grade in the organisation (i.e. responsible for the work of other people)?

PROMPT AS APPROPRIATE: Foreman, Sergeant, Office Manager, Executive Officer etc.

Yes - TYPE IN DETAILS

None

C12n. Roughly, how many people work at this person's work place, including yourself?

C12o. For how many people is this person responsible?

C12p. Does this person have any qualifications?

PROMPT AS APPROPRIATE: Apprenticeship, professional qualifications, university degrees, diplomas etc

C13. How many people are there living in this household, including yourself?

INCLUDE ONLY THOSE WHO SHARE FOOD WITH RESPONDENT OR A SHARE A KITCHEN/LIVING ROOM WITH RESPONDENT

IF MORE THAN 10 PEOPLE IN HOUSEHOLD, CODE 10

C14. And finally to which of the following groups would you say you belong?

White

Black Caribbean

Black African

Black Other

Indian

Pakistani

Bangladeshi

Chinese

Other Asian

Other ethnic group (CODE AND TYPE IN)

Don't know

Refused

SHOW CARD W

214. Thank you very much. That is just about the end of the interview. This has been a serious study - how worthwhile do you think it has been to take part?

Extremely worthwhile

Very worthwhile

Quite worthwhile

Not very worthwhile

Not at all worthwhile

Don't know

Refused

215. Is there anything we have covered that has upset you in any way?

Yes

No

Don't know

Refused

IF UPSET
216. Would you like to tell us anything about this?

CODE AND TYPE IN

No, nothing to say

Don't know

Refused

THANK RESPONDENT AND CLOSE

"I would just like to confirm that my name is from the British Market Research Bureau in London. All your replies will be treated in the strictest confidence.

INTERVIEWER: Signify that this interview is a true record and has been conducted within the Market Research Society Code of Conduct by typing in your interviewer number below.

YOU MUST ENTER YOUR FULL INTERVIEWER NUMBER AT THIS QUESTION (EVEN IF YOU HAVE TAKEN OVER SOMEONE ELSE'S ASSIGNMENT)

217. HOW MUCH INFLUENCE DO YOU FEEL ENVIRONMENT EXERTED ON THE ANSWERS GIVEN?

A lot
A little
None

218. WERE PARENTS PRESENT AT ALL DURING THE INTERVIEW?

Yes
No
Don't know

C15. NOW ASSESS SOCIAL GRADE OF RESPONDENT'S JOB

TYPE OF FIRM: %232.

JOB : %233.

EMPLOYMENT STATUS: SELF-EMPLOYED/EMPLOYEE

NO. OF PEOPLE AT PLACE OF WORK: %236/Don't know

NO. OF PEOPLE RESPONSIBLE FOR: %237/Don't know

QUALIFICATIONS: %238

POSITION/RANK/GRADE: %235

A
B
CI
C2
D
E
CODE LATER

C16. NOW ASSESS SOCIAL GRADE

TYPE OF FIRM: %244

JOB : %245

EMPLOYMENT STATUS : SELF-EMPLOYED/EMPLOYEE

NO. OF PEOPLE AT PLACE OF WORK: %248/Don't know

NO. OF PEOPLE RESPONSIBLE FOR: %249/Don't know

QUALIFICATIONS: %250

POSITION/RANK/GRADE: %247

A
B

C1
C2
D
E
CODE LATER

WHEN YOU ARE SURE YOU HAVE FINISHED THE INTERVIEW

PRESS ENTER